THE CROSS VS THE CRESCENT

THE CROSS VS THE CRESCENT

Religion and Politics in Tanzania
From the 1890s to the 1990s

Lawrence E. Y. Mbogoni

Mkuki na Nyota Publishers
P. O. Box 4246, Dar es Salaam
www.mkukinanyota.com

Published by Mkuki na Nyota Publishers Ltd
6 Muhonda St., Mission Quarter, Kariakoo
P. O. Box 4246, Dar es Salaam, Tanzania
www.mkukinanyota.com

Cover illustrated by Abdullah Gugu
Photos by D. M. Simba

ISBN 9987 686 62 1

In memory of my
Mother Amelia Chibesi

Table of Contents

PREFACE AND ACKNOWLEDGMENTS

The present work is the result of research that I undertook following the Mwembechai Mosque riots on 13 February 1998 which left two dead and considerable damage to private and public property. At the time of the Mwembechai crisis the problem was said not to be between Christianity and Islam but rather between the Government and the Muslim community in Tanzania. However, Hamza Njozi's book titled Mwembechai Killings, which was published in Canada in 2000, suggested that the crisis was political as well as religious. It was partly because I was dissatisfied with Dr. Njozi's limited historical context of the crisis that I embarked on my own research. In so doing I was guided by a hope that a broader historical context might help toward a better understanding of current relations between the two faiths in Tanzania.

It remains to express my gratitude to the numerous people and institutions for assisting me to accomplish this study. The story told in the following pages required research on three continents. I owe many thanks to archivists and librarians in the United States of America, the United Kingdom, and the United Republic of Tanzania. In particular I thank the archivists at the Public Record Office, Kew Gardens, London; the Rhodes House Library, Oxford; the CMS archives, University of Birmingham; and the Tanzania National Archives, Dar es Salaam, especially its Director, Mr. Peter Mlyansi. I must also thank Virginia Burwell, Celi Cellano, and Jackie Hill, the interlibrary loan staff at William Paterson University, who probably went beyond the call of duty to meet my requests for source materials at short notice. Without their assistance this study would have taken much longer to complete.

I must also thank Mrs. Beatrice Dale (nee Rwabushaija), for providing me with accommodation on several occasions when I was working at the Public Record Office in London. In Tanzania several people offered me help which enabled me to do my research with ease. Mr. And Mrs. Godwin Mbogoni provided me with accommodation and other comforts of home while I was in Dar es Salaam. My cousin, Robert Massimba, offered me company and transportation for which I am very grateful. Father Andrew Luanda facilitated my access to the parish archives at the St. Joseph's Cathedral, Dar es Salaam. Brother Kevin Dargan at Maryknoll, NY, facilitated the acquisition of

ix

Maryknoll archive sources which I would otherwise have not been able to get. Mr. Lulenga George Fumbuka bought and sent me a copy of Father John C. Sivalon's book, *Kanisa Katoliki na Siasa ya Tanzania Bara,* which I was unable to get in the USA. Mr. Mohamed Said sent me a copy of Tewa Said Tewa's unpublished manuscript on the history of Islam in Tanzania.

Professor Geoffrey Mmari, Vice Chancellor of the Open University, allowed me to look at a draft in his possession of research findings by the University of Dar es Salaam's Research and Education for Democracy in Tanzania (REDET). I noticed that several papers provide considerable empirical data about the correlation between religion, education and employment. The evidence of current imbalances in education and employment between Christians and Muslims is very well demonstrated. Hopefully this work will soon be published. With this knowledge, therefore, I decided to devote a chapter on the colonial experience for believers of both faiths as a way of providing a background to the present situation. Unlike REDET's research, my own research pays greater attention to the religious issues that have tended to divide Christians and Muslims in Tanzania.

As I grappled with and developed the ideas presented in this book I benefitted a lot from conversations with a number of colleagues and friends. Following the Mwembechai riots and killings there was a heated discussion by members of TANZANET, an Internet organization of Tanzanians living abroad, about what had happened. I learnt a lot from the contributions of Gertrude Malai (nee Ndesamburo), Saada al-Ghafry, Dr. Hassan O. Ali, Alhaj Yusufu Kalala, the late Dr. Rugatiri Mekacha, Dr. Joseph Mbele, Lulenga George Fumbuka, Dr. Seth Chachage, Dr. Willy Makundi, Agnetta Kamugisha, Kassim Abdullah, Jaha Juma Jaha, Dr. Selina Mushi, H. S. Othman, Emmanuel J. Muganda, Dr. Said Kapiga and Mlima Aziz. I also would like to thank in particular Professor Ali A. Mazrui and Professor Marcia Wright who read drafts of the work in progress and offered very constructive comments and suggestions. I am equally grateful to the publisher's anonymous reader for his or her insightful comments and criticism.

Finally, this work would not have been possible if it were not for the support of my family. To be sure, they had no input in the writing of this book. But I very much appreciate their moral support. Research for this book was conducted without the benefit of a research grant. Instead I depended upon my modest salary. Consequently, my wife, Margaret, and our children, had to endure economic hardship because I used money for their basic needs to travel to England and Tanzania to consult and collect source materials.

L. E. Y. Mbogoni

Wayne, New Jersey, USA
August, 2003

CHAPTER ONE

INTRODUCTION

Conflict is one of the most pervasive features of human existence. Humans have been known to turn on each other for all kinds of reasons. Karl Marx and his followers (Marxists) have postulated that all written history is the history of class struggles. Marxists argue that class differences represent the main driving force in history and are the major causes of conflict between people. In other words, for Marxists it is the contradictory totality of social economic relations which is the source of conflict in human history. Thus, in the Marxian scheme of things religion[1] is not by itself a problem that can lead to conflict. If anything, as Marx suggested, religion tends to obscure class differences. It acts as an opiate of the masses by dulling their consciousness against class injustices with promises of a good life in the hereafter.

Besides considering religion to be the opiate of the masses, Marx described religion to be "...the general theory of this world, its encyclopedic compendium, its logic in popular form, its spiritual point d'honneur, its enthusiasm, its moral sanction, its solemn complement and its universal basis of consolation and justification . . ." (Marx, 1973: 13). Even more important, Marx considered religion to be "the self-consciousness and self-esteem of man who has either not yet won through to himself, or has already lost himself again" (ibid.). For Marx, therefore, to believe in religion is to subscribe to false consciousness; to fight and die for one's religion is to fight and die for nothing. Nevertheless, as we well know, religious differences have been the cause of conflict and violence because followers feel very strongly about religion.

Marx externalized the causes of conflict in the form of social and economic class contradictions. The Bible, however, suggests that the source of human conflict is within us. James 4:1-2 reads:

> "Those conflicts and disputes among you, where do they come from? Do they not come from your cravings that are at war within you? You want something and do not have it; so you commit murder. And you covet something and cannot obtain it; so you engage in disputes and conflicts ..."[2]

1

Although the cravings alluded to above are in the things of this world (James 4:4), they are caused by selfishness which is a behavioral human weakness. The Biblical solution to such cravings is, therefore, not a class struggle but rather spiritual salvation (James 4:7). However, the Christian claim that the Bible has the answers to human problems has been challenged by other religions including Islam.

The struggle between Christianity and Islam for the salvation of humankind has been one of the most enduring conflicts in human history. It appears destined to remain until the end of time (Gilchrist, 1999: 6). As we will subsequently see in the course of this study, what has set Christians and Muslims at loggerheads are their religious beliefs, which are interwoven with intolerance. Theologically, each religion invites bigotry by claiming exclusive possession of final truth concerning the destiny and end of humankind, as well as sole authority and means for interpreting that end (Allport, 1973: 88). Moreover, each religion claims that its followers constitute the true community of God. For instance, whereas Catholicismbefore Vatican II believed there was no salvation outside of the Catholic Church, Muslims believe that infidels are accursed and destined for Hell because they have not submitted to the will of Allah.

In Tanzania, like elsewhere in the world, religious intolerance has gone hand in hand with religious prejudice. It will be demonstrated in this study that between the 1890s and the 1990s there was at work socio-cultural influences which predisposed the followers of Christianity to be prejudiced against Islam. The advent of European colonial rule tipped the scales in favor of Christianity in what was dubbed as a clash of cultures and civilizations. It is important to bear in mind that the Church as an institution was closely linked with the colonial structure in Tanzania.

Historically there have been three occasions when the followers of Christianity and Islam came into conflict against each other in Tanzania.[3] Christianity was first brought to Tanzania in the 16th century by the Portuguese. By then Islam was already established along the coast. The Portuguese were outright hostile to Islam and believed they were carrying on a "crusade" against the Muslim coastal city states of Kilwa and Zanzibar. Later, in the 19th century, the followers of Christianity and Islam clashed again when the Muslims fought first

2

against the imposition of German colonial rule and later against British rule. From the mid-1980s and throughout the 1990s there was an upsurge of both Christian and Islamic "fundamentalism" which was characterized by hostile public lectures known as *mihadhara* on both sides. This study focuses mainly on the second and third encounters.[4]

German East Africa was a large compact block of land in eastern Africa lying between the Great Lakes - Lake Victoria, Lake Tanganyika, and Lake Nyasa - and the Indian Ocean. It included the territory then known as Rwanda-Urundi. The acquisition of German East Africa was, of course, the result of the European scramble for Africa. As it was, the rules of the game laid down by the Berlin Conference of 1884/85 required that any colonial declaration of intent had to be supported by proof of signed treaties with local native authorities. It was for this purpose that toward the end of 1884 Dr. Carl Peters acquired, obviously by deception, signed treaties with the chiefs of Usagara, Ungulu, Uzigua and Ukami which were used as "proof" of German colonial claims. On 3 March 1885, the official gazette in Berlin revealed that an imperial charter had just been granted to a "German colonization company" to establish a "protectorate" in East Africa (Pakenham, 1991: 284). The colonisation company was the brainchild of none other than Dr. Carl Peters himself.

After World War I the territory of Rwanda-Urundi was taken over by Belgium and split into Rwanda and Burundi. The rest of German East Africa was renamed Tanganyika when the British took over its administration in 1919. Tanganyika Territory extended from 1°S to approximately 11°S and from 29°E to 45°E, and was about 740 miles long and 760 miles broad, with a coastline of about 550 miles. Offshore were the islands of Mafia to the southeast, and Zanzibar and Pemba. The latter two islands became a British "protectorate" in 1890 although its administration was carried on by the descendants of Seyyid Said, the Omani founder of the Zanzibar Sultanate.

The fact that German East Africa became a contending field between two of the monotheistic religions, Islam and Christianity, is not surprising. Despite some basic commonalities, the two faiths differ and disagree on matters of theologies, the essence of their Scriptures as well as the roles of their respective Prophets. Thus, a good portion of the study is devoted to discussing the religious disputes between

3

Christians and Muslims ranging from the authenticity of the Bible to the divinity of Jesus. These issues are of direct interest to students of religion and theology.

Students of Tanzania politics will find this study of interest because of the issues which it raises; one of which is the role of religion as a political force in Tanzania. The introduction of Islam and Christianity in Tanzania created one more cleavage in the fabric of Tanzanian society.[5] The Muslim riots of the last decade of the 20th century were indicative of the greater propensity of religion, more than ethnocentrism and racism, to encourage differences and conflict in Tanzanian society. Islamic revival and radicalism during the 1990s were partly due to increased contact (via the Internet) and growing opportunities for travel and study in Saudi Arabia and other countries of the Middle East. Muslim youth groups such as Ansar Sunna were organised by students attending universities in Saudi Arabia. Unlike their elders they subscribed to orthodox Islam and criticized practices such as maulidi celebrations, saint veneration and attempts to solve problems by theurgical means as un-Islamic (Chande, 1998: 217). They also sought to give voice to Muslim grievances against the state in new ways. The question which students of Tanzania politics may need to answer is what political role mosques and sheikhs will play in the twenty-first century as Muslims endeavour to mobilize along religious lines (Mohammed, 2002).

The title of this book is derived from the symbols of the two faiths, the cross and the crescent, which in themselves say something about differences between Christianity and Islam(Chapman, 1995: 7). On the one hand, for Christians the cross is a sign evoking a historical event basic to the history of salvation (Eliade, 1987: 161). As a symbol it represents the Crucification of Jesus who, by his death, redeemed mankind from the Original Sin.[6] Muslims, however, dispute the fact that the Crucification actually took place and do not believe God would have let Jesus die such a shameful death.

On the other, the crescent and star is the symbol of Islam. The moon plays a central role in Islam. Muslims follow a lunar calendar whose names are in Arabic and have specific meaning and significance. Thus the ninth month is known as Ramadhan, a month in which the Qur'an was first revealed and a month when Muslims are supposed to fast, starting at the first sighting of the new moon. Moreover, since a new moon is increasing, the crescent has come to symbolise Islam as a faith that is ever growing in strength. It is also said that when the Prophet Muhammad first arrived in Medina he was welcomed with a *kasida* likening him to a moon that had come to shed light to a darkened world.[7]

However, the crescent was also at one time the symbol of the eastern half of the Holy Roman Empire with Constantinople (Istanbul) as its capital.[8] When the Turkish Muslims conquered Constantinople in AD 1453 (and renamed it Istanbul) they also took over the crescent and used it as a Turkish symbol. According to Mallouhi, it was only in the nineteenth century that the crescent, usually together with a star, came to be regarded as the emblem of the Islamic faith (Mallouhi, 2000: 7).

Although Christians and Muslims in German East Africa held their religious beliefs in high esteem, they appear to have been contemptuous of anything that symbolised African traditional religious beliefs.[9] In fact, neither of the proponents of the two faiths acknowledged that Africans had anything resembling a religion.[10] Yet, as Mazrui aptly notes, "Long before the religion of the crescent or the religion of the cross arrived on the African continent, Africa was at worship, its sons and daughters were at prayer" (Mazrui, 1985: 838). Indeed, most if not all African societies had some idea of a Supreme Being to whom they attributed the power of creation as reflected in various African creation myths. However, African creation myths differ from the Christian or Islamic myths in their placement of God vis-a-vis human beings. Abraham Akrong explains the difference as follows:

> In the African creation myth, there is no assumed gulf between God and human beings on account of rebellion and disobedience. Therefore human beings do not stand before God in need of reconciliation as the only condition for salvation. Rather for Africans, the presence of God as the greatest ancestor of the human race, should be acknowledged and celebrated. Hence the acknowledgement [sic] of God as the pre-eminent supreme being invoked before any being in all libation prayers. Salvation for African traditional theology is therefore not a return to an idyllic pristine past or participating in the coming of a perfect world but a "this-worldly" celebration of the presence of God and all the relationships that nurture, protect and sustain life (Akrong, 1999: 132).

Whereas missionary disregard for African traditional religious beliefs reflected their European ethnocentric prejudices, their theological training did not equip them with knowledge for a better understanding of the very societies that they intended to convert. Even when they endeavored to study African cultures, "It was as if they were studying non-Christian cultures only to condemn them" (Shorter, 1988: 165). Consequently, mere condemnation of African beliefs would not suffice to convince people such as the Gogo to convert to either Christianity or Islam. As this aspect will be discussed more fully in chapter five, I need not enlarge on it here further than to say that missionary explanations of the Scriptures did not appear to make sense because the Gogo's cosmological view was very different from that of the missionaries.

Besides their ignorance of traditional religious beliefs most missionaries were also ignorant of Islam which they were supposed to combat. Whatever early missionaries said about Islam appear to have been influenced by their academic background and insufficient training. Most CMS missionaries to central Tanzania and elsewhere were not university graduates. The CMS training college at Islington which opened in 1825 was intended to prepare for Christian service men to whom the universities were practically closed because they did not meet university standards (Hodge, 1971-1972: 82). Those accepted at Islington could pursue either a short course of three or four terms (at the end of which the candidate graduated and was sent out as a lay missionary) or a three-year course.[11] By 1900 44 students had gone out as missionaries after attending the short course. Of these, 12 went to West Africa and 11went to East Africa.

Writing in 1900 about the kind of candidate that the short course was tailored for, the Principal of the Islington College noted that it was meant for "a man of elementary education, who takes ill to Latin and Greek, and whose mind moves too slowly at first for him ever to become a nimble logician or to adequately grasp philosophical arguments; but he must be a man of genuine force of character ..."[12] The three-year course, though described as "heavily loaded," appear to have been equivalent to a first year of study at university level (Hodges, 1971-1972: 88).[13]

Those graduating after the three-year course were ordained in London while those from the short course were not ordained in London but could be ordained in the field after passing the second language examination (Hodges, 1971-1972: 87).

The men trained for Holy Orders at Islington in the 1890s and early 1900s were not given much exposure to the beliefs of those whom they were to convert to Christianity. There is mention in the 1890s reports of "occasional short courses of a few lectures on the religions of the Near and Far East and India." However, as Hodges notes, such lectures do not appear to have occupied a very prominent place on the timetable at Islington, and there does not seem to have been any attempt to look at these religions in the context of the societies among whom they flourished (Hodges, 1971-1972: 91). Whatever was taught at Islington about Islam would not have departed from the then current popular view of Islam, which it was primarily the work of the devil and Muhammad was a "false prophet."

Chapter two looks at the confrontation between Christianity and Islam along the coast in German East Africa. The presence of Islam along the coast preceded that of Christianity by about twelve centuries. The exact date when Islam was introduced remains unknown. Some written sources suggest that the first Muslim expedition to the East African coast was sent there by the Ummayad Caliph Abd al-Malik ibn Marwan (685 - 705CE), under the leadership of the amir Musa al Khathami. It was followed in /66/7CE by a second expedition led by Yahya ibn Umar al-Anazi, an officer of the Abbasid Caliph al-Mansur (Cerulli, 1969: 208). These early expeditions were then followed by Muslim immigrants who established a chain of settlements from the gulf of Eden all the way down to Kilwa.

However, some local oral traditions suggest that Islam may have arrived much earlier when the Prophet Muhammad was still alive. According to one legend, the earliest immigrants from the Arabian Peninsula were members of the Madian tribe who had converted to Islam soon after Muhammad arrived in Medina. It is said that the Madians stayed only for a short time in the outskirts of Medina before they started migrating to East Africa (Tewa manuscript, nd, 7). The Madians are credited with establishing the earliest settlements such as Mogadishu, Shungwaya, Kilwa and Sofala. Needless to say, these early coastal settlements later became seaports and independent city-states. In the fifteenth century they were overrun by the Portuguese who were the first Christians to reach East Africa.

The Portuguese reached the East African coast in 1498. They were, however, more interested in plunder than in the propagation of

Christianity. In any case, after the Portuguese interlude there was no rival to Islam until the arrival of the first missionary at Zanzibar in 1844. Yet, despite the centuries of unrivaled opportunity for spreading Islam among the people of German East Africa Muslim influence remained mainly confined to the coastal areas. In the interior of German East Africa pockets of Islamic influence existed only where Arab and Swahili traders had settled, and along the caravan routes.

Therefore, the arrival of missionaries and their spread into the interior brought them face to face with Islam in places where Islam was already established as well as in new frontiers where Muslim traders were increasingly venturing. More specifically, Arab presence in the interior had paved the way for European travellers including missionaries. In 1888 the missionary A. M. Mackay acknowledged how Arab presence indirectly facilitated the spreading of the Gospel. He said:

> "...I feel safe to say, that generally speaking, wherever the European traveller in East Africa has ventured to penetrate regions hitherto unvisited by the Arab, he has found it impossible to *purchase* the right of passage, and has had to either fight his way or take refuge in flight ... Where the Arab has traded (I mean peacefully) the missionary may go any day; where the Arab has not ventured, the missionary must exercise the greatest caution in trying to go." (CMS G3 A5 O, 1888, no. 372, a memo by A. M. Mackay).

As we will see later, the establishment of German rule was, in turn, to facilitate the spread of Islam where Arabs had never ventured before!

Hostility between Muslim *ulama* and missionaries was inevitable especially when the *ulama* resorted to poetic propaganda to thwart Christian proselytisation. The poetry of the time presented the confrontation between Christianity and Islam as a conflict of cultures and civilizations. Both Islam and the Swahili culture it had given rise to were extolled as the best. However, as Lyndon Harries notes the battle between Western and Eastern civilization in East Africa was liable to be won by the West because Islam had nothing to offer Africans (Harries, 1954: 28).

To the contrary, in West and Central Africa the "civilizing" impact of Islam was exalted by the likes of Edward W. Blyden and Winwood Reade. For Winwood Reade the redeeming value of Islam accounted for the contrast between Muslim and "pagan" Africans in the Casamanche region of West Africa. He writes,

> Let us judge things by their results ... The African pagans and the African Mohammedans may be seen side by side on the same river - the Casamanche. The first are drunkards, gamblers, swine; as diseased in body as debased in mind. The later are practical Christians. They are sober; truthful; constant in their devotions; strictly honest. They treat kindly those who are below them; they do their duty to their neighbours (Quoted by Plessis, 1921: 5).

Likewise, in comparing the influence of Islam and Christianity on the African, Blyden discerned a more liberating influence on the part of Islam:

> Wherever the Negro is found in Christian lands, his leading trait is not docility ...but servility ...Individuals here and there may be found of extraordinary intelligence, enterprise, and energy, but there is no Christian community of Negroes anywhere which is self-reliant and independent...On the other hand, there are numerous Negro Mohammedan communities and states in Africa which are self-reliant, productive, independent, and dominant, supporting, without the countenance or patronage of the parent country, Arabia, whence they derived them [sic], their political, literary, and ecclesiastical institutions (Blyden, 1994: 12).

Blyden attributed the liberating influence of Islam to the absence of countenance or patronage from Arabia. He notes how on their own African Muslims erected mosques, kept up their religious services, and even supported itinerant clerics without financial support from Mecca. On the other hand, Blyden attributed the docility of African Christians to their dependence for financial support from Europe.

Reade and Blyden belonged to a larger literary camp known during the nineteenth century as the Islamicists. According to Thomas Prasch, "The Islamicist argument was rooted in extreme racism and, despite its approach to cultural relativism, remained firmly ethnocentric: Islam was an acceptable religion for Africa because both Islam and Africans were seen as lower forms, incapable of attaining the apex of Western civilization" (Prasch, 1989: 73). This Islamicist position was initially advanced by the Rev. Isaac Taylor in a sermon he gave in 1887. In his sermon, Rev. Taylor suggested that given the absence of civilized virtues in much of Africa Islam was better suited to the continent than Christianity. Many missionaries, who saw their role being challenged, denied that Islam could make any contributions.

In order to contextualise early Christian missionary hostility toward Islam it is necessary to understand the religious doctrine which informed the attitudes of European missionaries who went to East Africa at the turn of the twentieth century. Since the sources that inform much of this study are mainly Protestant, it is also necessary to know the historical context of the Protestant missionary enterprise.

The Protestant missionary enterprise at the turn of the twentieth century was the product of the Evangelical Movement whose language and substance of its preaching were naturally those of an orthodox evangelical doctrine (Addison, 1966: 289). What Addison describes as "The (Protestant) Plan of Redemption" or "The Economy of Salvation" is worth quoting *in extenso*:

> God created Adam in a state of innocense, but Adam sinned and fell. This Original Sin infected all his descendants, who therefore lay under the wrath of God. Only repentance and forgiveness could save them from everlasting punishment. To make this possible, God sent His only Son, Jesus Christ, who suffered on the cross the penalty due to human sin and thereby redeemed us through His blood. Vindicated and exalted through His Resurrection and Ascension, He now reigns as Lord and will one day return to earth as the Judge of all mankind at the General Resurrection. Meanwhile all men are steeped in sin and in dire need of pardon. This they can obtain by repentant acceptance of Christ the Saviour, through perfect faith in His redeeming power and in the promises of God. Those who so receive Him will be sanctified by His Holy Spirit and will receive the reward of heaven. Those who persist in rejecting Him will go to hell (Addison, 1966: 289).

Such was the interpretation of the Gospel which gave a strong emphasis on dogmas that were the opposites of Islamic fundamentals and easily antagonized Muslims (Addison, 1966: 290). Yet, as we will see in chapter three the introduction of Christianity in Dar es Salaam very much depended on the hospitality and goodwill of local Muslims.

Islam, of course, neither subscribes to the idea of Original Sin nor does it accept the concept of redemption through a Savior. The Deity of Jesus continues to be the greatest factor driving Christianity and Islam apart. Gilchrist aptly notes that: "What to Christians is the foundation of their belief - that Jesus is God's own Son who alone could redeem (them) from (their) sins and take (them) *into* heaven - is to the Muslims one of the greatest expressions of unbelief and the

one which, more than any other, is likely to keep them *out* of heaven ...
To Muhammad the belief in Jesus as the Son of God appeared to be
parallel to the pagan Arab belief that many of their idols, such as Al-
Lat, al-Uzza and Manat, were the 'daughters of Allah.' Idolatry, *per se*,
was to the Prophet of Islam an act of blasphemy, ascribing as it did
partners to Allah which was unthinkable and an affront to the very
glory of his being" (Gilchrist, 2002: 81-82).

Moreover, although Islam recognizes Jesus as a prophet it does
not subscribe to the idea that he was crucified and then resurrected.
However, Islam accepts that Jesus ascended to Heaven. As for who
gets to go to heaven Islam teaches that the prerogative is God's alone.
Despite these theological differences Christianity and Islam have one
thing in common namely the belief and recognition of the
Omnipresence of Almighty God. These commonalities and differences
are further explored in Chapter Four.

Besides their theological differences, Christianity and Islam also
differed in their initial modes of propagation in German East Africa.
From the beginning Christianity was propagated by missionaries while
Islam was not. Initially, however, early missionaries avoided open
confrontation with Islam. Later, the advent of colonial rule encouraged
Christian missionaries in German East Africa to adopt a more
confrontational attitude vis-a-vis Islam. This legacy of confrontation
and hostility persisted well into the post colonial period as witnessed
by the religious *mihadhara* which culminated in the Mwembechai riots
and killings of Muslims in 1998. This is, therefore, a historical study
of relations between Christianity and Islam in Tanzania whose
intention is to explain the underlying causes of the latent as well as
open hostility between the propagators of Christian and Islamic faiths
from the 1890s to the end of the twentieth century.

In his book titled *Mwembechai Killings* Hamza Njozi suggests
that the killings were the culmination of some conspiracy between
the Church and the Government; a twin alliance whose objective has
always been to marginalise and oppress Muslims in Tanzania (Njozi,
2000). Njozi suggests that at independence in 1961 Julius Nyerere
supposedly fashioned Tanganyika's doctrines and ideals according to
the teachings of his Catholic Church with the sole purpose of
marginalizing Islam.

According to Njozi, Nyerere was responding to the concerns

of the Christian clergy that "Islam was growing very fast in Tanzania, and that the growth of Islam would greatly weaken Christianity" (Njozi, 2000: 2- 4).

Although Njozi identifies the years between 1959 and 1966 to be the formative period when Christian political machinations against Muslims began, this study suggests that neither was this the first time that Christian missionaries in Tanzania were worried about losing out to Islam nor was it the first time that Christian missionaries received Government support in their struggle against Islam. Njozi appears to be unaware of the historical convergence of the interests of missionaries and the colonial government whose roots go back to the nineteenth century. Jane Smith succinctly notes that:

> The beginnings of Western colonisation of the rest of the world linked up with the urge to bring Christianity as a part of the outreach effort, and many examples can be given of the close relationship, and shared outlook, between missionaries and colonial authorities. The tasks of civilizing and evangelizing were seen as mutually supportive ...(Smith, 1998: 358).

Such was the case in German East Africa. Needless to say, the arrival of missionaries coincided with the advent of European colonialism. Consequently, missionaries tended to be identified with or even mistaken for imperial agents. Thus, when the coastal peoples rose up in resistance against German rule the targets of their anger and violence included missionaries and mission stations. However, later on colonial administrations provided an enabling environment for the growth of Christianity. By the early 1900s German authorities were so seriously concerned about the growth and vitality of Islam that they exhorted Christian missionaries to increase their efforts to combat its expansion and influence.

The genesis of this study was a heated dialogue which I had with Muslim members of an Internet group known as TANZANET following the riots at the Mwembechai Mosque on 13 February, 1998. It was reported after the riots that Muslims had spilt into the streets chanting "Takbir" and "Allah Akbar, Haiya al la Jihad." I floated a query on TANZANET asking whether the said Muslims were calling for a *jihad*. I wanted to know if their intention was to further the spread of Islam in Tanzania by the sword. I was immediately accused of unnecessarily alarming TANZANET members. An ardent Muslim member categorically objected to the idea of Islam being spread by the use of force. She said, "in Islam there is NO compulsion in religion." She said that the use of force to spread the Islamic faith was a myth and those who believe in such a myth are simply victims of malicious stories about the readiness of Muslims to kill those whom they cannot convert.

Jihad, it was also argued, can be to strive, endeavor to fight and struggle, which can be armed or unarmed. One contributor referred to the Qur'an chapter 9, verse 20[14] to drive home his point about the nature of jihads. He gave a translation of the verse by Abdullah Yusuf Ali to the effect that jihad may require fighting in Allah's cause in earnest and ceaseless activity, involving the sacrifice (if need be) of life, person, or property, in the service of Allah. Another Muslim TANZANET member wrote: *"Ama kuhusu Waislamu wa Mwembechai kutaka kuwasilimisha wote wasiokuwa Waislamu hilo sina habari nalo na sidhani kama ni jambo wenye uwezo nalo. Maana mtu hawi Mwislamu ila kwa kuamini imani ya Kiislamu. Na imani iko moyoni kiasi kwamba hakuna namna ya kumlazimisha mtu (kwa nguvu) kuwa nayo."*[15] The contributor also gave Abdallah Yusuf Ali's rendition of the meaningless use of force. Supposedly compulsion is incompatible with Islam which depends upon faith and will, and without faith and will Islam would be meaningless.

The above explanations of jihads and whether or not force can or cannot be used for conversions are obviously contradictory. I was at a loss as to which one to believe. I did not know at the time, not having read much of the Qur'an, that the verses which forbid the use of force were actually revealed earlier and were abrogated by verses that sanction the use of force, which were revealed later! Thus, Chapter 2: 256 which was revealed earlier at Medina says: "There is no compulsion in religion. The right direction is henceforth distinct from error. And he who rejecteth false deities and believeth in Allah hath grasped a firm handhold which will never break. Allah is Hearer, Knower."[16] But chapter 9 verses 5 and 20 which were revealed later at Medina abrogate the earlier restriction on the use of force. Chapter 9 verse 5 reads:

> "Then, when the sacred months have passed, slay the idolaters wherever ye find them, and take them (captive), and besiege them, and prepare for them each ambush. But if they repent and establish

worship and pay the poor-due, then leave their way free. Lo! Allah is Forgiving, and Merciful."

Chapter 9 verse 20, as we have already noted, calls for ceaseless activity which may involve sacrifice (if need be) of life, person, or property in the name of Allah. Other cases of abrogating and abrogated verses are dealt with in detail in chapter four which deals with early Christian polemic against Islam.[17]

However, at this juncture it will suffice to note why the question of abrogation has persisted and continues to be a vexing problem in Qur'anic studies. Abrogation is the English translation of the Arabic term *naskh*. According to Amin M. Sallam al-Manasyeh al-Btoush, the term *naskh* has a wider meaning than what is meant by "abrogation" in English (al-Btoush, 1994: 20). Ibn Kathir suggests that as used in Chapter 2 verse 106, it was intended as a refutation of Jewish criticism regarding the changes in the rituals of the Muslims (Quoted by Btoush, 1994: 74). Then there are those who interpret the use of *naskh* in Chapter 2 verse106 to refer to the abrogation of verses within the Qur'an itself. Thus according to Ash-Shafi'i, whatever Allah abrogated in the Qur'an, He did so "to make (things) lighter and more comfortable ... (Quoted by Semaan, 1961: 37).

Regardless of the different interpretations of *naskh*, Muslim scholars concur that the source of the abrogating verses is God Himself. In Chapter 10 verse 15 we read: "And when Our clear revelations are recited unto them, they who look not for the meeting with Us say: Bring a Lecture other than this, or change it. Say (O Muhammad): It is not for me to change it of my own accord. I only follow that which is inspired in me. Lo! If I disobey my Lord I fear the retribution of an awful Day." Their critics disagree, however. They raise a number of questions of which the following are just examples: Could God have given Muhammad difficult obligations without realizing the burden He was imposing on His believers? Since He is all knowing why did He not give the abrogating verses to start with? Did God make mistakes in some of His revelations which He later decided to correct?

According to Ash-Shafi'i, each revelation was right during its time: "So, those who (were Muslims) at the time such things were obligatory, showed their obedience both by observing them and by disregarding them whereas, those who were not (converted to Islam) when such things were obligatory, show their obedience by following the obligatory duty which abrogates the former" (Quoted by Semaan, 1961: 54). If each revelation was right during its time the removal, adjustment or revision of the abrogated verses, therefore, suggests that they had served and outlived their original intended purposes. In other words, the abrogating verses were more in accord with the changed circumstances of Islam during the span of Muhammad's life.

Evidently, the verses that permit the use of force, compulsion, and violence in the conversion of unbelievers were revealed at a time when circumstances required the use of force. Hitherto, freedom of choice (*ismah*) and personal responsibilities for such choice were the norms (An-Na'im: 1986: 204).[18] Punishment for disbelief was left to God (Chapter 2 verses 39, 89-90). Afterwards, because of the need to consolidate the unity of the newly created Muslim *umma* and the fact that "the Arabs were not mature enough to appreciate and live in accordance with those superior principles, the offer of freedom and responsibility was withdrawn" (An-Na'im: 1986: 204). Compulsion (*ikrah*) and guardianship was imposed (ibid., 204) and conversion from Islam forbidden (Chapter 4 verse 89). The recompense of those who fought against Allah and His Messenger was slaughter, Crucification, banishment, or the loss of their hands and feet *(Chapter 5 verse 33)*. In short, as Rodinson puts it:

> In Medina the preaching of supreme truths concerning divinity, the world and man, the call to the spiritual reform of the individual and the teaching of the history of divine intervention in the lives of men became less paramount. What was needed above all was to mobilise men's energies for immediate action, to denounce the enemy, reassure the armies of the faithful, justify the decisions taken, brand traitors and irresolute people for what they were, and give the community of the Faithful some rules by which to live . . ." (Rodinson, 1971: 217).

Moreover, in Mecca the unbelievers caused a powerless Muhammad to simply lament for their unbelief. Thus, in Chapter 23 verse 39 (which was revealed in Mecca) it is written: "He (Muhammad) said: My Lord! Help me because they deny me." However, in Medina after he had become powerful, his conduct toward the unbelievers changed. Several revelations told him to be harsh in his treatment of those who opposed him (Welch, 1999: 159). In Chapter 9 verse 73 (revealed in Medina) we read: "O Prophet! Strive against the disbelievers and the hypocrites! Be harsh with them. Their ultimate abode is hell, a hapless journey's end." Other Qur'anic verses establishing *the jihad*, holy war to spread the faith, and discrimination against non-Muslims and women were revealed later in Medina[19] (An-Na'im: 1986: 204).

The importance of abrogating and abrogated verses in the Qur'an is that the message of the Qur'an is not one and the same for all times. According to Mahmoud Muhammad Taha the Qur'an contains two messages (Taha, 1987), one of freedom and tolerance and another of compulsion and intolerance. Taha notes that Islam was first offered in tolerant and egalitarian terms in Mecca, where the Prophet preached equality and individual responsibility between all men and women without distinction on grounds of race, sex, or social origin.[20] But because that message was rejected in practice, and the Prophet and his followers were persecuted and forced to emigrate to Medina, the verses which called for restraint were later abrogated and replaced by those which called for and justified the use of force. However, Taha suggests that the abrogation or repeal of Chapter 2 verse 256 and other similar verses was temporary rather than final and conclusive[21] (Taha, 1987: 21).

The need to use compulsion was especially felt shortly after the death of Muhammad in 632. Following his death there was a widespread defection from Islam as well as the embryonic Islamic state with its center at Medina. It is interesting to note that the defectors found it necessary to attack the religious basis of the Islamic state, "not in the name of Christianity or any existing religion, but in the name of self-constituted Arab prophets" (Watt, 1961:226). Abu Bakr, Muhammad's father-in-law and successor, embarked on a number of military campaigns, known as the *riddah* wars, to stamp out apostasy and to re-enforce Islam. In 634, after two years of campaigning, Abu Bakr and the Muslims of Medina were able to bring the entire Arabian peninsula under Islamic influence (Esposito, 1999: 11). Further conquests were undertaken by Abu Bakr's immediate successors namely Caliphs Umar ibn-al-Khattab (r. 634-44) and Uthman ibn-Affan (r. 644-56).

Therefore, when Muslims today disavow the use of compulsion to convert nonbelievers to Islam they do so on the basis of Chapter 2 verse 256 and other verses which are known to have been abrogated by later verses which permitted the use of force. Likewise, the events of

11 September 2001 prompted many Muslims to disavow violence in an effort to repair what they considered the damaged image of Islam. Islam, they correctly said, means peace. What they did not say was that the peace of Islam, within the concept of *Dar al-Islam* (the land of belief), applies only within the borders of Islam; those outside it (i.e., those living in *dar al-kafr* or land of unbelief) are exempt from the peace (Nafziger and Watson, 2003).

However, the use of force in the name of religion has not been the preserve of Muslims alone. Christianity too has had its *jihads* which are famously known as "Crusades." During the Medieval Ages Christian armies marched against the Muslims and the Jews behind banners of the Cross.[22] As was the case with Islamic *jihads*, the Christian crusaders killed and were prepared to die for a cause they considered to be greater than the worth of a human life (Shorter, 1985: 53). Christian leaders such as Pope Leo IV (847-855 AD) made promises of heavenly reward for those who died in battle against the Muslims (Partner, 1998: 64). Pope John VIII, the successor of Leo, made similar promises and referred to those who died fighting the Muslims as "martyrs" (ibid., 65). This medieval sense of sacrifice in the name of religion was very much a part of the missionary endeavor in central Tanganyika where early missionaries were subject to harsh living conditions and many "sacrificed" their lives.

Chapter Five deals with the introduction of Christianity in central Tanganyika. In this region Islam had already taken roots especially in areas along the caravan routes. It was in these and other areas that missionaries endeavored to find ways of "defeating" Islam. As we will see, the arrival of the railroad further facilitated the spread of both faiths in the region and therefore intensified the competition for converts. What eventually gave the missionaries an edge over their perceived adversaries was the support of the German administration and a joint strategy especially between the Protestant denominations to win converts. Moreover, through the provision of education missionaries were able to attract potential converts which excluded a majority of Muslims who were suspicious of the proselyting role of mission schools. This was the genesis of the inequality between Muslims and Christians in accessing colonial education.

In Chapter Six we look at the experience of Christians and Muslims under European colonial rule. The chapter examines the role of British colonial education in the marginalisation of Muslims especially in salaried employment. In the early colonial times before World War I Muslims were the only literate people in the country and so they were able to gain posts in the civil service. In this period the Germans had introduced public schools in Tanga and Dar es Salaam which attracted mostly Muslim students. However, when the British took over the provision of education was entrusted to voluntary agencies most of which were run by Christian missionaries. Muslims were suspicious of missionary-run schools and most of them opted not to send their children there. Consequently, as a result of lack of education very few Muslims found their way into the colonial civil service.

Chapter Seven examines the interplay of religion and politics after independence. The chapter highlights Muslim relations and grievances against the post colonial state in Tanzania. The 1998 Mwembechai Mosque riots and the resulting killings of Muslims by the police are said to have been the culminations of a long history of government disregard of Muslim interests. The background to the riots was the new phenomenon of *mihadhara* (religious public rallies) in the propagation of Islam. Hitherto, I had read and believed that Islam in Tanzania had spread peacefully by way of the good example of the Muslims' way of life. People saw, liked, envied, and wanted to emulate the Muslims. I asked myself, what was the essence of this new phenomenon of public *mihadhara* in the name of Islam?

Chapter Eight deals with two controversies, namely the consumption of pork and the veiling of women. There is no evidence that the pig was ever domesticated in Tanzania before the arrival of Europeans. Domestic pigs were first introduced along the coast by the Portuguese in the sixteenth century. Later on missionaries kept pigs as a source of meat. The introduction of domesticated pigs and the consumption of pork does not appear to have been a source of conflict between Muslims and Christians before the 1990s. However, in 1993 the controversy over the status of pigs and the consumption of pork led to the demolition of pork butcheries by Muslims in Dar es Salaam. It is suggested that the causes of Muslim fury had more to do with "Islamic revivalism" than with health issues. Pigs were associated with Christians. Killing them or destroying butcheries where pork was sold was a symbolic statement against Christianity. Likewise, prior to the 1990s the veiling of Muslim women was not a matter of concern. The demand for female students to wear the *hijab* is examined and placed in historical context.

Chapter Nine focuses on the theological issues that generated misunderstandings and hostility between Christians and Muslims towards the end of the twentieth century. The *mihadhara* of the 1990s seemed to give a special urgency to the movement of Islamic revival in Tanzania insofar as they espoused the comparative disadvantage of Muslims in the job market and gave purposes to Muslim radicalization. They were, in other words, a reaction to the Muslim perceived predicament of marginality. However, the *mihadhara* appear to have had a twofold purpose: to demand equality in the job market and to seek the expansion of Islam by weakening Christian belief. But why did the *mihadhara* preachers resort to the idea of organizing open air rallies at this time? Equally important, why did they at this particular time seek to popularise and seek converts for Islam by publicly discrediting Christianity?

Explored also in chapter nine are the alleged Muslim blasphemies against Christianity. The Mwembechai riots occurred soon after Father Camillius Lwambano of Mburahati broadcast his protest to the Government about Muslim *kashfa* or blasphemies against Christianity. One alleged blasphemy was that Muslim preachers were publicly denigrating Jesus and saying that he is not the Son of God. According to Njozi, Father Lwambano's "emotionally-charged claims," which were broadcast over Radio Tumaini (owned by the Roman Catholic Church), were not only baseless but led to the catastrophic events of 13 February, 1998. It is alleged that Father Lwambano's broadcast forced the government to take severe measures against the alleged extremist Muslim preachers (Njozi, 2000: 32).

The concluding chapter highlights the main causes of hostility and misunderstanding between Christians and Muslims in Tanzania from the end of the nineteenth century to the end of the twentieth century. The main causes have been Christian-Muslim subversion of each other's faith; the exclusivity of both faiths that the other religion is not the way of salvation; and their different conceptions of God and of the way in which to serve Him.[23] Moreover, tension between Christians and Muslims was exacerbated by politics. One of the complaints by Muslims was that the Government, which they alleged was Christian-dominated, treated them as second class citizens. It is suggested that the solution to religious enmity between Christians and Muslims in Tanzania is unqualified religious freedom and tolerance. Tanzanians must also seriously address Muslim complaints about religious discrimination in the public sector.

CHAPTER TWO

ISLAM VS. CHRISTIANITY ALONG THE COAST BEFORE WWI

The presence of Arabs and other people of Middle Eastern descent along the East African coast has been dated from about the eighth century of the common era. These immigrants were responsible for the introduction of Islam in the various city-states which they established as centers of trade along the coast. In the sixteenth and seventeenth centuries the Portuguese attempted to destroy the Muslim city-states of Kilwa, Mombasa, Lamu, and Pate, whose sheikhs were put to death and their peoples heavily plundered "just because they dared to defend their faith and the freedom of their native soil" (Harries, 1954: 23). By the end of the seventeenth century the East African Muslims succeeded, with the help of the Oman ruler Ahmed bin Said, to drive the Portuguese from the whole coast north of Mozambique.

Omani influence in East Africa was later solidified by the transfer of Seyyid Said's capital from Muscat to Zanzibar in 1842. With that transfer began a new period in East African history that was dominated by the dynamics of the Zanzibar Sultanate. Seyyid Said laid claim to an enormous territory stretching for some 600 miles from what is today Somalia to Mozambique. His claim was, however, not effectively enforced due to inbuilt weaknesses in his government structure. The Rev. Krapf offers us a very valuable description of the nature of Seyyid Said's government. According to Rev. Krapf, Seyyid Said's navy was made of about twenty modern large and small vessels of war. Although they were a sight of imposing nature they were of little use because the Sultan's sailors did not know how to manage them (CMS, G 3 A 5/O/ 25, Krapf, "Further description of Zanzibar").

The Sultan's land forces stationed at Zanzibar were less impressive than his navy. The Sultan had a body guard of only fifty men. It appears that Seyyid Said could raise a small force from his Arab subjects who expected to be paid for their services. His garrisons at various places along the coast were manned by "a rabble of Arab Beduins and Beloodjees, who went in the Imam's service, in quest of money or from motives of rapine and sacking, for which the Sooahele

[sic] coast offers frequent opportunities" (Krapf, CMS G 3 A 5/O/ 25). Rev. Krapf notes that the discipline and military skills of the Arab and Baluchi soldiers stood at the lowest ebb, and did not allow the Sultan to conquer the countries situated a few miles from the seashore.[24] Their pay was scanty and proportioned to their miserable accomplishments. Equally denied of substantive pay were the various governors stationed at various coastal towns and settlements. The first rate governors of some places received only ten dollars per month as their wages. Since Seyyid Said could not pay his officials he left them to their own devices, as long as they kept things quiet.

According to Rev. Krapf, Seyyid Said was not disposed to spend money "for pursuits calculated to civilize his subjects and introduce a better system of government throughout." Apparently the Arab nobility placed no demands for such expenditure as long as he acted upon the Islamic principles (Krapf, CMS G 3 A 5/O/25). Despite Seyyid Said's laissez faire political system, Arab and Islamic influences held sway all along the East African coast. These influences were the result of developments that occurred following the ousting of the Portuguese from East Africa.

Harries notes that during the eighteenth century following the departure of the Portuguese there was a great resurgence of Islam throughout the East African coast:

> A literary revival reflected the moods of the times. A spate of songs, poems, romances and epics marked the spirit of liberation. Compositions like Seyyid Abdallah's *Al-Inkshafi* (The Soul's Awakening) were being read in the mosques throughout the coast. The minstrels' journeys were revived, at which the people heard the latest compositions. Epics, known as *tendi* or *tenzi*, literally 'acts', or as we say, plays, became popular; *among them were plays on the life of Christ, and the life of Job*, as well as upon the life and death of Muhammad, and similar religious themes written by Muslims for Muslims" (emphasis added) (Harries, 1954: 24).

If indeed Muslims wrote plays on the life of Christ, this was not necessarily indicative of Christian influences in their lives. Jesus, as many Muslims would readily point out, is a revered prophet known to them as *Nabii* Isa. However, this is not to deny some influences which may have resulted from contact with British naval reconnaissance vessels and American traders on the East African coast (von Sicard, 1978: 55). According to von Sicard, in the 1840s Captain W. F. W. Owen and R. P. Waters, the first American consul in Zanzibar, distributed Arabic translations of the Bible and the New Testament Arab elites. The recipients included the Governor of Lamu, Seyyid Seif bin Hemed, and the Governor of Pemba as well as many ordinary Muslims.

The first missionary to arrive in Zanzibar after the Portuguese had left was Rev. Johan Ludwig Krapf who was accompanied by his wife. When the Krapfs arrived in Zanzibar in 1844 they were cordially received by His Highness the Imam Sultan Seyyid Said (CMS C A 5/O/16/1, Krapf to Lieder, dated 13 February, 1844). We have already noted Rev. Krapf's observations about the nature of Seyyid Said's government. As a missionary he was impressed by the sway of Islam in Zanzibar itself. "The whole island of Zanzibar,' he noted, `has adopted the Mohammedan tenets, but the foreigners – Banians and white people – are not disturbed in their persuasions" (Krapf, CMS C A 5/O/16/25). Apparently Seyyid Said's administration was based on the Islamic *Sharia* legal code. According to Krapf, heavy theft was punished by cutting the left hand. A second theft forfeited the right hand. Murder was punishable by death, if the relatives of the victim asked the Imam for this punishment; if they sought to accept restitution the murderer was sentenced to pay 2,000 German crowns.

Evidently, Rev. Krapf did not see Zanzibar as a field of Christian proselytisation. His attention, like that of most missionaries who later followed with the exception of the Universities Mission to Central Africa (hereafter UMCA), was directed at the mainland separated only by a few miles of ocean from Zanzibar. It is in this regard that he noted the limited Arab success to Islamize the masses of African natives in the interior of Africa. He surmised the reason for this failure to be the Arabs' inability to "invade these countries with large armies and propagate their faith with fire and sword." Consequently, Rev. Krapf made a number of journeys to Tanga, Mombasa and Usambara with the objective of establishing mission stations there.

The Holy Ghost Fathers, a French Catholic mission, arrived in Zanzibar in 1868. They were followed by the UMCA missionaries (Anglican) in 1875. A year later the Church Missionary Society (Anglican) missionaries arrived. They were followed by the White Fathers (French Catholic) in 1878. The German missionary societies, Evangelisch-Lutherische Mission zu Leipzig and Evangelische Missionsgesellschaft fur Deutsch-Ostafrika, arrived in the 1890s. The reception of all these groups by the Sultans of Zanzibar was cordial with no indication of an outward animosity toward Christianity even though the Sultans were Muslims. Harries suggests that such tolerance may not have been possible if the Sultans did not belong to the more tolerant Ibadhi sect of Islam (Harries, 1954: 66).

However, the missionary freedom to proselytise had also been guaranteed by the *Treaty of Friendship, Commerce, and Navigation* of 1886 between England and Zanzibar. Although most of the 27 Articles of this treaty related to Rights and Tariffs, Article XXIII specifically guaranteed religious freedom. It reads:

> Subjects of the two High Contracting Parties shall, within the dominions of each other, enjoy freedom of conscience and religious toleration. The free and public exercise of all forms of religion, and the right to build edifices for religious worship, and to organise religious missions of all creeds, shall not be restricted or interfered with in any way whatsoever. Missionaries, scientists, as with their followers, property and collections, shall likewise be under the special protection of the High Contracting Parties (CMS G3 A5 O, 1888, no 372, Mackay memo.).

The then British Agent and Consul-General in Zanzibar, Colonel Charles Bean Evan-Smith, a devout Christian, had sufficient influence with the newly installed Sultan Khalifa to demand the later's adherence to the spirit of the above treaty.

Besides the goodwill of their Arab hosts early missionaries depended very much on the printed word to proselytise. Those were the days of what Martin Sturmer calls "unobtrusive" Christianization (Sturmer, 1998: 38). For this and other purposes different missionary groups started their own newspapers in Kiswahili. Among the earliest were the following: *Msimulizi* (1888) published in Zanzibar by the Universities Mission to Central Africa, *Habari za Mwezi* (1894) published at Magila on the mainland, *Pwani na Bara* (1910) and its two-page supplement *Mdogo wa Pwani na Bara* (1914) published by the Evangelische Missionsgesellschaft fur Deutsch-Ostafrika with printing offices in Dar es Salaam. The Catholics were latecomers in the newspaper business and the first edition of their newspaper *Rafiki Yangu* appeared on 1 January, 1910. By 1913 the readership of *Rafiki Yangu* was approximately three thousand (Mbiku, 1985:89).

In the first instance, the Kiswahili monthly *Pwani na Bara*, facilitated correspondence between African converts who were literate in Kiswahili. Oscar Gemuseus, the Rungwe Moravian educator, lauded the use of Kiswahili as the medium of instruction and was proud of its outcome: "After a few months my pupils were all able to give contributions to our Christian monthly paper, *Pwani na Bara*, edited in Dar es Salaam, which was a chain linking together all Christians of the whole colony" (Quoted by Wright, 1971: 126).

Much later especially after World War II the Church presses made some significant contribution in supporting African nationalism as well as combating communism. The Catholic newspaper, *Kiongozi*, supported the cause of the Tanganyika African National Union (TANU), the nationalist party which led Tanganyika to independence in 1961. In 1952 Munseri, a lay Christian from Bukoba in north west Tanganyika, launched *Bukya na Gandi* (Dawn with Fresh News), a weekly paper in English, Kiswahili and Kihaya. As a Catholic, Munseri was influenced by church propaganda and used his newspaper to counter communist influence (Anderson, 1977: 160).

Besides the contribution of newspapers in early evangelical work the translation and distribution of the Scriptures was equally essential in the furtherance of the Christian faith. First, the supply of the printed Word was indispensable to build up converts and train native teachers and preachers (Sugirtharajah, 2001: 168). Second, as we will see in chapter five vernacular Bibles and hymnals excited African converts at receiving the Word of God in their own languages.[25] The availability of such literature was, therefore, of great significance in the spread of Christianity especially in rural areas where most Christian missions operated.

However, the history and contribution of colporteurs in the evangelisation of German East Africa and later Tanganyika have yet to be written. According to von Sicard, the Lutheran missionary Johannes Kupfernagel was the first to realise the importance of colportage and how it would be a way to give some permanence to evangelical work. Von Sicard writes: "As a result he requested that an Agency of the British and Foreign Bible Society be established in Dar es Salaam to meet the demand for Indian, Arabic and Swahili Scriptures"[26] (von Sicard, 1970: 200). The request was turned down on the excuse that a subagency already existed at Mombasa.

Despite the aid afforded by the printed word the early propagation of Christianity among the Swahilis was an uphill battle. This is because the Swahili culture and its way of life were intricately tied to Islam and Islamic culture. Moreover, the introduction of Christianity which was closely followed by German colonialism triggered off a concerted literary criticism of both by Muslim *ulama*, learned men, and others who were literate in both Arabic and Kiswahili. Their main weapon was poetry which was written in both Arabic and Kiswahili. The use of the Kiswahili language was an important factor.[27] Delivered in the popular form of song-poems the dissemination of these oral texts of resistance sought to question the legitimacy of German rule and to undermine the influence of Christianity. In regard to the latter, the undermining did not have to be direct. Poems that praised Islam had a similar effect. Such was the case of Mgeni bin Faqihi's *Utenzi wa Rasi ' l Ghuli* written sometime between 1850 and 1855.[28] The poem, a translation of an Arabic epic, legitimises and celebrates the spread of Islam (Mbele, 1988). Its popularity was such that its reciters were invited to places as far as Kilimatinde, Tabora and Ujiji in the far interior of Tanzania (van Kessel, 1979: vi).

However, in the vanguard of Muslim criticism and resistance were poets like Abdul Karim bin Jamalidinni and Hemed bin Abdallah bin Said al-Buhriy. Jamalidinni's poem *"Shairi la Dola Jermani"* is described by John Iliffe as a "eulogy" (Quoted by Biersteker, 1996: 156). According to Biersteker, it is a eulogy in the sense of "praise of the dead." She suggests that the poem exalts Islam at the same time as it celebrates the "death" of Christian ideology and German rule (Biersteker, 1996: 156). Hemed al-Buhriy's poem *Utenzi wa Vita vya Wadachi Kutamalaki Mrima* presents the armed struggle led by Bushiri bin Salim as a *jihad* against the infidel Christian Germans. The following verses underscore this perception: [29]

Wakatunza Majahili	The Infidels studied
Taurati na Injili	The Torah and the Gospel
Vyuo vikawaratili	The books told them
kwingiliwa na wakaa	A great event was imminent
Walikuja wakangia	They came and entered
Na majibwa yao pia	With their great dogs too
Liwali akakimbia	And the governor
	had fled
asihimili	He could not bear to remain.
Basi wakaja Pangani	They came to Pangani
roho zili kasirani	Full of wrath,

nyumba wakaizaini	They fitted up the house
na mizinga wakatia	And laid cannon.
Na merikebu Maziwe	And the ship at Maziwe
mji wote unamiwe	The whole town was humbled
na Wazungu waingiwe	And the Europeans
mjini wakatembea	Strode about the streets.
Mji ukanyamazana	The town was silent,
pasiwe mtu kunena	No one spoke,
jamii ya waungwana	Not a free man
pasi mwinyi kutongou	Said a word.

Utenzi wa Vita vya Wadachi Kutamalaki Mrima mainly documents the invasion of coastal towns and their subsequent defeat by the Germans. It also presents German conquest as a religiously polluting experience for the vanquished Muslims.[30]

Although Buhriy's poem suggests that Bushiri's resistance against German rule was religiously motivated evidence shows that it was rather politically motivated. Indeed, at Tanga there was an outrage when some Germans accompanied by their dogs entered mosques during the month of Ramadhan. However, this was only the last straw. The real cause of agitation was German high-handedness, especially the imposition of a head tax, a burial tax and an inheritance tax. According to Thomas Pakenham, Bushiri "was a hot-headed Swahili sugar-plantation owner" whose clan, the Al-Harthi, had for centuries similarly defied the economic and political encroachment of the Sultans of Zanzibar (Pakenham1991: 346). However, Oliver notes that at the time of Bushiri's uprising the Sultan, Khalifa ibn Said, did his utmost to aid Bushiri at Pangani in 1888 and 1889 (Quoted by Martin, 1976: 168). Subsequently Bushiri was captured by the Germans and hanged in public.

However, in his war against the Germans Bushiri capitalised on the insecurity of all Europeans including missionaries. Contrary to suggestions that Bushiri and his followers acted with commendable restraint toward missionaries (Pakenham, 1991: 348), evidence from CMS archives shows that he and his supporters posed a serious danger to missionaries regardless of their nationality. Correspondence between the British Consul-General, C. B. Evan-Smith, and W. S. Price dated

25 January, 1889, mentioned the murder of a Mr. Brooks of the London Missionary Society and his fifty porters near Saadani (CMS, G 3 A 5/ O/84). The town of Saadani was under the control of Bwana Kheri, Bushiri's main accomplice. In January 1889 Suleiman bin Seif, another accomplice of Bushiri, attacked the mission station at Dar es Salaam, killed three missionaries, and made prisoners of four others (Pakenham, 1991: 348). The Benedictine missionaries at Pugu, some fifteen miles west of Dar es Salaam, were also attacked on 13 January, 1889. In this attack two Brothers, one Sister and a number of children were killed; others escaped into the bush but some were captured and taken hostage (Mbiku, 1985: 25).

Missionaries further inland were equally in danger from Bushiri and his accomplices. In January 1889 the missionaries in Ugogo learnt that Abdullah, the son of Bwana Kheri, had ordered all white people who ventured to the coast, whether English, French or German, to be murdered together with their African servants. The order caused African porters and mailmen in the employ of missionaries to desert. It was because of this hostile environment that the CMS headquarters in London gave consent to the British Consul-General at Zanzibar to organise the withdrawal of all its missionaries from the interior (CMS, G 3 A 5/O/84, C. B. Evan-Smith to the Missionaries at Mpwapwa and Mamboya, dated 2 February, 1889). The Bushiri uprising was followed by the Maji Maji uprising from 1905 to 1907. The war was a subject of poetic works by Swahili and Arab poets. Jamalidinni's poem titled *Utenzi wa Vita vya Maji Maji*[31] is not only a fine piece of literature itself, but it is also an interesting historical documentation of the war. However, Jamalidinni's ethnocentric, political and religious sympathies are obvious throughout the poem. The following verses are a good example:

> *Twalikaa tukilala*
> *na ndisha njema tukila;*
> *mara ikaja ghafula*
> *tukasikia habari*
>
> *Ya washenzi wamekhuni*
> *ni hivi waja bomani*
> *na silaha mkononi*
> *na miji kuyihasiri*

Na sote tukadharau
kwa habari ni kuu;
huwaje hata wao
kufanya mno jeuri?[32] (English version see end note 32)

Although Whiteley translates the word *washenzi* to mean pagans, Jamalidinni may not have implied that the "rebels" were pagans but rather that they were contemptible savages or uncivilized. In *Utenzi wa Vita vya Wadachi*, Buhriy, Jamalidini's contemporary, also used the term to describe upcountry rebel warriors in Pangani. As Glassman has noted, its meaning is closer to barbarian than pagan (Glassman, 1995: 241). Based on such meaning its use set the "rebels" apart from the civilized Arabs and Swahili like Jamalidinni. Both Jamalidinni and Buhriy's poems reflect an unmistakable element of prejudice which is essential in the production of difference.

In any case, some of those who participated in the Maji Maji war were Muslims, including some African jumbes and akidas, in whose case (as Jamalidinni must have known) the term *washenzi* would not apply.[33] However, for Jamalidinni the ethnic identity of the "rebels" and their savagery was more important than their religion because, as he notes in the poem, they attacked all foreigners including Arabs, Indians and Swahili who, as Jamalidinni notes in the first verse above, "were relaxing, resting, and eating well" when suddenly they heard the news that the Africans had "rebelled."

Furthermore, it is obvious that Jamalidinni's political sentiments were anti-Maji Maji as the following verses indicate:

Washenzi wameshitadi
dunia kuifisidi;
mupite wapi nukudi?
Nelezeni uzuri!

Tulizeni roho zenu!
Idumu hishima yenu!
Hatubakishi kipenu,
yote tutatia nari.

Basi, hapa nimeweka
maneno kuyatamka,
mangine nayakumbuka
niyapange kwa uzuri![34] (English version see end note 34)

In a number of verses Jamalidinni refers to the Germans as "Bwana wetu" (i.e., verses 55, 87, 307) or "our master," an indication that by 1905 the Arabs and Swahili along the coast had accepted German rule as a part of their political reality.

The contempt with which Jamalidinni held the "rebels" is expressed toward the end of the poem, obviously to leave the reader with no doubt about where he, Jamalidinni, stood. In verses 326-328 Jamalidinni writes:

Washenzi hawana akili!
Fukara hana rijali!
Wote watamkubali
kila alilo dhukuri.

WaMakonde na waHiyao
wamekosa roho zao
pamoja na wana wao
kupigwa faya nahari

Na kila mwenyi jina
abadani hakupona
kitanzi alikiona;
sasa amani sururi![35] (English version see end note 35)

Jamalidinni also singles out (in verse 330) one of the leaders of Maji Maji, one Omari Kinjalla (a Muslim), for a personal insult:

Mwana haramu Kinjara,
aduwa Ilahi Songera;
wametaka ubora
bilashi kujikhasiri![36] (English version see end note 36)

Although Jamalidinni did not consider religion, certainly not Islam, to be a factor in the Maji Maji resistance, Margaret Bates suggests that the resistance had some religious undertones. Bates notes that **the "rebels" referred to themselves as the** *askari ya mungu*, and felt that they were divinely sent to drive out the hated foreigners (Bates, 1957).

The religious mechanisms that the leaders of Maji Maji manipulated very effectively were highly indigenous. However, according to Sunseri (1999) competing interpretations of Maji Maji existed during the war; many of which, he suggests, were imbued with Christian symbolism and Biblical metaphors.[37] Sunseri also suggests that the influence of Christian symbolism and Biblical metaphors is evidence of substantial Christianisation in the Maji Maji area before 1905 (Sunseri, 1999). What Sunseri does not consider is the possibility that those involved in organising and fighting the war may have used Christian symbols and metaphors simply because these represented a connection to a universal narrative. As Landau notes, the process of translation of Christianity is a process of reformulating a symbolic language and therefore should be seen not in terms of equivalencies of meanings (Landau, 1995: 53 80).

Thus, although Maji Maji fighters saw themselves as *askari ya mungu* their God was not that of the Christians. Otherwise, their targets would not have included mission stations and European missionaries. The most famous of their victims was Bishop Cassian Spiess. Despite warning about the possible danger of an attack Bishop Spiess and his party of two sisters and two brothers set off from Kilwa on their way to Peramiho near Songea. As the party struggled to reach Liwale they were ambushed by "rebels" and killed.

According to Governor von Gotzen's account Bishop Spiess was murdered by Abdallah Mchimaye, one of the leaders of the *Maji Maji* fighters in Liwale. However, oral testimony recorded by R. M. Bell (MSS Afr. s. 452, Rhodes House Library) contradicts von Gotzen's account. The bishop was shot, not speared according to Governor von Gotzen's account, by a native named Kindamba Makupura. The Brothers were killed by Salim Kikoko and a slave named Mtendamema whereas the Sisters were killed by Nachogoya and Ntiranjara.

Liwale district appears to have been a hot bed of Muslim rebels. Besides Abdallah Mchimaye other Maji Maji leaders from the district were Omari Kinjalla and Abdallah Mpanda. Abdallah Mpanda, an elephant hunter, is said to have been the moving spirit of the war in the central area of Liwale district. His village, Kitandagora, was situated about twelve hours' walk from Liwale. Unfortunately we know very little about the religious and political motives of these Muslim leaders. It is therefore difficult to ascertain whether the killing of Bishop Spiess and his fellow missionaries had something to do with Muslim anti-Christian sentiments in central Liwale.

Elsewhere, however, such as in the Matumbi area there are indications that Islam may have been the moving spirit of the war, at least initially. Oral sources suggest that Ngameya, the Maji Maji leader in the Madaba area, was traditionally regarded by the Ngindo as a man who converted their tribe to Islam. It is said that for a short time before the uprising was suppressed, a number of teachers appointed by Ngameya had been at work spreading the faith. Mwinyi Hemed Lipupu, who later headed the Native Authority at Liwale, is said to have been one of these teachers (Bell, MSS. Afr. s. 452). Meanwhile, Muslims, heathens and Christians all joined the same cause but no matter what their religion all regarded that cause as a divine mission. According to Sunseri, the historiography of Maji Maji indicates strong influences from Abrahamic sources, both Christian and Islamic (Sunseri, 1999: 365).

In regard to the latter, Sunseri notes how Muslim traders, teachers, *akidas* and *liwalis* as well as Muslim plantation owners were all prominent in the Maji Maji outbreak region before 1905 (ibid., 368). Many of these Muslims of status and wealth cooperated with the Germans. However, there were those Muslims who were not beneficiaries of the new political dispensation under the Germans. These Muslims were predominantly African, poor and, unlike the wealthier Arabs, Indians and Swahilis, their religious practices were heavily influenced by African traditions. Many also belonged to Sufi orders. According to Lodhi and Westerlund (1997), many Sufis played an important role in the Maji Maji war: "The traditional African ideas of Kinjikitile, the leader of the uprising, were to an extent intertwined with Sufi ideas."[38]

Other leaders such as Kibasila at Kisangire in Zaramo country were also known to have given the uprising religious overtones (von Sicard, 1970: 179). Von Sicard writes:

> Already in early 1905 when Wentzel had asked Kibasila if he would want a school at Kisangire, he had turned it down on the grounds that he was a Muslim and had his Quar'an [sic] school there already. This Islamic element in the uprising led to a setback for the spread of Islam generally (ibid., 188). However, von Sicard does not offer details how or in what way the uprising put Islam at a disadvantage against Christianity.

As far as the German administration was concerned, Maji Maji was the handiwork of one of the colonial "bogeymen" namely "witch doctors." The main "witch doctors" were Kinjikitile Ngwale from

Ngarambe and his brother-in-law, Ngameya, from the village of Kitope in Upogoro. For the European missionaries, African "witch doctors" were seen as corrupting enemies of Christianity. Jamalidinni's poem about the Maji Maji "rebels" spoke to what may as well have been a popular perception of the Africans by most missionaries. To the early missionaries Africans did not lead normal lives and were morally corrupt, spiritually empty and materially very backward. Yet, missionaries believed that however degraded the Africans were, they were capable of salvation: "Such a perception [sic], viewed against the colonial portrayals of the time, which stressed the animal properties of Africans, was a decidedly positive one" (Sugirtharajah, 2001: 167).

Early Christian missionaries in Tanganyika, as elsewhere in colonial Africa, worried about their converts living within spiritually and morally corrupting communities. The missionaries, therefore, endeavored to isolate their converts in closed mission communities. However, in their isolation mission stations in areas affected by the Maji Maji uprising such as Maneromango, Lukuledi, Nyangao and Masasi became easy targets of the Maji Maji "rebels." The cases of Lukuledi and Nyangao are worth noting. On 27 August 1905 the missionaries at Nyangao heard that the Maji Maji fighters were closing in. Father Leo, Brother Cyprian and four sisters deserted the mission and sought refuge in the bush. When they were discovered, they fended off their attackers with only one gun which they had in their possession! According to Mbiku, their survival was miraculous because their attackers retreated for no apparent reason (Mbiku, 1985: 56). The only casualty was Sister Walburga who was later captured and killed by the Maji Maji fighters. Likewise, when Father Thomas Spreiter and his colleagues at Lukuledi heard that the people of Mchekenje wa Mititimo who had joined forces with Jumbe Mkuu's army were headed for Lukuledi they sought refuge in the bush because they had no ammunition. Later they fled to Masasi where they joined other missionaries on the run. They eventually succeeded to reach Mikindani where their safety was assured. Apparently what compounded the vulnerability of the mission stations at Nyangao and Lukuledi was the fact that they were neither fortified nor well armed.

On the contrary, mission stations to the north of the areas affected by Maji Maji had been fortified in anticipation of possible attacks especially by slave traders. Mhonda, the first inland mission of the Holy Ghost Fathers, near Morogoro, was built in 1877 and fortified in 1881. In 1880 the Holy Ghost Fathers opened Mandera, halfway to Mhonda, which was turned into "a practically impregnable fortress" in 1883 (Anderson, 1977: 12). Yet, despite their secure locations these missions and others to the north of the Maji Maji area faced a different threat namely unrelenting Islamic propagation which was apparently very successful in some areas.

In 1897, Hilarion, one of the longest serving catechists at Mhonda, and a number of Christians converted to Islam. Hilarion was later appointed *akida* to Kibambawe near the Rufiji Rapids, the source of the water used in the Maji Maji war. Was Hilarion the mastermind behind Bokero and Kinjekitile? Stollowsky, who at the time was a District official at Mohoro and was partly involved in investigating who was behind the uprising, strongly believed that Hilarion may have had a hand in the idea, if not the planning, of the uprising. What he says about Hilarion is worth quoting at length:

> Kibambawe (or Kungulio) was the home of the old brigand Hilalion, who used to extort *hongo* from the caravans and had been expelled by the government from the Ngulu area. A former mission pupil who had been trained as a native priest, he spoke French and Latin reasonably well and was in other ways educated to a level that was unusual among our natives. In the early 1880s he had, so to speak, usurped the throne of Ngulu, using the Christianity in which he had been painstakingly educated as the foundation for his rise to a position of power and dominion. From the pious missionary Hilarion, there emerged a thoroughly unscrupulous heathen potentate Hilalion, who with unusual dissimulation and cunning had elevated the crudest materialism of the native to despotic dignity. After the establishment of German rule in East Africa, he had been clever enough to show unfailing respect to the stronger power, and so fatten himself at the government's expense. The economy of his kingdom, which had formerly depended on caravan *hongo*, gradually came to depend exclusively on a discreet embezzling of the official hut tax. I am not acquainted with the precise reasons for his eventual transfer from his usurped kingdom in Ngulu to the post of sultan and *akida* in Kungulio. It was certainly a most ill-advised move, for Hilalio had long been ripe for the chain gang or the gallows, where he would doubtless have ended up during the rebellion, had a premature and natural end not kindly spared him such a fate. At the end of March 1905, while on a visit in Mohoro, he was suddenly taken seriously ill and died (Stollowsky, 1988: 695).

Although Stollowsky's anecdotal evidence about Hilarion's involvement in the planning of Maji Maji is convincing it remains unclear what Hilarion expected to gain personally or otherwise from the Maji Maji war. The Maji Maji war appears to have been a turning point in the process of Christianisation in the affected areas. William B. Anderson writes:

> In Peramiho area in South-west Tanganyika, where Maji Maji had raged most fiercely and where the parish priest had been killed, the number of Christians rose from 500 to 5,000 in the following ten years. In southern Tanganyika the Berlin Society's 4 mission stations among the Nkonde expanded to 21 out stations and 88 preaching points, almost all manned by new converts (Anderson, 1977: 60).

Among the acclaimed successes were the baptismal of Ngoni Maji Maji leaders including Nkosi Gama Mputa who was given the name Hadrian. Their baptismal encouraged others to follow their example.

Yet the work of proselytizing was made more difficult by the ravages of war. Mission buildings and gardens had been destroyed. Also many people had either died or sought refuge in the wilderness; thousands had their farms and houses destroyed and were threatened by famine. At Songea even after the war had ended the District Officer deliberately continued the scotched earth policy which exacerbated famine conditions. The efforts of Father Johannes to intervene by securing and distributing food aid alleviated the suffering. But his attempts to seek the Governor's intervention failed and led to his own expulsion (Mbiku, 1985: 64)

Equally interesting was the emergence of a new Benedictine philosophy which sought to reorient missionary work in the Maji Maji areas. In 1908 Abbot Norbert, the leader of the Benedictines who was visiting Songea when the war broke out, published a booklet titled "Euntes in mundum universun" (Quoted by Mbiku, 1985: 70) in which he pointed out that it was not enough to help the poor, feed the hungry, heal the sick and care for the orphans; that such activities would not heal the wounds caused by the Maji Maji war. He explained that the only way that would bring hope and success in spiritual work was to raise people's living standards. He encouraged the missions to become models of modern farming to peasant communities around them, to encourage them to secure modern farming implements and seed, to provide financial assistance to those who wanted to purchase livestock or start orchards; as well as to encourage the establishment of organisations which would buy and sell produce at fair prices. Abbot Nobert also suggested that Christians could be encouraged to open communal farms which they would work willingly without any compulsion. As we will later see in chapter seven, this idea was very much akin to farming as expressed by Thomas More in his *Utopia.*

In the Maji Maji areas and elsewhere the Benedictines aimed at circumventing rivalry from other Christian sects as well as from Muslims. In regard to the latter Abbot Nobert wrote: "Islam is ready to conquer East Africa. All areas along the coast are under its sway. In the lands of the Pogoro and the Hehe Muslims are spreading their faith. Even in remote areas ... there are reports that Islam is gathering momentum, nobody knows the reasons or who are responsible for its spread" (Quoted by Mbiku, 1985: 78). One strategy that the Benedictines endeavored to use was to open as many schools as they could. It was not an easy task considering that in some areas such as Ifakara Muslims refused to let them do so. At Ifakara due to many years of competition the school strategy assumed unprecedented importance. In 1913 Father Joseph Damm wrote: "It is obvious that those children who attend school recant Islam, and those who do not, boys and girls, accept Islam" (Quoted by Mbiku, 1985: 78). A year later he wrote again: "Without there being a mission (and its schools), Islam would have captured this entire area. Now its strength is compromised, and since Qur'anic teachers have less ability, they have relocated" (ibid.)

Likewise the Catholics had a hard time trying to reestablish their mission at Kipatimu, about one hundred and seventy miles to the south of Dar es Salaam. Prior to the outbreak of the Maji Maji war Kipatimu mission was considered to be a Christian island in a sea of Islam. Apparently the Ngindo and Matumbi who were the main ethnic groups in the area were not receptive to Christianity. Before the war only a few Matumbi had been converted to Christianity. Here as at Ifakara and other areas the strategy after the war was to use schools to attract potential converts. But local Muslims were suspicious of these schools and either refused the missionaries permission to build them or did not allow their children to register. School attendance was further compromised by truancy, famine, child labor and relocation to areas away from Kipatimu. The outbreak of World War I made school attendance even worse, a situation which lingered long after it was over. By 1968 there were only about 2,200 Christians, in a population of about 60,000, who were mostly Matumbi that lived near Kipatimu (Mbiku, 1985: 123).

To the north of the region affected by the Maji Maji war missionaries encountered, both before and after Maji Maji, different difficulties. One of these was organized Muslim propaganda which made proselytization difficult. Among other things Muslim propagandists claimed that in Hell the Christians would be used as firewood for the burning of other infidels (Anderson, 1977: 58). Although in Uzaramo and other areas the most uncompromising propagandists were illiterate Muslims,[39] equally effective criticism of Christianity was offered by Muslim *ulama*. The latter questioned the sacred nature of the Christian Scriptures; the Crucification and Resurrection of Jesus; and the Divinity of Jesus. As we will see later in chapter eight, these issues were also at the center of Muslim-Christian debates during the 1980s and 1990s. Since most *ulama* lived in urban centers where Muslims predominated it was there that Christianity was strongly challenged. Partly because of the predominance of Islam in the towns, most denominations, with the exception of the Christian Missionary Society (C.M.S.) and the Catholics, avoided urban centers. The beginnings of Christianity in Dar es Salaam involved proselytization among Muslims as well as evangelism among the non-Muslim Africans. Dar es Salaam, therefore, offers an interesting case study of the encounter between Islam and Christianity in an urban setting.

However, before we venture to look at the struggle for African souls between Islam and Christianity in Dar es Salaam, it is noteworthy to consider another crisis which the German administration faced in 1908. In that year the District Commissioner of Lindi reported and warned Governor von Rechenberg about the circulation of a letter popularly known as the Mecca Letter. Receivers of the letter were supposed to make eight copies and mail them to eight different people. It was in essence a chain letter. Although the letter was imbued with religious overtones its exegesis was, in fact, anti-German rule.

Current evidence suggests that the Mecca Letter was the brainchild of Mohammed ibn Khalfan al-Barwani, otherwise known as Rumaliza. At the time Rumaliza was residing in Zanzibar but he also had many family members in the Kilwa and Lindi areas. Rumaliza had been involved in slave raiding as well as ivory trading, the former in partnership with Hemed ibn Mohammed alias Tippu Tip. When they fell out Rumaliza was able to contest in a Dar es Salaam court for ownership of property jointly owned with Tippu Tip within German East Africa. But Rumaliza had lost considerable property in Lindi which had been confiscated by the German authorities. Moreover, the fact that his former trading preserves were now under German rule meant that he no longer enjoyed the near monopoly he had before. Thus Rumaliza's purpose in broadcasting the Mecca Letter was to instigate opposition to German rule with the hope of ending it.

However, Rumaliza's political objective had to be clothed in religious garb. Its millennial terminology and its attacks on whatever was not orthodox were intended to unify the diverse Muslim community against the Germans. According to Bradford Martin, Rumaliza himself may have entertained the idea of leading the resistance movement had a successful uprising taken place on a suitable scale (Martin, 1976: 171). The Mecca Letter's religious overtones did not deter Governor von Rechenberg from suspecting its political motives. Martin notes that in one of his dispatches to Berlin Governor von Rechenberg observed:

> Even if no dangers have arisen from this movement, it would be wrong to ignore certain questionable phenomena. The Muslim coastal population has made no effort since the Bushiri Rising to oppose the new order of things. At the same time the religious tolerance of Europeans was unknown, and the Muslims feared a government which would act along the lines of the saying *cuius regio eius religio*, in the Islamic manner. But in the last twenty years, they have become convinced that German rule does not signify any limitation of Islamic belief... However, the contrivers and propagators of the letter have obviously taken as their point of departure the idea of exciting the Muslims against the regime and assuring them of pagan support... The idea of playing off the Bush Negroes under Muslim leadership against the Europeans is based on the realization that the Rising of 1905 failed over two things: 1) the lack of communications, organisation, and leadership among the mutinous tribes, and 2) because of the loyalty of the colored troops... Through the participation of the Muslim population in such a movement, the fidelity of the largely Muslim' *askaris* could be shaken. The events at Lindi point directly at such an intention (Martin, 1976: 172).

Needless to say, the Mecca Letter exacerbated the administration's suspicion of Islam as a front for political agitation. Furthermore, German suspicion was aroused by what appeared to them to be a high frequency in mosque attendance. Arab and Swahili Muslims are said to frequent the mosque more than any other public place (Hadjivayanis, 1999). Besides providing the possibility of interaction with other Muslims, the mosque served other purposes as well. According to Hadjivayanis: "The Mosque, throughout the long history of East Africa, has served as the place of composing Kasidas, writing poetry, and organizing the Tarika. It is in fact the Tarika in the Muslim world that provided the vehicle for the devotees to organized resistance against colonialism." In regard to the Mecca Letter affair, Martin offers convincing evidence how the Qadiriyya brotherhood was instrumental in its circulation in areas such as Bagamoyo, Mpwapwa and Tabora (Martin, 1976: 159).

CHAPTER THREE

CHRISTIANITY ENCOUNTERS ISLAM IN EARLY COLONIAL DAR ES SALAAM

Evidently missionaries who arrived in German East Africa in the late 1880s and early 1890s were beneficiaries of cordial and friendly relations with Zanzibar's Muslim rulers that had been established by their predecessors such as Johan Krapf. On the one hand, Seyyid Said's assistance to missionaries like Krapf was calculated and a matter of personal interest and gains, i.e., for the development of his domains. He figured that he could gain something by having friendly relations with Europeans regardless of whether they were missionaries or traders. On the other hand, the tolerance of Zanzibar's Muslim rulers was occasionally abused as was the case with the conversion of an heir apparent to the Sultan, who was baptized as Andrew da Cunha. According to von Sicard, the Sultan "was disgusted and angry and said that the priest who had been responsible for this outrage would pay dearly for it" (von Sicard, 1970. 54). However, we do not know whether the Sultan's threat was effected. Besides the case of Andrew da Cunha, there is also the celebrated case of Emily Ruete, one of the daughters of Seyyid Said who eloped with a German businessman and after marrying him she converted to Christianity.

The Lutheran 'Berlin III' Mission, also known as the Evangelical Mission Society for German East Africa in Berlin (hereafter E. M. S.), started work in Dar es Salaam in 1887.[40] A year later the Benedictine Missionaries of St. Ottilien who belonged to the Catholic Church arrived. The Roman Catholics would later become the largest denomination in the city (Anderson, 1977: 155). According to Anderson, in 1920 only one and one half of the population were Christians. In 1960, before independence, 20% were Christians. In 1973 at least 40% were Christians (Anderson, 1977: 157). Given the rapid expansion of Catholic parishes in Dar es Salaam in the early 1970s there is reason to believe that Catholics constituted the majority of the 40% of Christians in Dar es Salaam. In this period the Catholic Church opened new parishes in Kunduchi and Kurasini (1970), Mwananyamala and Ukonga (1971), Kibaha (1972), Kigamboni, Mburahati and Ubungo (1973).

41

The founding of the E. M. S. was closely tied to the same colonial interests that influenced the formation of the German East Africa Company (hereafter G. E. A. Co.). The two initially operated in more or less similar fashion. Consequently, to the people living along the German East Africa coastline, the behaviour of their personnel seemed to be abhorrently the same. This partly explains the criticism of both Christianity and German colonialism by the *ulama* as noted above in regard to the poems written about *Vita vya Wadachi*. Subsequently, the work of the E. M. S. was handed over to the Berlin Mission Society in 1903 (von Sicard, 1970: 54). Prior to 1903 Lutheran missionary work focused more on providing care to newly freed slaves and their families as well as providing medical services which included the personnel of the G. E. A. Co. It was after 1904 that evangelical work was given more emphasis.

The first Lutheran missionary in Dar es Salaam was Rev. Johann Greiner who arrived at Dar es Salaam from Zanzibar on 2 July 1887.[41] At this time Dar es Salaam was still a small fishing village despite efforts by Sultan Majid in the 1860s to make it his summer resort. His successor, Sultan Barghash, neglected the place and entrusted its affairs in the hands of an *akida*, one Muhammad bin Suleiman, and a *liwali* named Said bin Abdallah under whose authority were a number of local African headmen. The failure of Seyyid Majid's grandiose plans gave rise to local beliefs that the place was cursed (Father Le Roy, quoted by von Sicard, 1978: 60). It was also presumed that if a Christian mission were to be established in Dar es Salaam the curse would be broken. The population of Dar es Salaam at this time was approximately 2,000 which included an estimated 200 Indians and 150 Arabs. The rest were Africans of which the Zaramo predominated.

Once Greiner was settled, he endeavored to purchase a piece of land on which to build his mission-station. The piece of land that Greiner favored, located near the present site of the State House, was part of a coconut plantation which was mortgaged by Mwinjuma bin Shomvilhaji to one Abdallah bin Said for 1000 Persian reale. According to E. C. Baker, Mwinjuma bin Shomvilhaj was descended from Diwan Mgungurugwa bin Abubakar, Mshomvi, who ruled at Ununio, beyond Kunduchi on the old Dar es Salaam/Bagamoyo road *(Tanganyika Notes and Records*, 23: 47). Since Mgungurugwa had no movable property to bequeath his progeny, he provided for their future by settling them at various places on the coast where they could profit by the royalties paid on ambergris and the *mkadi* screw pine which was valued for its strongly scented flowers. At these various places Mgungurugwa's descendants ruled as *diwans*. According to Baker, Mwinjuma bin Shomvilhaj was the *diwan* of the Mzizima Washomvi who prior to the advent of German rule lived on the northern side of the entrance to the harbor then known as Magogoni (Baker, MSS Afr. r. 84, Rhodes House Library).

In order to buy the piece of land that he wanted Greiner needed permission from the Sultan in Zanzibar. The *liwali*, being the local representative of the Sultan[42], made a recommendation to the Sultan in favour of the purchase. After purchasing the land Greiner made a trip to Zanzibar where he employed the services of three masons, a carpenter named Musa and an overseer named Suet (Suedi?). In order to clear the land Greiner employed local labour. In this regard, it is important to note that the work of establishing the first mission-station in Dar es Salaam actually depended on the labour of people who by faith were Muslims. But why would Muslims participate in the construction of a church and other mission buildings belonging to a faith that was opposed to Islam? Was it a case of *mtumikie kafiri upate mradi wako?*[13] Unfortunately available sources do not shed light on such sentiments.

In the course of clearing the land Greiner encountered several problems. One of the problems was that the local labourers were reluctant to cut down the coconut and baobab trees on the construction site. Sigvard von Sicard explains this reluctance to have been due to two factors. On the one hand, the local people were reluctant to cut down coconut trees because the coconut was a very valuable multi purpose tree.[44] On the other, they were reluctant to cut down the baobab trees because these were considered to be the "trees of life" because they were associated with spirit forces. According to von Sicard, only by prodding and cajoling were the labourers made to clear the land (von Sicard, 1970: 64).

We do not know what Greiner made of the local beliefs about baobabs and spirit forces. He probably considered such beliefs to be an indication of nothing else other than superstitious heathendom. However, those who have read Chinua Achebe's *Things Fall Apart* may recall how the missionaries in Umuofia were given a piece of land in the fictional Evil Forest which they had to clear to build their church. Everyone expected the missionaries would come to a bad end because of exposure to the malevolent forces inhabiting the Evil Forest. When nothing happened, some started to question whether there were indeed evil spirits in the Evil Forest. Others believed the missionaries must have had stronger guardian spirits. In either case, the experience sowed seeds of doubt about the potency of evil forces and contributed toward the first conversions to Christianity.

We also do not know if the cutting down of baobab trees contributed to a change of attitude by the Muslim Zaramo toward their "trees of life." What we do know is that this was the first encounter between Christianity and local traditional beliefs. Most Zaramo believed in a Supreme Being, *Mulungu*, who was associated with rainfall. However, the Zaramo also venerated their ancestors. Most prayers were directed to familial spirits because religion among the Zaramo was a family affair. Every family was responsible for appeasing its ancestral spirits for which shrines were built. Ancestral spirits served as a liaison between the living and the Supreme Being. This was an important role. The Zaramo believed that major calamities and misfortunes were caused by *Mulungu* to whom one could not appeal directly but indirectly through one's ancestral spirits.

The Zaramo also believed that misfortune could be caused by malevolent spirits. The spirits had each their favourite places where they usually remained, such as trees (the baobab being one), springs and bodies of water. In order to determine the proper course of action necessary to appease a displeased ancestral spirit or one of the malevolent spirits, a spirit medium was consulted. The spirit medium, a *mganga*, would invoke the spirit using particular formulae. It should also be noted here that whereas the Christianisation of the Zaramo did not allow them to continue to relate to Zaramo beliefs about spirits, their Islamization did not deter them from assimilating some of their ideas and practices into Islam. The Africanisation of Islam by the Zaramo included the Islamization of some of their rites such as *kupunga pepo*, the exorcism of a spirit possessing a person, which resonated with Islamic beliefs about evil spirits and jinns. To the Zaramo such religious eclecticism made sense because it was a practical safety net.

Eventually, Greiner was able to have the land cleared of coconut and baobab trees and construction started. Greiner, his staff and proteges were able to move into the new premises on 21 August 1888. Since early missionaries were forced by circumstances to be self-supporting in terms of provisions, Greiner's immediate task was to start a farm on which he raised local cattle for milk, chickens and pigs for eggs and meat respectively, and coconuts as a source of some revenue. It is not clear whether or not at this time the rearing of pigs and the consumption of pork caused any tensions between the missionaries and their Muslim neighbours. However, as we will later see, the rearing of pigs and the selling of pork during the 1990s became one of the causes of tension between Christians and Muslims in Dar es Salaam.

The employment of local labour for the construction of his mission-station gave Greiner the opportunity to interact with the local Muslims and to speak to them about spiritual matters. According to von Sicard, Greiner was soon popularly referred to as the "German Pastor" and people sought him out for spiritual discourse (von Sicard, 1970: 62). Although the nature of Greiner's conversations with the Muslims remains unknown, we can surmise that the interaction was probably mutually respectful. Unfortunately the beginnings of missionary work were abruptly brought to a halt by Bushiri's uprising which forced Greiner to evacuate his mission and depart for Zanzibar on 13 January 1889.

Following the successful quelling of the Bushiri uprising Dar es Salaam was declared the capital of German East Africa in 1891. Consequently, its new status turned Dar es Salaam into a beehive of activities which attracted an ever increasing number of immigrants from surrounding areas as well as further inland. Despite the growing population of Dar es Salaam the Christian community remained significantly small and was actually drastically reduced by a number of deaths. By 1893 evangelistic work remained confined to the grounds of the mission-station. In the meantime there arrived in 1890 a new competitor in the name of the Benedictine Fathers. In the face of such competition the Lutherans attempted to seek influence in areas near and around Dar es Salaam which hitherto they had neglected. Their evangelical work took them into predominantly Muslim communities such as Magogoni. What the missionaries encountered in these communities was not outright hostility but imperviousness to the Christian message due to what von Sicard calls "ingrained Islamic thought-patterns" (von Sicard, 1970: 87). By 1900 only 16 adults[45] had been baptized after undergoing the necessary catechetical preparations.

Among other reasons why Dar es Salaam proved to be a barren area for Lutheran evangelistic work was Islamic propaganda against Christianity as reflected in the poetry of Buhriy and others. Upon taking over from E. M. S. the Berlin Mission Society endeavoured to come up with new strategies especially to confront the influence of Islam in the urban setting of Dar es Salaam whose population in 1904 was estimated to be 20,000 inhabitants, the majority being Africans. Von Sicard gauges the influence of Islam in early colonial Dar es Salaam by the number of mosques which in 1904 were estimated to be 16, four large and twelve small ones (von Sicard, 1970: 177).

However, the number of mosques in itself does not mean that Dar es Salaam Muslims were devout practitioners of their faith. One is reminded of Dr. David Livingstone's 1866 indictment of Muslim residents of Mikindani to the south of Dar es Salaam. According to Sir John Gray Dr. Livingstone did not especially entertain a high opinion of the Arab residents:

> The Arabs here are a wretched lot physically, thin, washed-out creatures – many with bleared eyes ... They are low coast Arabs, three-quarters Africans and, as usual, possess the bad without the good qualities of both parents. Many of them came and begged brandy, and laughed when they remarked that they could drink it in secret, but not openly (Gray, 1950: 32).

Like the Mikindani Arabs who craved brandy, Zaramo Muslims imbibed *tembo*, an alcoholic drink tapped from the palm tree. Thus, their drinking coupled with beliefs in spirits and other supernatural forces made the Zaramo nominal rather than devout Muslims. However, even as nominal Muslims the Zaramo proved difficult initially to be converted to Christianity.

The Berlin Mission Society's proposed strategies to confront Islam are further dealt with in chapter four. Suffice it to note here that the German administration suggested among other things that encouraging natives to keep pigs could be a means toward lessening the spread of Islam (Joelson, 1920: 108). Besides attempts to proselytize by preaching the Word, the Lutheran evangelical endeavours in early colonial Dar es Salaam included health and educational work. In regard to the provision of education the initial objective was to enrol newly freed slave children. A part of the Anglo-Zanzibar Treaty of 1873 stipulated that children freed by the British navy were to be distributed among the various missions along the coast. Von Sicard notes that during one of Greiner's visits to Zanzibar in December 1887, he was asked to take care of some children who had recently been freed. The request necessitated the building of a school to cater to these children's education needs. The first teacher of the school was Gobau Desta from Ethiopia. Whether from the beginning the school was used as a medium of Christian apologetics is difficult to determine due to the unavailability of school syllabi. But it is not farfetched to visualize a situation where the children would have learnt the alphabet together with some of the ABCs of Christianity.

We have already noted how Lutheran proselytization in Dar es Salaam produced limited results. Even after work was expanded to Kisarawe and Maneromango the number of converts remained very small at first. Thus by July 1903 the Lutherans recorded a total of 234 baptized and 29 waiting to be baptized in all their work areas namely Dar es Salaam, Kisarawe and Maneromango (KKKT, Dayosisi ya Mashariki na Pwani, 1992: 3). By 1937 those baptized numbered 1, 418 while those waiting to be baptized totaled 133 (ibid., 3). A part of this later proselytizing was done under "new management" after the Bethel Mission took over from the E. M. S. (Berlin III) in 1903.

In Dar es Salaam the Bethel Mission also inherited the newly inaugurated Azania Front Lutheran Cathedral. The stimulus for its construction came from none other than Governor von Soden who was willing to facilitate the availability of public land for this purpose. Due to financial difficulties construction did not take place during von Soden's administration and the plot of land reverted back to the public domain. A new plot was later found close to the harbour. The foundation stone was laid on 18 May 1899 when the E. M. S. was under the Rev. Otto Roloff. The architectural design was done by the Government chief architect. However, unlike Greiner, Roloff did not employ Muslim carpenters and masons. These services, including those of the foreman named Israel Lukoa, were provided by African Christian converts from the Maneromango mission-station. All the workers engaged in construction work lived at Magogoni, which by this time was a Lutheran estate.

Whereas the German administration facilitated the availability of public land for the construction of the Azania Front Cathedral, Kaiser Wilhelm's household donated a piano, three large church bells (still functional to date) as well as the colourful windows embellished with Biblical images. The three windows on the eastern side above the altar depict Jesus' Birth, Crucification and Resurrection. The round window on the northern side show the Emperor at prayer and the one on the southern side shows Jesus saving Peter from drowning. The inauguration day on 2 May 1902 was a public holiday. Invited guests from Zanzibar were transported to and fro free of charge onboard the *Danifer*, a Government boat (KKKT, Dayosisi ya Mashariki na Pwani, 1992: 7).

At this juncture let us shift our focus from the Lutherans to another group of early missionaries in Dar es Salaam, namely the Catholic Benedictine Missionaries of St. Ottilien. Like the Lutherans, they arrived at Dar es Salaam from Zanzibar on 22 January, 1888. This was eighteen years after the first Catholic mission had been established at Zanzibar in 1860.[46] The Benedictine missionaries who arrived at Dar es Salaam included one priest, Father Boniface Flehschutz aged twenty-seven and leader of the group, one seminarian, eight Brothers and four Sisters, all being less than forty years of age. The seminarian, Brothers and Sisters were individually skilled in carpentry, masonry, tailoring and shoe making, teaching, nursing and domestic science (Mbiku, 1985: 19).

According to Mbiku (1985) Father Flehschutz had been instructed by the Benedictine leader, Father Andrew Amrhein, not to establish a mission on the coast but rather a little further inland where the influence of Islam was likely to be minimal. It was also believed that the Lutheran missionaries who had already established themselves at Dar es Salaam would probably have resented seeing a Catholic mission established so close to theirs. Therefore, the Benedictine missionaries scouted the areas near Dar es Salaam with the help of Captain Leue the Commandant of Dar es Salaam. They soon chose to establish themselves at Pugu, some fifteen miles west of Dar es Salaam. Whether the influence of Islam at Pugu was minimal or not is difficult to ascertain. But it appears that the local people welcomed the missionaries and after some lengthy negotiations the missionaries were able to buy land for their new mission-station. However, the Bushir war soon forced them to abandon Pugu.

Following the defeat of the Bushir uprising Father Flehschutz accompanied by Brothers Joseph and Fridolin were recalled from Germany and arrived in Dar es Salaam in early December 1889. This time Father Flehschutz decided to stay and establish a mission-station in Dar es Salaam. Two dilapidated buildings were bought and renovated for residential quarters. Later on farms were bought at Kurasini, Msimbazi and Mbagala where the Brothers raised cassava, paddy, corn and reared donkeys, cattle, sheep, goats and pigs. When the Capuchin Fathers took over in 1921, the Msimbazi farm was the largest with 300 cattle, 200 pigs and 13 donkeys.

From their home base in Dar es Salaam the Benedictine Fathers focused to spread the gospel in the southern parts especially in the Lindi area. Thus on 2 February, 1895, they were able to open a new mission-station at Lukuledi. By 1903 the Lukuledi mission was ministering to a little more than one thousand converts. Besides Lukuledi another mission was established at Nyangao in 1896. Nyangao was about sixty miles from Lukuledi on the road to Lindi. In both places schools were opened and soon hundreds of pupils were attending being taught how to read as well as listening to religious instructions. These out stations depended very much on the Dar es Salaam mission to organize supply caravans. Some of these caravans would have forty, sixty or even one hundred porters. Yet there is no evidence that attempts were made to convert such porters.

Evangelical work in Dar es Salaam gathered momentum under the guidance of Father Maurus Hartmann who arrived in Dar es Salaam on 24 June, 1894. Two years later Father Hartmann was able to get a plot of land from the Government for the construction of a church. The land was free but was given on condition that the building to be built on it had to be impressive and beautiful (Mbiku, 1985: 41). After a fund-raising trip to St. Ottilien in late 1896 the construction of St. Joseph's Cathedral was started on 5 December, 1897 and was completed in 1902. The cathedral was built in "Gothic style with a spire and a pleasant door-way formed of triple pointed arches and a decorative circular window over them" (Casson, TNR, 7, 1970: 182).

Thus the construction of the two Christian cathedrals in Dar es Salaam, with their spires piercing the blue sky, dramatically changed its skyline (See photographs below). Although the oldest mosques at Kitumbini, Kisutu, Magogoni and Msasani-Magofuni were relatively simple buildings, both the Lutheran and Catholic cathedrals were imposing structures by the standards of the day. Situated in commanding positions in front of the harbour, the two cathedrals witness with silence to the religious life of early colonial Dar es Salaam. As structures they represent a great effort of a new building age in Tanzania's colonial history. They structurally epitomize the history of Christianity etched in stone. Their sheer sizes reflect the anticipated large congregations from a growing urban Christian community.

In design the cathedrals were imitations of European architecture, but built with stone and brick, the materials most readily available in Dar es Salaam. A sense of permanence is unmistakable in their thick walls whereas aspiration and enthusiasm soar like the African eagle into heaven in the pointed arches and towering spires. The spires carry aloft that unmistakable symbol of Christianity, the cross. As we have already noted, for Christians the cross is a sign attesting to a historical event that took place approximately two thousand years ago, namely the Crucification and death of Jesus the Christ. Although we do not know how early missionaries in Dar es Salaam explained the symbol of the cross, it is pertinent to ask how Africans, especially the early converts, reacted to this visual symbol of Christianity. In spite of the unavailability of narratives which attest to early African reactions to the cross and its meaning of salvation, we can speculate that they probably reacted the same way that people had reacted during the first century of Christianity. In reference to non-Christian reactions to the symbol of the cross and its message of salvation, *The Encyclopedia of Religion* notes:

> ...the image of a god abandoned to a shameful punishment and nailed on a cross was not likely to arouse enthusiasm. On the contrary, such an image created serious difficulties in the eyes of pagans, who were unable to resolve the apparent contradiction of a crucified god who in so dying became a savior.

However, to the persecuted early Christians the cross stood both for the trials of life to be born by following Christ as well as for Christ's saving act. From the second century onward both meanings were given outward expression in the sign of the cross, i.e., the tracing of the cross on forehead and breast, which became a profession of faith. Subsequently, this practice, as well as the tracing of the cross in blessings, became a part of the liturgy (Meagher, 1979: 950). The practice of carving or painting the cross as an artifact came later and resulted in the veneration of the cross. To some Christians, however, the veneration of the cross and other religious images was deemed unacceptable, if not repugnant.

In Europe Christian opposition to image veneration led to iconoclasm, which is the breaking of images considered to be idols. In colonial Africa some separatist churches such as that introduced by Simon Kimbangu, in what is today the Democratic Republic of Congo, tended to downplay the significance of the cross. Ali Mazrui notes that the huge Kimbanguist Temple at Nkamba has no cross inside the building (Mazrui, 1986: 153). Mazrui explains the absence of the cross inside the Temple to be the result of Kimbanguist adherence to the first commandment against graven images and idolatry. But another reason why the cross plays a significantly more modest role in the Kimbanguist movement is because Simon Kimbangu was considered by his followers to be their equivalent of Jesus: a Black prophet and God's messenger to the Black races. Unlike Jesus, however, Kimbangu was not crucified but rather died in a colonial jail cell.

In Europe the Church reacted to iconoclasm by clarifying the differences between the *latria* and *dulia* forms of veneration. *Dulia* veneration, distinct from *latria* veneration reserved only for God alone, was considered by the Council of Nicaea II in 787 CE to be acceptable. It included representations, in whatever form, of the Crucification; figures on sacred vessels or vestments; icons of Christ, Mary, the angels, and saints. Expressions of veneration, then and now, include the kissing and incensation of images, placing lights and candles before them. One unexpected consequence of *dulia* veneration over the ages has been its association with superstitious beliefs. The phenomenon of weeping icons and statues especially of Mary, but also of Jesus and the saints, is a relatively commonly reported "supernatural" occurrence. What is of particular interest is that the substance of the "tears" is not water but olive oil.

Another phenomenon has been the appearance of Apparitions of the Virgin Mary and of Jesus. In 1988 St. Mary's Catholic primary school, Aking in Akamkpa Local Government area of Cross River State, Nigeria, became a center of attraction when an image believed to be of Jesus appeared on the wall of the school. The image, clad in white garments with a lamb on the right hand and a staff in the left hand, had light shining around it. Reports said the picture disappeared

51

after 10 minutes but stayed for several hours on the wall of an elementary 3A classroom on a second appearance. People from all walks of life thronged the school premises to have a glimpse of the mysterious image on the wall which remained like a television screen throughout the period (*The Nigerian Chronicle*, Cross River State, Nigeria, 3 October 1988).

Early Christians in Dar es Salaam and elsewhere most likely understood the intent of the Church's teaching on venerating religious images. Nevertheless, like their counterparts elsewhere they more than venerated these images, sometimes attributing to them all sorts of supernatural powers. Even today, some Christians will wear a cross on a journey in the belief that it will protect them from, say, injury or even death in a serious automobile accident. Christian students have been known to wear crosses while taking their examinations in the belief that the cross will help them pass the examinations. During his middle school days in the early 1960s this author was aware of a popular belief among Catholic students that the Eucharist would bleed if pricked with a needle!

By and large, it is likely that early Christians in Dar es Salaam, like their counterparts in other parts of Africa, were ridiculed by Muslims for venerating the cross and other religious images. Enrico Cerulli notes how Muslim popular poetry in Amharic-speaking areas of Ethiopia was used to ridicule Christian beliefs. In regard to the veneration of sacred images, and especially the cross, one poem's stanza runs as follows:

> The question of the Christians: I do not understand it, no!
> They hammer a piece of wood and dress it with silk.
> O stupid Christians! O stupid Christians!
> They hammer a piece of wood and then they say to it
> "Forgive me!" (Cerulli, 1969: 213)

Research on Swahili poetry in early colonial Dar es Salaam would do much to illuminate the prevailing popular Muslim conceptions of Christian symbols such as the cross.

However, Dar es Salaam Muslims themselves had their own religious symbols and other representations which they held in high esteem. One of these is the crescent moon, *hilal*, a symbol (often accompanied by a star) which actually predates Islam by several thousand years. Information on the origins of this symbol is difficult

Fig. 1: St. Joseph's Cathedral, Dar-Es-Salaam, Tanzania,
built between 1897 - 1902.

Fig. 2: Magomeni Mapipa Mosque, Dar es Salaam, Tanzania. Built in the late 1990s

to ascertain, but most sources agree that the crescent and star symbol was used by peoples of Central Asia and Siberia in their worship of sun, moon, and sky gods. It was not until the beginning of the Ottoman Empire that the crescent moon and star symbol became affiliated with the Muslim world.[47]

The religious significance of the new moon crescent is hinted in the Qur'an, Chapter 2 verse 189 which reads: "They ask thee about the new moons; say: They are fixed times for the people and for the pilgrimage." Thus, for ages the practice has been for Muslims to search the evening sky for the sight of the new moon in order to ensure that the rituals of the different lunar months are satisfactorily observed (Mazrui, 1986: 140). However, it is important to note that the prophet Muhammad himself never used the crescent as a symbol. The adorning of mosques with crescent finials came much later after the death of Muhammad. This practice appears to have already started when in the eleventh century the Cathedral of Ani was converted into a mosque and the cross on its dome was replaced by a silver crescent (Lewis, et. al., 1986: 383). Likewise the dome and minarets of the Mosque of the Umayyads in Damascus were decorated with crescent finials.

Besides the crescent, Muslims in early colonial Dar es Salaam like their counterparts elsewhere had for ages venerated Qur'anic calligraphy. Qur'anic calligraphy is not only revered but it is used in place of the depiction of living things as decorations. The notion that the depiction of living things is forbidden in Islamic art is derived from Qur'anic injunctions against idolatry. Thus, as Blair and Bloom note:

> God is worshipped directly without intercessors, so there is no place for images of saints as there is in Christian art. Muhammad was God's messenger, but unlike Christ, Muhammad was not divine. His deeds – not his person – represent the ideal to which Muslims aspire. Unlike the Bible, little of the Qur'an is narrative, so there was little reason to use illustrated stories to teach the faith (Blair and Bloom, 1999: 230).

Blair and Bloom conclude that in time the lack of motive and opportunity to use illustrated stories hardened into law, and the absence of figures became a characteristic feature of Islamic religious art. Thus few depictions, if any, of people can be found in mosques and other buildings intended for religious purposes (Blair and Bloom, 1999: 230).

In early colonial Dar es Salaam the Africanization of the religion of the crescent included the veneration of objects that were anathema to orthodox Islam. Thus, the reverence of Qur'anic calligraphy led to the production of amulets containing scraps of paper with Qur'anic messages. An amulet, called *hirizi* in Kiswahili, was believed to ward off evil forces.[48] Beliefs about evil forces abounded. As we have already noted, at the time of the arrival of Rev. Greiner it was popularly believed that Dar es Salaam was a cursed place and people hoped that the building of a mission station would probably annul the curse! What is equally significant is that Muslims who believed in evil spirits were in no position to criticize Christians for engaging in *shirk* such as the attribution of Divine-status to Jesus.

Indeed, the very fact that Muslims in early colonial Dar es Salaam believed and feared evil spirits was contrary to Islamic teaching that they fear none but God (Chapter 9 verse 18). One could say that in seeking protective powers in amulets, charms and other portents Muslims equated the power of such evil spirits to that of God when in fact such spirits were not supposed to have either existence or power save under God (Cragg, 1959: 113). In early colonial Dar es Salaam Muslims were either not aware of the Qur'an's warning (Chapter 4 verse 48) that "Whoso ascribeth partners to Allah, he hath indeed invented a tremendous sin" or sincerely believed they were not engaging in *shirk* by engaging in superstitious practices. In general, as Pouwels notes, their conversion was more of a reorientation of spiritual solemnization which did not require wholesale abdication of their ancient beliefs and rituals (Pouwels, 2000: 254).

Yet if Islam is not only what God requires but what believers do then the state of Islam in early colonial Dar es Salaam was probably far from the ideal. What was it that limited the realization of complete submission to God as Islam really means? Was it something environmental or circumstantial and thus also political? The opportunity to be validly what a Muslim should be requires an Islamic political order. As Cragg notes:

> The faith must fashion and control the state. The state must be the instrumentality of the faith. The creed presupposes rule: government enables obedience. Man in Islam can only truly be himself when the appropriate Islamic conditions in the state are realized around him (Cragg, 1959: 124).

It goes without saying that the imposition of German and later

British rule was a serious circumstantial obstacle to Islam in Tanganyika as it was beneficial to Christianity.

Other significant differences between Christianity and Islam in early colonial Dar es Salaam were their different styles and days of worship. If by making the sign of the cross a Christian affirmed his belief in the Trinity, a Muslim's postures at prayer (especially *kusujudu* or prostration) were an affirmation that there is no god except God. Besides the requirement to pray five times a day, Muslims held major congregational prayers on Fridays. However, sounds of the muezzin only clashed with the ringing of church bells on sundays when Christians turned out for prayers. It was under German rule that Sunday was made a day of rest for everybody. There is no evidence that Muslim employees either protested against resting on Sunday or demanded that Friday be equally made a resting day.[49] Unlike Christianity, Islam does not recognize any particular day of worship as a day of rest, including Friday. Indeed, in Chapter 62 verses 9-10 we read: "O ye who believe! When the call is heard for the prayer of the day of congregation, haste unto remembrance of Allah and leave your trading. That is better for you if ye did but know. And when the prayer is ended, then disperse in the land and seek of Allah's bounty, and remember Allah much, that ye may be successful."

Muslims unlike Christians must leave their shoes at the door before they enter the mosque. It is uncertain when the Muslim practice of removing shoes before entering a mosque began (Cragg, 1959: 26). However, it appears to be an ancient Semitic practice associated with reverence. Thus, in Exodus 3: 5 we read: "Come no closer! Remove the sandals from your feet, for the place on which you are standing is holy ground." And in the Chapter 20 verse 12 we read: "Lo! I, even I, am thy Lord. So take off thy shoes, for lo! thou art in the holy valley of Tuwa." It therefore must have amazed Dar es Salaam Muslims to see Christians entering their churches with shoes. Did the Christian practice put off potential converts from among the ranks of Muslims? Unfortunately the sources are silent on this matter.

Finally, tension and hostility between Christians and Muslims in early colonial Dar es Salaam came to the fore on closer contact. The Lutheran missionaries, for instance, showed little sensitivity to Muslim sensibilities by requiring all those who settled on mission land, including Ng'ambo which is now Kigamboni, to follow regulations which clearly favoured a Christian way of life. Most of those who settled at Ng'ambo were Sukuma and Nyamwezi Muslims. They were attracted to Ng'ambo by the area's very fertile land. Of particular interest were the regulations that forbade residents from cultivating their farms on sundays; regulations that prohibited the building of shrines for spirits including *kinyamkela*[50] as well as engaging in spirit exorcism, *kupunga pepo*; regulations that criminalized the taking of Zaramo and Islamic oaths as well as and regulations that forbade Zaramo initiation rites, *jando*, and Islamic instruction (von Sicard, 1970: 228-9).

On the other hand, Muslim African landlords in early colonial Dar es Salaam discriminated against prospective Christian tenants. Such discrimination especially affected Christians from upcountry who came to work in Dar es Salaam. It was on the intervention of Bishop Frank Weston of Zanzibar that the Government allocated a plot of land in Kariakoo specifically for Christians to build their residential quarters. This area came to be known as "Mission Quarters." With Church assistance about forty residential houses were built between 1923 and 1926. In the middle of this "village" was built a small church in 1929/30 which was named St. Francis. In what was considered hostile environment, the need for collective support led to the formation of the Roman Catholic Dar es Salaam African Association in 1934. Its main objective was to organize and spiritually strengthen all Catholics in the Kariakoo area (Mbiku, 1985: 99).

Meanwhile, the population of early colonial Dar es Salaam remained predominantly Muslim. Therefore, Muslim interests directly or indirectly influenced how public officials behaved as well as Government policy on religious matters. Such influence is evident in the Government's handling of an affray between Muslims and Christians at Matombo, Morogoro in early July 1933. On the night of 5 July 1933, the night of the birth of Prophet Muhammad, Muslims belonging to the Askariya and Qadiriyya brotherhoods were in a procession to Matombo for the purpose of celebrating *Maulid* and performing *Dhikr*.[51] The former is a celebration of Muhammad's birthday and the later is an occasion devoted to the remembrance of Allah by reciting his various names. The Qur'an says, "Allah's are the fairest names. Invoke Him by them." Also Allah is said to promise to take care of those who remember Him after the early morning and evening prayers.

Dhikr can be performed loudly in public or silently in private. The Muslims at Matombo were performing the loud type of dhikr by repeatedly and in loud voices chanting "La Ilaha Illa Llahi Muhammad Rasul Llahu."[52] It happened that the road they used passed by the Holy Ghost Fathers' mission. As they approached the mission chanting "La Ilaha Illa Llahi Muhammad Rasul Llahu," a priest stopped and asked them, "Why do you pass here making a noise and uttering dirty words?" The Muslims supposedly apologized and were allowed to proceed. They had not gone far when they were confronted by two other priests accompanied by some of their followers. The priests and their followers endeavoured to stop the chanting of the Muslims (TNA 21715).

According to the Acting Commissioner of Police what followed is not altogether clear, but it seems that the Muslims were set upon and beaten, some of them severely. One Muslim who was partially blind in one eye was blinded in the second eye in the ensuing melee. When the case was brought before the District Officer (D.O.) he found the missionaries and one African Christian guilty of interfering with a procession and unlawful assembly. In his report to the Provincial Commissioner (P. C.), the D. O. noted that although the Muslims were tactless and almost provocative in passing the Mission buildings reciting the *Dhikr*, "they were in no way responsible for the affray that took place" (D.O. to P.C., dated 22 Sept., 1933, TNA 21715).

The D. O. was of the opinion that the conduct of the two priests found guilty was deserving of the greatest censure. "Not only did they make no attempt whatever to control their Christians when they were brawling,' he said, 'but they failed to report the occurrence to me" (ibid.). He believed that had a higher authority in the Church approached the Muslims immediately after the incident to apologize and offer compensation, "Feelings would never have run high amongst the Mohammedans and the case could easily have been settled out of court." (ibid.).

In order to create a better feeling between the Christians and Muslims at Matombo the D.O. recommended the removal from the area of the two White Fathers. He proposed also that in the future the reciting of *Dhikr* on that part of the road which passes the Mission be prohibited to prevent the recurrence of any such unfortunate incident. According to the P. C. the missionaries at Matombo were dissatisfied "not so much with the conviction as with the severity of the sentences, "in which, they felt, the District Officer was influenced by the attitude of the local Mohammedans"[53] (P. C. to Chief Secretary, dated 25 Sept. 1933, TNA 21715). Father Gattang, the Acting Administrator of the Mission, objected also to the recommendation of the D. O. that the priests concerned in the affray should be removed to another area. However, despite their dissatisfaction they were unwilling to appeal "as they wished to avoid any recrudescence of the quarrel and any increase of the Mohammedan hostility against them" (ibid.). As we will shortly see, they need not have worried because intervention came from an unlikely source.

Official reaction in Dar es Salaam to the affray at Matombo was one of alarm. Upon learning about the incident the P. C. as well as the Acting Commissioner of Police and the Chief Secretary became very concerned that Muslims in Dar es Salaam would react negatively. This fear was made the worse when it was discovered that printed copies of a letter from some Morogoro sheikhs were being circulated in Dar es Salaam. It was feared that the objective of the letter was to agitate Dar es Salaam Muslims to fight for their brethren in Morogoro who claimed their Muslim dignity had been affronted by Christians without reason (Juma Kawambwa, et. al., to M. O. Abasi, letter dated 11 July 1933, TNA 21715).

The Morogoro D. O.'s suggestion to abolish *Dhikr* triggered off exchanges between high-level officials in Dar es Salaam. It was observed that *Dhikr* had lately become popular and numerous groups had been formed, "each under the leadership of a 'Sheikh' [sic], who [was] usually an African having some knowledge of Moslem Holy Writ, sufficient at any rate to impress his followers" (TNA, 21715). The concern of officials was whether the influence of these 'Sheikhs' over their converts and adherents was desirable:

> Some are men of no substance who, under the guise of religion, appear to make a business of Thikri [sic] and hold considerable sway over their followers, and who themselves are more often than not drawn from the less attractive sections of the community. It is perhaps a matter for consideration whether or not after ascertaining the views of responsible Mohammedans here and elsewhere in East Africa, the public performance of these irregular Thikri ceremonies should be

restricted as, it is understood, they are in Zanzibar. While it is the policy of Government not to interfere with any form of religious observance not actively repugnant to morals or a public nuisance, the fact should not be lost sight of that the influence of these groups over their followers may not be purely religious. These groups are likely to turn into societies, not necessarily anti-social in aims but certainly not conducive to good order (TNA, 21715).

Despite official concerns about *Dhikr* the fear of Muslim negative reaction to its abolition caused officials in Dar es Salaam not to go along with the D. O.'s recommendation to abolish its performance at Matombo.[54] Moreover, Government officials in Dar es Salaam did not want to appear like they were interfering with religious freedom. It was to this effect that Circular No. 2 of 1933 concerning *Dhikr* was issued. The Circular directed Provincial Commissioners and the Commissioner of Police to handle cases concerning *Dhikr* by means of the provisions of the existing law, that is to say, Sections of 30 to 33 of the Police Ordinance.

Apart from the above administrative handling of the Matombo incident, matters took an interesting judicial turn when Mr. Justice Hearne reviewed the case some months later. Justice Hearne did not concur with the magistrate that the Holy Ghost Fathers had planned to interfere with the procession. Justice Hearne did not believe that three priests and two African followers would have planned to obstruct a procession of religious enthusiasts of 80 to 100 persons (*Tanganyika Standard*, 24 October 1933, TNA 21715).

Another issue that concerned Justice Hearne was whether the Muslims had the right of procession as well as the right to use the road that passed through the Mission. His interpretation of the law was as follows:

A religious procession, like the rest of the public, has no doubt the right to pass on the highway. But there is no peculiar right known to the law as the right of procession: and the circumstances attending a procession may entitle other users of the road to object to an excessive noise, or to any particular feature of the procession occasioning a nuisance without contravening the law (ibid.).

Moreover, Justice Hearne found that the Muslims perjured themselves when they denied that they carried sticks and that they hit one of the priests and a native Christian.

On the basis of the above legal technicalities Justice Hearne quashed the convictions and sentences of four of the accused. He also directed that the fines paid by them be refunded. He, however, found one African Christian guilty of having thrown stones at the Muslims. His conviction and fine of Shs. 50 under Section 119 of the Penal Code was upheld but his conviction under section 72 was quashed. It is not known how the Muslims in Morogoro and Dar es Salaam reacted to the revision of the findings of the Magistrate's court.

CHAPTER FOUR

EARLY CHRISTIAN POLEMIC IN KISWAHILI AGAINST ISLAM

One missionary strategy of combating Islam was to publish Kiswahili books and manuals which specifically aimed at critiquing the teachings of Islam in favour of Christianity. In this chapter we focus on two early books by Rev. J. Murray Mitchell and Rev. Godfrey Dale. The issues that these two authors deal with in their books indicate that there was already an ongoing dialogue between the followers of Christianity and Islam in German East Africa about the differences between the two faiths. Mitchell's book entitled *Shuhuda za Dini ya Kimasihia pamoja na Kupeleleza Kidogo Dini ya Isilamu*[55] was published in 1905. Mitchell's intended audience was the literate African who, he says, due to the availability of books was becoming more knowledgeable about the world. Despite the increasing availability of books Mitchell lamented the ignorance of the literate African about religious matters and the significant differences between religions. As the earliest publication and because of the nature of its criticism of Islam *Shuhuda za Dini ya Kimasihia* is worth of close and detailed scrutiny.

Mitchell starts by noting that people may disregard differences of nationality, colour, race and culture. What they cannot disregard are differences of religion (Mitchell, 1905: 4). The basic question which Mitchell intends to elucidate upon is whether all the different religions can equally be true, their differences of doctrines and teachings notwithstanding. Mitchell believes that his own religion (Christianity) is the true religion: "If we (Christians) follow the true religion, then those others must believe in the wrong and erroneous faiths" (Mitchell, 1905: 5).

First and foremost, Mitchell attempts to prove the authenticity of the New Testament and to show why it is believable to Christians. He notes that the Apostles Matthew and John were disciples of Jesus and eyewitnesses to the things they narrate about in their gospels.[56] The gospels of Mark and Luke, he says, were written by close companions of the Apostles Peter and Paul respectively. Moreover, Mitchell argues that given the fact that the things that Jesus is said to have done were done in public, the absence of eyewitness accounts which deny what the Gospels say happened suggests that these miracles happened (ibid., 15 - 43). He accepts the authenticity of the miracles performed by Jesus because there are no narratives of the time which deny that such things ever happened. According to Mitchell, hostile Jewish scholars of the time such as Celsus acknowledged that these miracles happened albeit attributed them to magic and the power of Satan. Mitchell notes that even the *Antiquities of the Jews*, vol. XVIII, no. 4, acknowledges Jesus and his power to do miracles.[57]

Furthermore, Mitchell notes that the prophesy of Jesus is not only authenticated by the miracles that he performed but also by his teachings as well as the things he said would come to pass and did. For Mitchell the most amazing prophesy in the Bible is about the spread of Christianity over the entire world (ibid., 76). Jesus said: "And I, when I am lifted up from the earth, will draw all people[58] to myself" (John, 12: 32). Similar to this prophesy are the instructions Jesus gave to his eleven disciples when he appeared to them after his resurrection: "Go into the world and proclaim the good news (or gospel) to the whole creation" (Mark, 16: 15).

By and large, Mitchell attempts to provide proof that the Bible is indeed the Word of God. He writes: "If we look at the internal evidence which authenticates Christianity, we must look at the accolades (*sifa*) of the religion itself. We do not ask, how did this message come? Who brought it? But we ask, what is this message? Is it the message we should know comes from God?[59] Is this His true religion?" (Mitchell, 1905: 79). Mitchell suggests that determination of Christianity as the true religion can be done in two ways: "*Kwanza, twaweza kuipima kwa yale tuyajuayo ya Mngu, na kuangalia kwamba yamkini imetoka kwake Yeye. Pili, twaweza kuilinganisha na mambo ya watu tuyajuayo, na kusema kwamba ndiyo kazi ya bin-Adamu au sivyo*"[60] (ibid., 79).

According to Mitchell, Christianity was not inspired by human beings. He notes that the Jews, who at the time of Jesus were under Roman rule, expected a Messiah who would deliver them from Roman oppression. When Jesus told Pontius Pilate that his kingdom was not of this earth (John 18: 36), the statement was interpreted by the majority of Jews as a repudiation of the role of the messiah in the realization of Jewish national aspirations. In this regard, it is important to understand the political conditions under which Jews at the time of Jesus lived and the aspirations which their oppression stirred up.

Samuel Sandmel, the "Biblist" scholar, notes that Jews of the time of
Jesus believed that a Messiah would do three very important things:

> "he would destroy the power of Rome; he would inaugurate a dynasty
> of the proper line, that of David, in place of the improper
> Hasmoneans, who had usurped the throne, and the even more
> improper Herodians. Also, since Jews were scattered throughout the
> then known world, the Messiah was expected to spur and enable the
> exiles to return to Palestine (Sandmel, 1973: 32). Thus, according to
> Sandmel, the Jews who did not accept Jesus as the Messiah "rejected
> the claims because the expectations did not materialize. The power
> of Rome was not broken, the Davidic line was not restored, the
> scattered were not miraculously restored to Palestine; day-to-day life
> went on as before" (Sandmel, 1973: 33).

Most Jews also resented Jesus likening himself with God. John
10: 22-33 reads: "At that time the festival of the Dedication took place
in Jerusalem. It was winter, and Jesus was walking in the temple, in the
portico of Solomon. So the Jews gathered around him and asked,
'How long will you keep us in suspense? If you are the Messiah, tell
us plainly.' Jesus answered, 'I have told you, and you do not believe.
The works I do in my Father's name testify to me ... The Father and I
are one.' The Jews took up stones again to stone him. Jesus replied, 'I
have shown you many good works from the Father. For which of
these are you going to stone me?' The Jews answered, 'It is not for a
good work that we are going to stone you, but for blasphemy, because
you, though only a human being, are making yourself God.'" According
to Sandmel, whereas Jews may accept the figurative use of the term
"Son of God," as in Deuteronomy 14: 1, they vehemently are opposed
to any literal meaning which ascribes the Sonship of God to Jesus
alone (Sandmel, 1973: 37).

Moreover, the theological divide between Judaism and
Christianity is said to have deepened due to the teachings of Paul.
Paul's ministry resulted in what has come to be known as Pauline
Christianity. Although both Judaism and Christianity believe that there
is such a thing as the will of God, they differ in their understanding
of how that will has been revealed to humans and how humans can
execute it. The followers of Judaism believe that they can execute the
will of God by abiding to Mosaic Law.[61] Pauline Christianity, however,
believes to the contrary. Paul taught that laws and regulations could
impede one's fidelity to God's will. He instead preached that only a
believer's "faith" rather than "works" could lead to salvation (Sandmel,

1973: 132). As we will see later, Paul's teachings were not pleasing to Jews only but also to Muslims.

By and large, the schism between Jesus and his followers and other Jews is said to have been politically motivated. Muhammad Ata ur-Rahim writes:

> The conflict between the Jews and the followers of Jesus was started by those Jews who had adapted Moses's message to suit their own ends, and who feared, quite correctly, that to support the followers of Jesus would inevitably lead to their losing the wealth, power and the position which they enjoyed. The pact which the upper echelon of Jews had made with the Romans, to safeguard their vested interests and privileges they had enjoyed for centuries, had necessitated their departing even further from the guidance they had been given ...Thus it was that a follower of Jesus accepted Jesus while a Jew rejected him (ur-Rahim, 1977: 55)

Yet the very first Christians were Jews who professed their faith despite the dangers of persecution this exposed them to. Roman rulers were first opposed to Christianity and persecuted anybody who professed the faith. However, the believers persevered and in the end the Roman empire became Christian; which in itself, according to Mitchell, is a miracle (Mitchell, 1905: 82).

Furthermore, Mitchell says that it is what the Bible says that validates it as coming from God. He points out that the life of Jesus is narrated by four different Apostles and neither contradicts the other in any significant way.[62] The book of Acts of the Apostles also provides further information about Jesus and the first Christians. He argues that they have all been scrutinized and they have been found not to contradict or differ from each other in their testimony.[63]

According to Mitchell the testimony of the Qur'an, much as the source is the same person, is contradictory in many places. The chapters revealed in Mecca are different, if not contradictory, to those revealed in Medina (Mitchell, 1905: 85). In analyzing Islam, Mitchell suggests that there are differences between Islam as taught by Muhammad and Islam as we know it today (ibid., 157). He writes:

> The religion practised by his followers now is not the one he introduced; and to give him due respect, we must not attribute to him silly and wrong things believed by his followers. All that Muhammad taught is not in the Qur'an. Four pillars of Islam are mentioned - 1. The Qur'an, 2. Sunna, 3. Hadith, and 4. The Pilgrimage.[64] The most

important pillar is the Qur'an...If this pillar (the Qur'an) is made to
fall the whole religion falls (ibid., 157-8).

In the remainder of his book Mitchell attempts to show how
Islam cannot be the true and ultimate religion as its followers believe.
Mitchell starts with what he calls Muhammad's problematic life.[65] He
notes that unlike the accounts about the life of Jesus, there are no
eyewitness accounts about the life of Muhammad (ibid., 159). The
most important authoritative sources about Muhammad's life such
as Al-Tabari (d.922 AD), Ibn Hisham (d. 825 AD), Al-Waqid (d. 819
AD), and Ibn Saad (d. 842 AD) were not contemporaries of
Muhammad. What they wrote about Muhammad was gleaned mostly
from oral testimonies whose validity is problematic.[66] Therefore, in
his view what we know about Muhammad may not be entirely true.

Mitchell notes that the problem of sources about Muhammad's
life applies even to the Qur'an itself. He points out that the Qur'an
was passed on by Muhammad to his followers over a period of twenty-
three years. His followers either memorized or wrote what he recited
to them. Those who wrote parts of the Qur'an did so on whatever
material available to them including pieces of skin, on stones and
lamb shoulder blades. The preservation of what was written was also
supposedly haphazard, a factor which may have caused the loss of
parts of the Qur'an (Mitchell, 1905: 160).

Two years after Muhammad's death Abu Bakr ordered that all
parts of the Qur'an, written or memorized, be collected and put
together. This was the first attempt to come up with a single written
version of the Qur'an. Seventeen years later, Uthman commissioned
four experts to compile a more agreeable version of the Qur'an from
the original copy which was in the custody of Hafsa, one of the
Prophet's wives and Abu Bakr's daughter. Subsequently, more copies
were made from Uthman's commissioned version and all copies deemed
to be erroneous were collected and put out of circulation.

Mitchell questions the validity of the Qur'an on the basis of
the various attempts to compile an agreeable version from the oral
sources. He notes that Shiite Muslims say that in the process of
compiling the Qur'an ten portions (sehemu kumi) were removed by
Uthman, which comprised a quarter of the Qur'an[67] (ibid., 161).
Moreover, Mitchell suggests that Muhammad himself during his
lifetime changed a lot of things in the Qur'an.[68] Some of these

assertions were recently reiterated by a correspondent in the *An-Nuur* newspaper (which is Muslim owned) of 2-8 October 1998. This correspondent notes that according to Sahih Al-Bukhari, the Caliph Omar once said:

> "If it was not for fear that people would say Omar has added (something) in the Qur'an I would have written the Rajm chapter by my own hand." The same correspondent says that according to Al-Bukhari, chapter 92 verse 3 in the original Qur'an used to read "Wadh Dhakari Wal Unthaa" but later Muhammad's Companions read it as "Wamaa Khalaqadh dhakara wal unthaa."

Mitchell goes on to show that Muslim claims that the Qur'an is the Word of God do not take into consideration its many contradictions. He asks, could God have later forbidden those things that he earlier had allowed? He suggests that even Muhammad himself was aware of these contradictions. In order to take care of this problem Muhammad came up with the idea of abrogation: Chapter 2 verse 106 reads, "Such of Our revelations as We abrogate or cause to be forgotten, We bring (in place) one better or the like thereof. Knowest thou not that Allah is Able to do all things?" Mitchell estimates that such abrogated verses number about one hundred and twenty-five. He gives the following as examples:

> Chapter 16 verse 11 reads: "Therewith He causeth crops to grow for you, and the olive and date-palm and grapes and all kinds of fruit. Lo! herein is indeed a portent for people who reflect."
>
> Chapter 2 verse 219 reads: "They question thee about strong drink and games of chance. Say: In both is great sin, and (some) utility for men; but the sin of them is greater than their usefulness..."
>
> Chapter 5 verse 90 reads: "O ye who believe! Strong drink and games of chance and idols and divining arrows are only an infamy of Satan's handiwork. Leave it aside in order that ye may succeed."
>
> Chapter 16 verse 11 which was revealed at Mecca was abrogated by Chapter 2 verse 219 and Chapter 5 verse 90, both revealed at Medina.[69]

According to Mitchell, the chapters revealed at Medina are more strict, legalistic and uncompromising than those revealed at Mecca. This is, however, of minor consequence to Mitchell than the fact that the Qur'an says things that the Bible does not say. He cites several examples as follows:

Chapter 5 verse 114: "Jesus, son of Mary, said: O Allah, Lord of us! Send down for us a table spread with food from heaven, that it may be a feast for us, for the first of us and for the last of us, and a sign from Thee. Give us sustenance, for Thou art the Best of Sustainers," and verse 115: "Allah said: Lo! I send it down for you. And whoso disbelieveth of you afterward, him surely will I punish with a punishment wherewith I have not punished any of (My) creatures."

Chapter 4 verse 157: "And because of their (Jews) saying: We slew the Messiah, Jesus son of Mary, Allah's messenger - They slew him not nor crucified him, but it appeared so unto them; and lo! those who disagree concerning it are in doubt thereof; they have no knowledge thereof save pursuit of a conjecture; they slew him not for certain,' verse 158, "But Allah took him up unto Himself. Allah was ever Mighty, Wise." Chapter 61 verse 6: "And when Jesus son of Mary said: O Children of Israel! Lo! I am the messenger of Allah unto you, confirming that which was (revealed) before me in the Torah, and bringing good tidings of a messenger who cometh after me, whose name is the Praised One.[70] Yet when he hath come unto them with clear proofs, they say: This is mere magic."

For Mitchell, the Qur'an's denial that Jesus was not crucified and did not die on the cross strikes at the very heart of Christianity, which believes that Jesus died for the sins of the world. The denial negates the Christian idea of salvation and the role of Jesus in the reconciliation of humans to God after their fall from God's grace. He also sees such a denial as presupposing that the entire New Testament and its teachings are erroneous and misleading. Surprisingly, however, Mitchell does not address the claim by Muslims that an entire gospel, that of Barnabas, was expunged from the New Testament not only because it tells about things as they really happened but foretells the coming of the Prophet Muhammad.

The mystery surrounding the Gospel of Barnabas is that only three or four original copies are known to exist. That Muslims have an Arabic copy of Gospel of Barnabas is well known (Axon, 1902). It is also no secret that Muslims have used the Gospel of Barnabas as a formidable instrument against Christianity. Needless to say, "Christian scholarship sees the *Gospel of Barnabas* as a forgery, probably dating from the sixteenth century, the work of a Christian convert to Islam or (more plausibly) of a Muslim writing in the shadow of the Inquisition" (Hansen and Twaddle, 1995: 211).

Whether the Gospel of Barnabas is a forgery or not Muslims have capitalized on what it supposedly says, which supports their religious viewpoint. In the following quotation from the Gospel of Barnabas Jesus disputes his divinity as Son of God and foretells the coming of the Prophet Muhammad:

> And when Jesus had ended his prayer, the High Priest cried with a loud voice, 'Stay, Jesus, we want to know who thou art, for the quiet of our people.' He answered, 'I am Jesus of Nazareth, born of Mary, of the stock of David, a mortal man, and fear God, and seek his honour and glory.' The High Priest said, 'It is written in the book of Moses that God is to send the Messias [sic], who will come and declare the truth, and will bring mercy with him, and therefore we desire thee to tell us, if thou art the Messias whom we expect?' Jesus said, 'It is true that God has promised, but I am not he: for he was created before me.' The High Priest said, 'By thy words and signs we know that thou art a prophet and a saint of God; and therefore I intreat [sic] thee in his name and for his sake, that thou tell us how the Messias will come.' Jesus answered, 'As God liveth, I am not that Messias which the tribes of the earth wait for, as God promised by our father Abraham, saying, In thy family I will bless all tribes. But when God shall take me out of the world, Satan will again promote this cursed sedition, making the wicked believe that I am the Son of God. My words and doctrine will be corrupted, insomuch that scarce thirty faithful shall be found. Then will God have mercy on his people, and will send his messenger into the world, by whom he hath created all things: and he will come from the South with power, and will destroy Idolaters, and take away from Satan the empire that he has over men, and will bring the mercy of God and salvation to those that shall believe him. Blessed are those that shall believe him.' (Quoted by Axon, 1902: 446).

In the following quotation we hear Jesus mention Muhammad by name and say that he is no where near in comparison to Muhammad:

> 'I that am unworthy to loose his shoes have had the favour to see him.' The President, High Priest, and Herod said, 'Disturb not thyself, Jesus the saint of God, for in our time there will be no more sedition: for we will write to the holy senate of Rome, that by an imperial decree none may call thee God.' Jesus said, 'I am not comforted with this... But my consolation is in the coming of the Messenger of God, who will destroy all false opinions concerning me...
>
> And above all my comfort is, that his faith shall have no end, but shall be inviolable and preserved by God... The High Priest said, 'What will the Messias be called, and how shall his coming and manner

of life be known?' Jesus answered, 'The name of the Messenger of God is Admirable; for God himself gave it him after he had created his soul and placed it in celestial brightness. God said, Observe Mohammed, for I will for thy sake create paradise and the world with a great number of creatures, of which I make thee a present: so that whosoever shall bless thee shall be blessed, and whosoever shall curse thee shall be cursed. And when I shall send thee into the world I will send thee for my messenger of salvation, and thy words shall be true; so that heaven and earth shall fail, but they shall never fail in thy law. Mohammed is his blessed name.' Then the multitudes lifted up their voices and said, 'Send us, O God, thy messenger; come presently, O Mohammed, for the salvation of the world.' (Quoted by Axon, 1902: 447).

In regard to the Qur'an's assertion that Jesus himself foretold the coming of Muhammad, Mitchell says the assertion arises from a confusion of the word *Paraklitos* with *Periklutos*. In John, 14: 16 Jesus said: "And I will ask the Father, and he will give you another Advocate,[71] to be with you forever. This is the Spirit of truth, whom the world cannot receive, because it neither sees him nor knows him. You know him because he abides with you, and he will be in you."[77] According to Mitchell, the advocate or helper translates as *Paraklitos* but when changed to the Greek it reads as *Periklutos*. In the later sense it translates as Famous which in Arabic is similar to the meaning of Ahmad. In Arabic the name Muhammad takes the same meaning. Mitchell further notes that what Jesus promised his disciples was the eternal assistance of the Holy Spirit rather than the coming of another Prophet in the name of Muhammad.

However, besides referring to the Gospel of Barnabas for proof of the foretelling of the coming of Muhammad, some Muslims, including Sheikh Ahmed Deedat of South Africa, have alluded to Deut. 18: 18 to be equally supportive of their thesis. But they appear to read verse 18 out of context. To get the full sense of what kind of prophet is prophesied here one has to read verses 15 through 22 as follows:

The Lord your God will raise up for you a prophet like me from among your people; you shall heed such a prophet. This is what you requested of the LORD your God at Ho'reb on the day of the assembly when you said: "If I hear the voice of the LORD my God anymore, or ever again see this great fire, I will die." Then the LORD replied to me: "They are right in what they have said. I will raise up for them a prophet like you from among their own people; I will put my words in the mouth of the prophet, who shall speak to them everything that I command. Anyone who does not heed the words that the prophet shall speak in my name, I myself will hold accountable. But any prophet who speaks in the name of other gods, or presumes to speak in my name a word that I have not commanded the prophet to speak - that prophet shall die." You may say to yourself, "How can we recognize a word that the LORD has not spoken?" If a prophet speaks in the name of the LORD but the thing does not take place or prove true, it is a word that the LORD has not spoken. The prophet has spoken it presumptuously; do not be frightened by it."

First, Deut. 18:18 does not refer to any specific prophet. The prophesied prophet, to be appointed by God, would lead the children of Israel. Moses was aging, and God was speaking of the transition to come following Moses' death. Second, a prophet "like" Moses simply meant that the prophet would be as dedicated and committed as Moses was. However, as it happened Joshua replaced Moses as leader of Israel, but Joshua was not a prophet.[73] Hence the knotty question of whom the replacement prophet would be. According to Deedat, strong similarities between Moses and Muhammad,[74] and the fact that the unlettered Muhammad transmitted Allah's Word verbally, are proof that it was he and no other prophet that was prophesied in Deut. 18:18 (Deedat, 1976).

In his booklet titled Is Muhammad Foretold in the Bible? John Gilchrist counter-argues that similarities between Moses and Muhammad do not help to identify the prophet predicted by Moses. (See Gilchrist at <http://www.answering-islam.org/Gilchrist/muhammad.html>). This is because there are, likewise, compelling similarities between Moses and Jesus.[75] According to Gilchrist, one of the crucial factors in really determining the identity of the prophet who was to follow Moses is genealogy. The genealogy of Muhammad, who is claimed to be an "Ishmaelite," puts him outside the line of succession after Moses.[76] Moreover, Gilchrist notes, Jesus who was from the tribe of Judah was uniquely like Moses because he, unlike Muhammad, also performed miracles.[77] Thus Gilchrist reiterates what Mitchell said almost a hundred years ago.

Despite the controversial nature of Mitchell's book it appears to have elicited no responses from Swahili Muslim scholars at the time. However, the publication of Mitchell's book seems to have motivated other missionaries to emulate his example. One such missionary was none other than the Rev. Godfrey Dale who belonged to the Universities Mission to Central Africa and worked in Zanzibar from 1889 to 1925. Rev. Dale's numerous works include *Tafsiri ya Kurani ya Kiarabu kwa Lugha ya Kisawahili*, *Maisha ya Muhammad* and *Khabari za dini ya Kiislamu kwa mukhtasari pamoja na maelezo ya ikhtilafu zilizopo kati ya dini ya Kiislamu na ya Kikristo* (Summary remarks about the religion of Islam together with an explanation of the existing differences between the religion of Islam and the religion of Christianity). Here we will focus more on *Khabari za dini ya Kiislamu* which was published in 1909.[78]

According to Rev. Dale *Khabari za dini ya Kiislamu* was written at the request of African Christian teachers in Zanzibar and on the mainland who wanted a simplified text that explained the basics of Islam. In writing *Khabari za dini ya Kiislamu*, however, Rev. Dale went beyond the call of duty. In this book he does indeed explain in simplified terms the basic teachings of Islam. But he also compares Islam to Christianity, a comparison which must have been intended for no other reason than to enable Christians to rebut Muslim criticism of Christianity as well as to offer their own criticism of Islam. One of the Muslim criticisms dealt with by Rev. Dale is the unacceptability of the Trinity to Muslims. Although Rev. Dale does not explicitly cite the Qur'anic verses which repudiate the Trinity, these are two verses in chapter five of the Qur'an which we cite here in full. Verse 73 reads: "They surely disbelieve who say: Lo! Allah is the third of three; when there is no God save the One God. If they desist not from so saying a painful doom will fall on those of them who disbelieve." Verse 116 reads: "And when Allah saith: O Jesus, son of Mary! Didst thou say unto mankind: Take me and my mother for two gods beside Allah? He saith: Be glorified! It was not mine to utter that to which I had no right..." The following verse reiterates the Oneness of Allah.

Rev. Dale suggests that insofar as the concept of the Trinity is concerned Muhammad's attempt to refute it was misguided and he did not understand its meaning. Rev. Dale's reading of verse 116 cited above apparently convinced him that Muhammad understood the three parts of the Trinity to be God, Jesus and the virgin Mary; that Christians are taught that there are three gods. On this issue Rev. Dale concludes that: *"Waislamu wakisema maneno haya hudhani wanakanusha dini ya Kristo, lakini hawajui kuwa wanafanya kosa lililo dhahiri kwa kila Mkristo anaejua*

73

dini yake"[79] (Dale 1909: 20). Later on in the book Rev. Dale explains the meaning of the Trinity in relation to what he calls Muslim misconceptions of the birth, and hence divinity, of Jesus.

In *Khabari za dini ya Kiislamu* Rev. Dale also describes and analyzes the meaning and the role of jihad in the spread of Islam. He defines a jihad as fighting against unbelievers, in order to Islamize them or to make them obedient or to exterminate them if they do not accept Islam, and to try and remove all religions so Islam may have no competitors (ibid., 67). He says, Muhammad said: "Paradise is under the shadow of the sword." And that "To fight for Islam is obligatory until the Last Day" (ibid., 67). Rev. Dale notes correctly that initially the use of force in conversion was forbidden; that Muhammad even ordered his followers to tolerate mistreatment and suffering when they were still a nascent community in Mecca. The latter view is supported by Chapter 103 verse 3 which reads, "Save those who believe and do good works, and exhort one another to truth and exhort one another to endurance." However, when Muhammad relocated to Medina and got the assistance of the people of Medina he allowed his followers to fight those that caused them injury. Eventually Muhammad ordered his followers to go and fight even those that had caused them no injury, instructing them that the verses that had hitherto forbidden fighting in the name of Allah had been abrogated by those ordering Muslims to force people to accept Islam. Rev. Dale notes that early Muslims went to battle twenty seven times by order of Muhammad, and that Muhammad himself participated in warfare nine times.

According to Rev. Dale, Muslims were obligated to fight against three categories of people, namely (a) all unbelievers who did not accept Islam or pay tax, (b) all those living in Muslim lands, who disobeyed or did not pay tax, and (c) Muslims who did not obey the Imam, and all who caused war. If Muslims conquered any land, they were supposed to allow the vanquished to chose one of the following: (1) to become Muslim, and if they agreed then they would be treated equally with other Muslims, (2) to pay a specific tax called *jizya*,[80] and if they did they would be known as dhimmi, and could follow their own religion although they would not be permitted to build houses of worship, and (3) those who refused to pay *jizya,* as a result of which their wives and children would be sold into slavery, and the men killed (Dale, 1909: 67-68).

The source of *jizya* is Chapter 9: 29 which reads: "Fight against such of those who have been given the Scripture as believe not in Allah nor in the Last Day, and forbid not that which Allah hath forbidden by His messenger, and follow not the Religion of Truth, until they pay the tribute readily, being brought low." Although interpretations of this verse vary, the significance of *jizya* was to offer protection to non-Muslims especially if they were minorities. This is succinctly expressed by Larhmaid:

> From the very beginning, the normative vision of Muslim identity developed through the assumption of including non-Muslim minorities who would pay Jizya to the Imam. The concept of the Imam evolved as signifying the spiritual role of a Muslim who exercises as well a secular authority, including the collection of jizya. The Qu'aran [sic] specifies that Jews and Christians of conquered territories must pay money to demonstrate their submission to Muslim powers. According to the Hadith and the Sunna...[81] the Prophet himself exercised his secular power by making a pact with the Jews of Medina. The term Imam developed in the time of the four Khalifes. When the Arabs of the Arabian peninsula conquered new territories, it necessitated the adoption of a legal status for the Christians and Jews who were living under the guardianship of a Muslim chief. Thus, the exercise of power in lands surrendering to Islamic law had always gone beyond the practice of faith and its conservation. It also necessitated the protection of non-Muslims who paid money in a symbolic encounter that signified the submission to a legitimate authority holding both religious and political power (Larhmaid, 2001: 1-2).

Rev. Dale explains that dhimmi had to pay jizya in person. And when one paid, a Muslim would symbolically strike him on the neck, saying, "Pay, you enemy of God." Dhimmi were also expected to dress differently, not to sit when a Muslim was standing, to give right of way to Muslims, and if a dhimmi blasphemed Muhammad they had to be killed. Rev. Dale concludes that all these orders reflected what Muslims thought of Christians under their authority. He was grateful that in his day Muslims in Zanzibar were not able to follow these religious orders regarding relations with people of other religions. As we noted in chapter one, although the sultans of Zanzibar were Muslims they welcomed and treated the missionaries well. Among other things they were allowed to build churches and they were not called upon to pay *jizya*.

Rev. Dale further explains how Muslims have always perceived the world which they divide into Dar-al-Harb and Dar-al-Islam. The former is the land of war, any land which is not ruled by Muslims (Dale, 1909: 69). However, he notes that Dar-al-Islam may be considered as Dar-al-Harb if the country is not ruled according to Islamic laws, or if it is not separated from a land of Dar-al-Harb by another Muslim country. In the later case the Imam may decide to maintain good relations with the neighbouring unbelievers. But should a chance avail itself that the Muslims may conquer their neighbours the Imam can declare war after informing the unbelievers of his intentions. If they agree to be ruled by the Muslims without fighting, and to pay tax (kharaja), then their land cannot be taken from them. Paradoxically, Rev. Dale did not attempt to apply these concepts to Zanzibar or to explain whether her Muslim rulers considered Zanzibar to be Dar-al-Islam or Dar-al-Harb.

Furthermore, Rev. Dale notes in *Khabari za dini ya Kiislamu* that apostasy is not easily tolerated by Muslims[82] (Dale, 1909: 70). If a believer forsakes Islam that person must be brought before the Imam and told to rejoin the faith. The person must be bound for three days after which time if they persist in their decision they must be killed. A female apostate cannot be killed but must be bound until she rejoins the faith. A man who deserts Islam forfeits his marriage and his wife is not obligated to seek divorce. However, Rev. Dale does not say what happened to Muslims in Zanzibar who may have converted to Christianity as the result of his own missionary endeavour.

In the second half of *Khabari za dini ya Kiislamu* Rev. Dale deals with imaginary dialogues in which a Christian is confronted by a Muslim who criticizes Christian beliefs. One such dialogue deals with the issue of the Crucification of Jesus. According to Rev. Dale, the basis of Muslim belief that this did not happen is that God could not have let His prophet suffer unnecessarily. He therefore secretly rescued him without his mother and followers knowing it. Moreover, Muslims think that Crucification would have been a very shameful experience for a prophet of Jesus' caliber.[83] Rev. Dale insists that Christians have valid reasons to believe that the Crucification happened just as much as Muslims believe that Muhammad fasted during the month of Ramadan and insist on following his example. He poses some hypothetical questions: what if someone tells a Muslim that

Muhammad only appeared to fast but was actually secretly nourished by God without his wives or his Companions knowing. Would the Muslim believe such an allegation? Why do Muslims believe that God let Muhammad be injured and almost killed in the battle of Uhud, but He would not let Jesus die on the Cross?

Another imaginary dialogue concerns the issue of the Resurrection of Jesus. Rev. Dale notes that because Muslims do not believe that Jesus was Crucified they do not accept that he was Resurrected. He notes that Muslims are waiting for his death and believe that when Jesus comes back and eventually dies he will be buried in Medina where a tomb has already been prepared for him. However, it is curious that Rev. Dale does not discuss the idea of the Resurrection in Islam.

Islam rejects the Christian belief in the Resurrection of Jesus which is based on a historical event that is believed to have happened about 2,000 years ago. The rejection is partly drawn from the Gospel of Barnabas. In the following quotations from the Gospel of Barnabas we are told how Jesus escaped death and who died in his place:

> Judas came near to the people with whom Jesus was; and when he heard the noise he entered into the house where the disciples slept. And God, seeing the fear and danger of his servant, ordered Gabriel and Michael and Rafael and Azrael to carry him out of the world. And they came in all haste, and bare him out of the window which looks towards the south. And they placed him in the third heaven, where he will remain blessing God, in the company of angels, till near the end of the world.
>
> And Judas the traitor entered before the rest into the place from which Jesus had just been taken up. And the disciples were sleeping. And the wonderful God acted wonderfully, changing Judas into the same figure and speech with Jesus. We, believing that it was he, said to him, 'Master, whom seekest thou?' And he said to them, smiling, 'Ye have forgotten yourselves, since ye do not know Judas Iscariot.' At this time the soldiery entered; and seeing Judas so like in every respect to Jesus, laid hands upon him, & c.
>
> They carried him to Mount Calvary, where they executed criminals, and crucified him, stripping him naked for the greater ignominy. Then he did nothing but cry out, 'O my God, why hast thou forsaken me, that I should die unjustly, when the real malefactor hath escaped?' I say in truth that he was so like in person, figure, and gesture to Jesus, that as many as knew him, believed firmly that it was he, except Peter... (emphasis in the original, Quoted by Axon, 1902: 447-8).

However, Islam accepts Resurrection as something that will happen to all living things and that it is within the power of Allah, as the Qur'an says, to cause life to cease and new life to begin. In Chapter 75 verses 3-4 we read, "Thinketh man that We shall not assemble his bones? Yea, verily. We are Able to restore his very fingers!" In Chapter 17 verses 49-52 it is written, "And they say: When we are bones and fragments, shall we, forsooth, be raised up as a new creation? Say: Be ye stones or iron Or some created thing that is yet greater in your thoughts! Then they will say: Who shall bring us back (to life). Say: He Who created you at first. Then will they shake their heads at thee, and say: When will it be? Say: It will perhaps be soon; A day when He will call you and ye will answer with His praise, and ye will think that ye have tarried but a little while."

On the issue of why Christians believe Jesus to be the Son of God Rev. Dale wanted to help African teachers to reply to Muslims, every time they would be asked about this. He starts with an observation about what Muslims mean when they talk about "Son of God." He observes how pre-Islamic Arabs believed that their deities Al-Lat, Uzza and Manat were daughters of God. He also notes that such beliefs angered Muhammad because they did not only envision a God with human qualities but One who begat only daughters.

Pre-Islamic beliefs about a God with human like qualities are repudiated in the Qur'an, Chapter 6 verses 100-102: "Yet they ascribe as partners unto Him the jinn, although He did create them, and impute falsely, without knowledge, sons and daughters unto Him. Glorified be He and High Exalted above (all) that they ascribe (unto Him). The Originator of the heavens and the earth! How can He have a child, when there is for Him no consort, when He created all things and is Aware of all things? Such is Allah, your Lord. There is no God save Him, the Creator of all things, so worship Him. And He taketh care of all things." According to Rev. Dale, when Muslims say, *"Mungu hazai wala hazaliwi,"* they are thinking of human birth. But Christians do not think in those terms and certainly not like the way pre-Islamic Arabs thought. Moreover, Rev. Dale suggests that some statements which are in the Qur'an show Christians other erroneous ideas that Muslims have about Jesus. Muslims believe that he did not exist in any form before he was conceived in the Virgin Mary's womb. They believe his birth was miraculous because he did not have a father. Muslims point out that Adam had no father or mother but was created from nothing. Likewise, they say, Jesus was born miraculously, was created out of nothing. God said be, and he was (Dale, 1909: 108).

Thus Muslims believe that Jesus ought to be called the word of God.[84] It is on this basis, says Rev. Dale, that Muslims criticize Christians; they think Christians are saying that God took a wife and begot a Son. However, Rev. Dale reiterates that this is not what Christians are saying when they refer to Jesus as the Son of God. "Indeed, if this is the meaning of the birth of Jesus as written in the Qur'an, those words (in the Qur'an) are proof that God did not write the Qur'an,[85] because God cannot falsely accuse someone that they believe something they do not. We do not believe that God begot in this manner, and we also do not believe that God begot a Son after a certain time."

In *Khabari ya dini ya Kiislamu*, Rev. Dale takes the divine nature of the Bible as given. He proceeds from this premise to provide Biblical evidence that when Christians say that Jesus is the Son of God they are simply repeating what God Himself said. Thus, according to Matthew 3: 17: "And a voice from heaven said, 'This is my Son, the Beloved, with whom I am well pleased'" Rev. Dale also cites Luke 1: 35; Mat. 26: 64; and John 5: 25, 9: 35, 11: 4 among others for evidence of the divine nature of Jesus which, he says, "is enough to show that our Lord has been given this name in all the four Gospels; and this is what those who wrote the Gospels believed" (Dale, 1909: 113).

Rev. Dale goes on to suggest the reasons why Jesus was called the Son of God. First, it is because Jesus knew the secrets of people he did not know, not only their current ones but also of the past and future. He also could tell what happened somewhere even though he was not there such as in the case of the death of Lazarus, and especially the money in the mouth of a fish as narrated in Matt. 17: 27. Second, he was referred to by this name because of his teachings. According to Matt. 7: 29 and John 6: 68-69, Jesus taught as someone with authority. Third, he was called the Son of God because of the miracles that he performed. Rev. Dale notes that unlike other prophets before him Jesus performed these miracles without having to pray too hard and long, and did so with authority as though he had control over all creatures, fish, trees, the ocean, wind, bad spirits and water (Dale, 1909: 114). Not only did Jesus heal the blind, the deaf, the lame, those with leprosy, those who could not speak, the paralyzed, and hunchbacks but in the end he resurrected himself to show his power over death and the grave. Finally, Jesus prophesied about things to come, such as how he would die, how he would rise from the dead, how he would ascend to heaven, the coming of the Holy Spirit and the burning of Jerusalem by the Romans.

In contradistinction with the divine and prophetic nature of Jesus, Rev. Dale questions the divine and prophetic nature of the other five major prophets namely Adam, Noah (Nuhu), Abraham (Ibrahim), Moses (Musa) and Muhammad. In regard to Muhammad, Rev. Dale says he was not *maasum*, that is not without sin (Dale, 1909: 120). However, this is not disputable because the Qur'an says so. In Chapter 57 verse 19 we read "So know (O Muhammad) that there is no God save Allah, and ask forgiveness for thy sin and for believing men and believing women. Allah knoweth (both) your place of turmoil and your place of rest."[86] Chapter 58 verse 2 says: "That Allah may forgive thee thy sin that which is past and that which is to come, and may perfect His favour unto thee, and may guide thee on a right path." What is controversial is what Rev. Dale says about sinful prophets in which group he includes Muhammad. According to Rev. Dale, prophets who had committed sin could not have brought salvation to others (Dale, 1909: 117). And of all the prophets only Jesus is acknowledged to have been sinless, which in the eyes of Rev. Dale elevates Jesus above all others as the true Savior. He writes:

> *Kwamba Isa Masihi alikuwa hana dhambi yo yote, kwa hiyo aliweza kutupatia ghofira, na kuwa kafara kwa dhambi zetu, mwenye haki kwa ajili yao wasio na haki, na aweza kutuonyesha njia ya utakatifu, maana yeye mwenyewe ni njia hiyo, na aweza kutuombea daima, maana yuko kwa Mungu, mwenye haki...*[87] (Dale, 1909: 125).

Toward the end of *Khabari za dini ya Kiislamu* Rev. Dale questions the claim by Muslims that Muhammad is the last and the greatest of all prophets, surpassing even Jesus. The finality of Muhammad's prophethood is mentioned in Chapter 33 verse 40 where we read: "Muhammad is not the father of any man among you, but he is the messenger of Allah and the Seal of the Prophets; and Allah is ever Aware of all things." Muhammad is supposed to be the seal or the last of the prophets because by his coming and the revelation of the Qur'an Islam was completed in every respect as declared in Chapter 5 verse 3, "This day have I perfected your religion for you and completed My favour unto you, and chosen for you as religion AL-ISLAM."

According to one Hadith, Muhammad himself supposedly explained and clarified the meaning of "seal" of the prophets. He said: Prophethood has been just like a Palace, which was being built throughout the ages: yet the Palace was incomplete, for the space for a single brick was left blank in it. So remember, I am the last brick, which has completed the Palace of Prophethood. Assuredly, there will be no prophet after me (Bukhari and Muslim quoted by Tariq, 1973: xiv). However, Rev. Dale notes that Christians do not accept Muhammad as a prophet, and even if they did they would follow Jesus instead of Muhammad because of what Jesus did. What is more important, Rev. Dale says that of all the prophets Jesus stands in his own category and, therefore, he and not Muhammad is the last and the greatest of all prophets (Dale, 1909: 128).

It is interesting to note that the contention that Muhammad could not have been the last prophet was later taken up by Sheikh Amri Abeid Kaluta, a Tanzanian follower of a branch of Islam known as the Ahmadiyya.[88] He questions the interpretation of the Arabic title *Khatama Nnabiyina* in the Qur'an in reference to Muhammad. Sheikh Kaluta suggests that in accordance with rules of Arabic grammar and syntax *Khatama Nnabiyina* ought not to be translated as the last prophet. The correct translation he says should rather be the seal, the jewel (?), or the best of the prophets. He also notes that when the word *Khatama* is followed by a word signifying plurality such as *Nnabiyina* it cannot mean the end.

Sheikh Kaluta's translation of *Khatama Nnabiyina* was vehemently denounced by Muslims some of whom called him an infidel. A correspondent, one Hassan Msamy of Mombasa, writing in the *Mwongozi* issue of 5 August, 1957, had this to say about the grammar and syntax of *Khatama Nnabiyina*:

> *nahaw ni mawazo ya kibinaadamu yaliyo vumbuliwa na Abul-aswad, ili kuwafundisha watu wa mataifa mengine lugha ya Kiarabu kwa urahisi. Kadhalika na hiyo Kuran ni maneno ya Mungu yaliyoshuka zamani kabla nahaw haijaanza kuvumbuliwa. Kwa hiyo kizushi huyu anawezaje kuwa na haki ya kudai lazima neno lo lote la Kuran lifasiriwe kwa kufuata mpango wa nahaw, na hali Kuran ni maneno ya Mungu (?)...Nahaw haikhalifu Kuran wala Kuran haikhalifu Nahaw.*[89]

Msamy goes on to suggest that the meaning of *Khatama Nnabiyina* agrees with the meaning of another statement made by the prophet himself which he gives as *La Nabiya Baady*.

For mainstream Muslims any denial of the finality of the prophethood of Muhammad touches a very sensitive nerve especially if the denial is by someone who considers himself to be a Muslim. Anyone who denies this alleged revelation is considered a *kafir*. For ardent Muslims like the renown Dr. Muhammad Iqbal, such denial by Ahmadiyya Muslims threatens to return them to the religious uncertainties of pre-Islamic Magian culture which prevailed in much of Western Middle Asia. Iqbal writes:

> The concept of Magian culture, according to modern research, includes cultures associated with Zoroastrianism, Judaism, Jewish Christianity, Chaldean and Sabean religions. To these creed-communities the idea of the continuity of prophethood was essential, and consequently they lived in a state of constant expectation... The result of the Magian attitude was the disintegration of old communities and the constant formation of new ones by all sorts of religious adventurers. It is obvious that Islam which claims to weld all the various communities of the world into one single community, cannot reconcile itself to a movement which threatens its present solidarity and holds the promise of further rifts in human society (Speech in Tariq, 1973: 92)

Apparently, Iqbal was unaware about the finality of prophethood in Christianity which he placed together with those other religions that still await the coming of the "real"Messiah. Insofar as Iqbal understood that the finality of prophethood means that with it all personal authority in religious life must come to an end he was very close to the teaching of Christianity. With Christianity there is no salvation except through Jesus Christ. This position was reaffirmed in a Vatican theological document entitled "On the Unity and Salvific Universality of Jesus Christ and the Church" which was issued in 2000. On the basis of this document the Vatican rejects equality of faith between world religions and reiterates the doctrine that non-Christians are in a "gravely deficient situation" regarding salvation. Of course, the Muslims have always objected to such a claim and their objections are based on Chapter 2 verse 105 which says: "Neither those who disbelieve among the People of the Scripture[90] nor the idolaters love that there should be sent down unto you any good thing from your Lord. But Allah chooseth for His mercy whom He will, and Allah is of Infinite Bounty."

Whereas *Khabari za dini ya Kiislamu* was very critical of Islam, it appears not to have caused an uproar in the Muslim community the same way that his translation of the Qur'an into Kiswahili did. Rev. Dale's *Tafsiri ya Kurani ya Kiarabu* was published in 1923 (Dale, 1923). In the preface Rev. Dale tells us that the purpose of the translation is to make the Qur'an accessible to Padres, teachers and Christians living among Muslims to enable them to understand what Muslims say the Qur'an says. He also notes that there are some people who questioned whether it was safe to make the translation available to African Christians. He himself says he was not afraid of doing so: *"Mkristo aisomae Kurani baada ya kuijua Injili, akiipenda Kurani kuliko Injili, mfano wake ni mtu apendae taa ya mafuta, ijapokuwa aweza kupata taa ya umeme"*[1] However, he commends his Christian readers to weigh seriously what they read in the Qur'an against what is said in 1 John, 4: 1, viz. "Beloved, do not believe every spirit, but test the spirits to see whether they are from God; for many false prophets have gone out into the world. By this you know the Spirit of God: every spirit that confesses that Jesus Christ has come in the flesh is from God, and every spirit that does not confess Jesus is not from God. And this is the spirit of the antichrist, of which you have heard that it is coming; and now it is already in the world."

After warning his readers about false prophets Rev. Dale suggests that they may wish to pay particular attention to those chapters in the Qur'an that mention Jesus, Zachariah, Mary, the Holy Spirit, the Cross, Suleiman, David and Joseph as well as references in the Qur'an about jinns, marriage, divorce and concubinage, revenge, and jihad, etc. He asks the readers to consider whether such statements can come from God. Rev. Dale goes on to say that although Muslims are taught to accept the New Testament and other Scriptures, they do not know that this is impossible because what the Qur'an teaches is contrary to the teachings of the New Testament (Dale, 1923: viii).

In the preface to the *Tafsiri ya Kurani ya Kiarabu* Rev. Dale poses several questions. How can Muslims believe that God sent the New Testament (Injil) when, in fact, the Qur'an negates it on fundamental matters such as the Crucification? Can God contradict or correct Himself? Since Muslims believe that Jewish and Christian Scriptures have been distorted, concealed, misinterpreted, misplaced or otherwise tampered with, can they show the originals which are correct? How can one distort, conceal, misinterpret, misplace or delete statements or words that have never existed?

It also appears that Rev. Dale's skepticism about the Qur'an being the Word of God is derived from things that he believes do not make any sense, spiritually as well as logically. According to the Qur'an, God asked, "O Jesus, son of Mary! Didst thou say unto mankind: Take me and my mother for two gods besides Allah?" Rev. Dale uses this verse to query why God would say this:

> *Ninyi (Muslims) mnasadiki kuwa Kurani ni maneno ya Mungu. Basi Mungu alimwuliza Isa haya kwa sababu gani? Kama Mungu alijua kwamba Isa hakusema hayo, ya nini kumwuliza? Kama hakujua, siye Mungu. Na tena, Je! Mungu aliona kama hivyo ndivyo wanavyoamini Wakristo? Kama ndivyo livyoona, Mungu alikuwa hana khabari. Kama alijua ya kuwa sivyo wanavyoamini, ya nini kuuliza?"* (Dale, 1909: 113).[92]

Equally illogical to Rev. Dale is the matter of abrogated verses or verses which appear to him to be human rather than divinely inspired. In 1913 Rev. Dale delivered one of four lectures in the Christ Church Cathedral, Zanzibar, in which he questions the concept of abrogation. He is skeptical of the claim that the Qur'an is an exact replica of an original Book, word for word, which is in heaven. He, therefore, queries whether the abrogation of verses in Qur'an is an indication that God can change His mind. Apparently Rev. Dale had posed this question to some Muslims in Zanzibar. According to Rev. Dale, the answer he got was that the circumstances which necessitated the abrogations were determined from eternity. There was therefore a verse for the original circumstances and a verse for the altered circumstances.

On the same matter of verses we are reminded of the controversy that Salman Rushdie's novel *The Satanic Verses* caused in the late 1980s. The novel takes its title from an incident in the Prophet Muhammad's early prophetic life when the polytheistic citizens of Mecca persuaded him to add two verses to the Qur'an to give angelic and intermediary status to Al-Lat, Al-Uzza and Manat, their favorite pre-Islamic goddesses. The Prophet complied (Rushdie, 1988: 124). Later the Prophet Muhammad expunged these verses, saying they had come from the Devil. The abrogating verses 19-22 in Chapter 53 read: "Have ye thought upon Al-Lat and Al-Uzza and Manat, the third, the other? Are yours the males and His the females? That indeed were an unfair division." Rushdie also questions whether the revelations that the

Prophet Muhammad received were indeed from the archangel Gibreel (Gabriel).

Likewise Rev. Dale was not entirely convinced that God was behind the abrogations. Rather he ventured to say that the Prophet Muhammad changed the verses either to correct himself or to suit prevailing circumstances. Rev. Dale gives the example of Chapter 4 verse 95 which, he says, originally read: "Those of the believers who stay at home in the time of Jihad are not in the sight of God as those who go to war." He says when the Prophet was asked, 'What if they are blind?', he asked for the shoulder blade upon which the words were written, had a spasmodic convulsion, and made Zaid add the words "free from trouble." The new verse then read: "Those of the believers who stay home free of trouble in the time of Jihad are not in the sight of God as those who go to war" (Dale, 1913: 42).

Needless to say, Rev. Dale's polemics were considered to be hostile to Islam. Some Muslims believed that a Christian priest could not come up with a correct translation of the Qur'an. It is therefore not surprising that his *Tafsiri ya Kurani ya Kiarabu* was received in certain Muslim circles with suspicion, if not outright hostility. It was such suspicion that led the eminent Muslim scholar, Sheikh Al-Amin bin Ali Mazrui[93] of Mombasa, Kenya, to embark on a Kiswahili translation of the Qur'an in 1936. He not only intended to translate the Qur'an but also to offer his own commentaries like Rev. Dale had done. Unfortunately, Sheikh Mazrui was unable to complete this task in his lifetime. What he was able to do was to translate Chapters One and Two, and a part of Chapter Three.

One of the reasons why Sheikh Mazrui was unable to complete his translation is that he was discouraged by the eminent Muslim scholar, Sheikh Muhammad bin Abdul-Alim As-Siddik. Sheikh As-Siddik happened to be visiting Mombasa in 1936 and when he met Sheikh Mazrui he asked him if he had any intention to translate the Qur'an into Kiswahili. Sheikh Mazrui told him that he had already started the translation because he wanted to correct Rev. Dale's translation. Sheikh As-Siddik asked him to consider the consequences of his own translation. He is reported to have told Sheikh Mazrui:

> *Dale ajulikana kuwa ni padri wa Kikristo. Kwa hiyo hapana Islamu yoyote atakayeshughulika na kuisoma tafsiri yake. Lakini utakapoirudi itakubidi unakili maneno yake, uyatie katika tafsiri yako ili upate kuyavunda. Hapo maneno ya Dale na upotofu wake yatawafikilia Islamu kwa wasita wa tafsiri yako. Na humjui ni yupi atakayeathirika kwa maneno yake*[94] (Mazrui, 1980: xi).

It remains unclear why Sheikh As-Siddik believed ordinary Muslims would not have wanted to read Rev. Dale's translation. What is clear, however, is that Sheikh As-Siddik was apprehensive regarding the consequences of criticizing Rev. Dale's translation. He feared that Sheikh Mazrui's translation and critique would help to transmit what Sheikh As-Siddik considered to be Rev. Dale's erroneous and misleading ideas about the Qur'an. Sheikh Mazrui must have taken the advice seriously because he never mentioned Dale's work in his own translation or the accompanying commentaries.

Despite the suspicions of some Muslims, Rev. Dale's translation of the Qur'anic text was acknowledged as no mean feat by Muslim authorities in Zanzibar (von Sicard, 1978: 62). Indeed, a careful comparison by the author of Rev. Dale's translation and Sheikh Mazrui's translation shows only minor differences either in the translation of some Arabic words or some phrases in the Qur'an. For instance, a comparison of their translations of Chapter One (Suratul Faatikah) shows how they are very much the same. On the left is Rev. Dale's translation and on the right is Sheikh Mazrui's translation:

Kwa jina la Mungu, mwenye huruma, mwenye rehema.	*Kwa jina la Mwenye-ezi-Mngu*
Sifa zote zina Mungu,	*Mwingi wa rehema,*
Bwana wa ulimwengu,	*Mwenye Kurehemu.*
Mwenye huruma, Mwenye Rehema,	*Kila sifa njema ni ya Mwenye-ezi-Mngu,*
Mfalme wa siku ya hukumu.	*Bwana wa viumbe.*
Twakuabudu wewe, twakuomba wewe	*Mwingi wa rehema,*
msaada.	*Mwenye Kurehemu.*
Utuongoze katika njia iliyonyoka;	*Mwenye kumiliki Siku ya Malipo.*
njia ya wale uliowapa neema, si wale	*Wewe peke Yako twakuabudu na*
Uliowaghadhabikia, wala wale waliopotea.	*Kwako peke Yako twaomba msaada.*
	Tuongoze njia iliyonyoka.[95]

The only difference is the translation of Bismillah, which Rev. Dale translates as *Kwa jina la Mungu* whereas Sheikh Mazrui adds the emphasis *Mwenye-ezi* which means Almighty. In his accompanying commentary Sheikh Mazrui notes that without this emphasis the concept of God in Arabic is used to refer to a pre-Islamic god or gods who were not Almighty.

Besides the attempt to "correct" Rev. Dale's translation of the Qur'an, Sheikh Mazrui responded to the Christian polemics with his own polemical works entitled *Uwongozi wa Kimasihiya na wa Kiislamu*

(1944) and *Dini ya Islamu* (1939).[96] According to Randall Pouwels, "Sh. Al-Amin was convinced of the universality of Islam" (Pouwels, 1981: 341). Pouwels notes that in *Dini ya Islamu* Sheikh Mazrui challenged Rev. Dale's criticisms of Islam "by listing the praises of various European intellectuals for Islam and by providing lists of numbers of Europeans and Americans themselves who were devoted Muslims" (ibid., 341). Needless to say, the above polemic exchanges were not very conducive for peaceful coexistence between Christians and Muslims in German East Africa and later in Tanganyika. One of the few reported confrontations from the 1890s between Christians and Muslims took place at Umba, north of Tanga, regarding the nature of Christ, and what von Sicard calls "an unpalatable, and seemingly unchristian polemic comparison between the evil and impure life of Muhammad and the holy and blessed life of Jesus" (von Sicard, 1978: 61).

Thus the Christian-Muslim dialogue about the nature and origin of their Scriptures, the nature of their prophets and their relation to God, issues which later during the 1990s became a source of much contention and violence, had already been defined by the beginning of the twentieth century. In fact Rev. Dale discussed these issues publicly with Muslims in Zanzibar in what may have been the precursor to the 1990s *mihadhara*. The only difference is that at the end of the twentieth century Muslim scholars were the ones who resurrected these issues. The Christian clergy were initially reluctant to respond to the Muslim charges about the false nature of Christianity in general and the Trinitarian controversy in particular.

It is not surprising, therefore, that the central issue that animated Christian-Muslim dialogue in the 1990s was whether or not Jesus is the Son of God. In a long letter to the Attorney General of Tanzania, Abu Aziz put in writing what *mihadhara* preachers were expressing verbally (Njozi, 2000: Appendix I). Aziz contends that Jesus is not the Son of God and Muslims cannot be accused of blasphemy because they are simply expressing what the Qur'an teaches. Aziz also questions the Divinity of the Bible and alleges that critical scrutiny of the Bible reveals a multitude of inconsistencies and discrepancies which have inimical implications to Christianity. Of particular interest is Aziz's assertion that "the 'Christianity' which evolved from St. Paul severed virtually all connection with its roots and can no longer be said to have anything to do with Jesus ... (who) unequivocally adhered to the Law of Moses" (Njozi, 2000: Appendix I, 175-176). Aziz quotes from Paul's Letter to the Galatians (2: 16) in which Paul says "a person is justified not by the works of the law but through faith in Jesus Christ."

Muslims, like the followers of Judaism, are not pleased with what Paul taught especially regarding the role of faith and works in bringing humans closer to God. By criticizing works Paul hit at the core of both religions which believe that works can enable a believer to execute the will of God. In Judaism a person can live a righteous life by abiding to The Laws of Moses and in Islam by abiding to the Shariah. Amplifying what Paul taught about the fallacy of works Martin Luther notes:

> It does not help the soul if the body is adorned with the sacred robes of priests or dwells in sacred places or is occupied with sacred duties or prays, fasts, abstains from certain kinds of food, or does any work that can be done by the body and in the body. The righteousness and freedom of the soul require something different, since the things which have been mentioned could be done by any wicked person. Such works produce nothing but hypocrites...Furthermore, to put aside all kinds of works, even contemplation, meditation, and all that the soul can do, does not help. One thing, and only one thing, is necessary for Christian life, righteousness, and freedom. That one thing is the most holy Word of God, the gospel of Christ, as Christ says, John 11 [:25], "I am the resurrection and the life; he who believes in me, though he die, yet shall he live" (Luther, 1960: 279).

Thus for Christians the soul can do without works but it cannot do without faith in the Word of God, the gospel of Christ. The above theological issues between Christianity and Islam were resurrected by *mihadhara* preachers during the 1990s. We will return to these issues in chapter eight.

To conclude, although the polemics of missionaries like Dale and Mitchell infused other missionaries with a spirit of triumphalism the struggle against Islam proved to be a daunting one. In the following chapter we focus our attention on the introduction of Christianity in Central Tanganyika, in the region known today as Dodoma. In Central Tanganyika the competition for converts would ultimately end in a stalemate. The attitude and approach of missionaries especially those belonging to the Christian Missionary Society (C.M.S.) were that they had to do whatever they could to stem the tide and keep the influence of Islam from flooding the land of the Wagogo.

CHAPTER FIVE

THE CROSS VS THE CRESCENT IN 19TH CENTURY CENTRAL TANGANYIKA

The presence of Muslims in central Tanganyika preceded that of Christian missionaries by about a century and a half (Rigby, 1966: 268). Like elsewhere in Africa, however, the spread of Islam into central Tanganyika was "less often the product of direct effort or conscious propaganda than the inevitable by-product of other activities" (Addison, 1966: 256). These other activities included trading whereby Arab and Swahili traders acted more or less as "unofficial missionaries" of Islam.[97] They helped spread Islam by the example of their lifestyle and the pride they took in their religion.[98] Blyden makes a similar observation regarding the spread of Islam in West Africa which was linked to the trading activities of the Mandingo and Fula. He writes: "Whenever they go, they produce the impression that they are not preachers only, but traders; but, on the other hand, that they are not traders merely, but preachers" (Blyden, 1994: 13).

However, in German East Africa the government also inadvertently helped to spread Islam into the interior of Tanganyika. How this happened is explained in a lengthy memorandum by Karl Axenfeld, mission inspector of the Berlin Missionary Society, which he wrote from Mufindi in the Southern Highlands of Tanganyika in July 1912. On the one hand, Axenfeld reiterated that because of German dependence on the service and language expertise of Muslim subordinate officials,[99] "great numbers of coast [Muslim] people accompanied the Europeans and gradually entered with them into the inland districts, even into those that, lying far from the old caravan - roads, were hardly reached by former Arab-traders" (CMS G3 A8/01, 1912). On the other, he noted that the accompaniment of Europeans by coast Muslims gave the impression that "the coast Mohamedans [sic] were superior to [locals] and stood high in the European favour. Thus the opinion that 'Moslem' was the term for the educated man, while 'shenzi' meant the man open to derision,[100] was confirmed and helped to spread Mohamedanism [sic]."[101]

Axenfeld also noted that the demand for well-educated natives induced government to open schools in which religion was not taught.

This system of schools did from the outset help to strengthen the monopoly of coast Muslims. Supposedly, a perusal of the lists that were kept at the government schools in Tanga and Dar es Salaam, which showed where former pupils were stationed, indicated to Axenfeld "with terrifying clearness in what degree the government schools spread an islamized (and) islamizing upperclass of natives over the whole colony"[102] (CMS G3 A8/01, 1912).

According to Axenfeld, the Muslim monopoly of the civil service was compounded by government policy which discouraged the opening of government schools in districts where mission schools already existed.[103] Although government promised that in such districts Christians could be taken into the civil service, this promise was subsequently of little or no efficacy, "because the Missions were not able to present as many boys as were required" (CMS G3 A8/01, 1912). Moreover, the Missions needed the more educated members of their congregations for their own church and school service. Furthermore, the whole system of Protestant schools was built upon the foundation of utilizing the tribal dialects, while government required officials who were fluent in Swahili.

Axenfeld further reiterated in his 1912 memorandum that despite official discomfort with the predominance of Muslims in civil service positions, in the colonial army and in other higher native positions, government was "at a loss as regards remedy of this misproportion [sic]." He went on to suggest that:

> The only thing Government can do (and they seem inclined to do it) is to subsidize the Mission schools more liberally (and) thereby to help the Missions to train Christian teachers who speak a good Swahili (and) if required also teachers for government schools, traders, soldiers etc. The training of such people, however, can only be undertaken by the Missions.

> If they fail to do their duty in this respect, or if they do it dilatorily, or if they fail doing it on a broad enough scale, Government would be quite justified partly blaming the Missions for the progress the islamization of the country makes (CMS G3 A8/01, 1912).

Subsequently, CMS schools at Buigiri and Mvumi in central Tanzania began to educate Africans for service in the colonial administration (Maddox, 1999: 158). By the 1920s a good number of clerks who worked for the Native Authorities under the system of indirect rule came from CMS schools.

Paradoxical as it may seem, mission education was not a guarantee for employment in the private sector. Apparently in the early days there was a general aversion by the average European to the mission boy. Joelson attributes this strange fact to four factors: "Firstly, because he (was) so often untrustworthy in action and in speech; secondly, because he (was) lazy; thirdly, because he (gave) himself airs of superiority; and fourthly, because he (was) inclined to curry favour" (Joelson, 1920: 89). According to Joelson, the characteristics that most annoyed the European were the last two. Such condescending paternalism later became a source of concern as the forces of nationalism gathered speed. Yet, as early as 1918 Bishop Frank Weston had warned fellow missionaries against their negative attitudes toward Africans (CMS Acc. 262/Z 4/2, "White Man and Black").[104]

Many of the early converts who also became literate sought to serve the Church. This was certainly the case with Andereya Mwaka (CMS, Acc. 212 F 12/9, "The Story of Andereya Mwaka," by Rev. Henry Cole). According to Christopher Mwaka, before Andereya was baptized in 1885 he was known as Mwakamubi Makanyaga (Christopher Mwaka, interviewed July 9, 2002). Andereya's father was the chief of Ibwaga, which is a few miles east of Kongwa. Christopher Mwaka narrated to me that sometime in 1885 Andereya left home to follow his father who had been summoned at the *boma* at Mpwapwa. On arrival at Mpwapwa he was told that his father had already left for home. When Andereya was returning home by way of Chamhawi, he was abducted by a Swahili slave trader. People who saw the abduction reported it to the local chief named Mapanjilo. Mapanjilo sent his men to ransom Andereya and the other children whom the Swahili trader was about to send to Bagamoyo.

Subsequently Andereya's father demanded the return of his son but chief Mapanjilo refused. War between the two chiefs was imminent when Rev. Henry Cole intervened and compensated chief Mapanjilo. Andereya was allowed to go home while the other children remained with Rev. Cole becoming the nucleus of his church school. According to Christopher Mwaka Rev. Cole later requested permission from chief Makanyaga for Andereya also to attend school at Cisokwe. Rev. Cole was given permission to take Andereya with whom he later developed a very close relationship.

When the Coles went to England on furlough in 1889, they took Andereya with them, as a nurse to their newly born baby. According to Rev. Cole, Andereya's month long stay in England "opened his eyes to the wonders of civilization." He further notes: "What he had seen he turned to good account on his return, and people came from all around to see the wonderful man who had been all the way to 'Ulaya' [Europe] and back without sustaining any broken bones, or a change of skin, or a loss of identity. This was *ipoto* (a miracle) indeed!" Why did the Gogo expect Andereya Mwaka to sustain broken bones, a change of skin, or a loss of identity by virtue of having been to Europe?

Like people elsewhere in Africa, the Gogo endeavoured to comprehend their initial encounters with Europeans within existing cultural frameworks. That one of them had gone to Europe and come back "without sustaining any broken bones, or a change of skin, or a loss of identity" was, in their eyes, a miracle of miracles. As David Northrup notes, placing Europeans geographically was initially much more of a problem for most Africans, let alone to decide if the homeland of the *wazungu* (Europeans) was a place like Africa or something of a quite different order (Northrup, 2002: 19). Andereya Mwaka's return from Europe and the sensation it caused is similar to the return from Portugal of the first four Kongolese who had been taken hostage by the Portuguese explorer Diogo Cao in 1483. Northrup writes:

> The return of the four in 1485 was a key event in the formation of Kongolese perceptions of the Portuguese. The manikongo [the king of Kongo] welcomed the four "as though they had seen them resuscitated from under the earth," a phrase, as anthropologist Wyatt MacGaffey points out, that resonated with significance in the context of Kongolese cosmological beliefs about the world of the living and the world of the dead ... To the Kongolese, as to many other Africans, Europeans looked like people whose skin had been painted with white pigment, the color of the underworld ... Thus the welcome given to the repatriated hostages was one accorded to persons returning not from a distant land otherwise like their own, but from a place incomparably different: the underworld of the dead" (Northrup, 2002: 19).

Subsequently, through his influence Andereya Mwaka's three brothers also became Christians, with the eldest later being appointed a chief under the Native Authority ordinance. A younger brother later got a good government post. Andereya Mwaka himself went on to attend "Huron" Training College at Kongwa, was ordained in 1922 and became a success story for the Church.[105] He took his priestly orders in 1924 and was later appointed a Canon when the Cathedral of the Holy Spirit at Dodoma was consecrated in 1933. According to Rev. Cole, Andereya's intimate knowledge of the character of his Gogo brethren, together with his tact and intelligence, conspired to make his ministry very fruitful at Dodoma. Unfortunately he was soon incapacitated and passed away on 1 September, 1935.

The career of Canon Andereya Mwaka also reminds one of the career of the West African Bishop Samuel Ajayi Crowther. He too was an ex-slave who not only became a Christian but was the first African to become a bishop of the CMS. Like Canon Andereya Mwaka, Bishop Crowther used his intimate knowledge of the character of his Yoruba brethren to make his ministry a great success. Bishop Crowther's polemical sermons in Yoruba were felt to be more damaging to traditional religion than those preached by the white man in English (Okafor, 1992: 59).

The contest between Christianity and Islam for Gogo souls was not limited to the pulpit, however. The provision of health services was a part of the evangelical endeavour in central Tanzania. A 1946 Diocese of Central Tanganyika memorandum on medical policy makes this connection plainly clear: "Our ultimate aim is to win men to God by showing them the love of God in Christ through the medium of medical work" (CMS, M/Y/A 8 1934-1947). The memorandum further states: "There should be regular teaching for all in-patients and ante-natal cases waiting at the Hospital. Live dressers and nurses are the best evangelists. When these are not available an endeavour should be made to obtain help of an outside evangelist or Bible woman. Persons not only capable of preaching and teaching, but also of dealing personally with patients, are required" (CMS, M/Y/A 8 1934-1947).

A patient's encounter with Christianity was extended upon discharge. It was recommended that a record of all patients who showed a positive response to the Word should be kept so that they could be followed up: "When a responsive patient returns to his village which is very distant from a church, a district superintendent should be informed in the hope that an Evangelist might be placed in that village.

An attempt should also be made to reach such outlying villages by medico-evangelist safaris. Such safaris should be made by a European accompanied by one or more of the hospital staff. They would camp one or more days in the village, carrying out evangelistic, as well as mdeical [sic] work"(CMS, M/Y/A 8 1934-1947).

Therefore, the choice of sites where health facilities were to be located was of strategic importance. On the eve of World War II, the Diocese of Central Tanganyika owned and operated hospitals and health facilities at Berega, Kongwa and Mpwapwa in eastern Ugogo, Buigiri and Mvumi in central Ugogo, and Kilimatinde and Makutupora in western Ugogo. Mvumi, located about twenty-six miles southeast of Dodoma, had a Government registered Nurses' Training School and a training school for dressers. It was the only Base Hospital in the Diocese. Its importance is reflected in the ever increasing numbers of patients it catered to over the years as the figures below show.

Year	1932	1936	1940	1945
General In-Patient	112	172	372	807
Maternity	32	310	223	252

The missionary endeavour in central Tanzania was also greatly facilitated by the opening of the Central Railway Line. The railway reached Dodoma in 1910. To the Gogo, the Reverend T. B. R. Westgate noted, the year 1910 was "the year of the railway" (CMS G3 A8/01, Westgate, Annual Letter, 30 November, 1910). According to Westgate, the arrival of the railway in Dodoma was physically and psychologically a momentous event. Psychologically, the railway was a marvel that surpassed all previous marvels that the Gogo had already seen such as carts, trucks, wagons, motor cars, and bicycles. Physically, its construction "afforded another impressive object of European strength and ability." In Westgate's opinion, the combined effect on the Gogo was so shattering it is worth quoting him at length:

> Things hitherto looked upon as impossible and consequently incredible, have come to pass, and one cannot but wonder what the permanent effect may be. The broad wound across the face of the giant forest, the murdered acacias and baobabs, the rocks, rocky eminences, and boulders annihilated with dynamite, the humbled hills and exalted valleys, the bridged ravines, chasms and rivers, the long snake-like road-bed, the sleepers, the rails, and the wonderful

"masini" which pants and puffs and hisses and squeals, backs up, goes forward, devours wood and water and black "stones" and vomits black smoke into the face of heaven - these are some of the things which have appeared before the eyes of this ancient and primitive people with the *startling suddenness of a vision* and as yet they have scarcely recovered from the shock(op. cit.).

The arrival of the railway in Ugogo immediately expedited the transit of personal and Mission goods. Missionaries returning from furlough reached central Tanganyika in two days of traveling from the Coast, a journey that before the advent of the railway "occupied three weeks with its attendant risks from mosquitoes and miasma" (CMS G3 A8/02, Rees and Baxter, "Report of the Ussagara-Ugogo Mission," 1910). The cost of porterage was greatly reduced since porters were only hired for shorter distances from nearby stations.

The construction of the Central Line also facilitated the spread of Islam and the Kiswahili language in German East Africa. Sunseri, for instance, notes that coastal Muslim *walimu* (teachers) and Christian missionaries from inland stations actively proselytized among the railway construction workers, "competing for the hearts and minds of workers" (Sunseri, 1998: 567). The symbiotic relationship between Islam and Kiswahili was seen by the Germans to be doubly subversive because both could be used at the same time to agitate against German colonial rule. The German administration dealt with the "danger" of the spread of Islam that was bound to the spread of Kiswahili by "dis-Islamizing" the later. According to Charles Pike, Carl Meinhof, a prominent German linguist of the time, proposed that Kiswahili be de-Islamized by replacing the Arabic script, which had been used for centuries in writing Kiswahili, with the Roman script and Arabic loan words with German terms (Pike, 1986: 224). However, the adoption of Kiswahili as the official language was apparently impressed upon the Chancellor, Otto von Bismarck, by the Bremen Conference (Wright, 1971: 7).

In an attempt to gain a competitive edge against Islam the Reverend D. J. Rees of the CMS and Pastor Karl Axenfeld of the Berlin Missionary Society met in London in 1910 to discuss a joint strategy in German East Africa.[106] It is unclear at whose initiative this meeting was arranged;[107] it was, however, of vital importance to both albeit for different reasons. The CMS was facing an acute shortage of missionaries due to declining enrolment at Islington and a decrease of funds which led to the closure of the College in 1912 (Hodge, 1971-1972: 95). So any endeavour that would help their enterprise in central Tanzania was liable to be seized upon eagerly. It should also be noted that such a joint strategy was in line with the endeavour of modern ecumenism.[108] What was unusual, though, was the apparent lessened sense of antagonism between Englishmen and Germans.[109]

At their London meeting Axenfeld upraised Rees about the concerns of the Imperial Governor of German East Africa, Freiherr Albrecht von Rechenberg (1906-1912), regarding the spread of Islam and what the Governor believed the missionaries, regardless of their denominations or nationality, needed to do (CMS G3 A8/02, 1910: 1). According to Axenfeld, the Governor was very concerned about the spread of Islam in German East Africa (GEA) especially along the Central railway which reached Dodoma in 1910. The Governor's advise to all missionary societies operating in GEA was that they should "concentrate their chief efforts upon the important centres along the railway route, and not upon districts more remote" (ibid.). Thus, from early on a strategy between the government and missionaries was conceived to defeat Islam in Tanzania.

In Germany Governor Rechenberg's concerns about the spread of Islam in German East Africa caught the attention of Carl Heinrich Becker[110] whose article "Materialen zur Kenntnis des Islam in Deutsch-Ostafrika" was published in the German periodical *Der Islam*, II, 1911, while the author was teaching at the Hamburg *Kolonialinstitut* (Becker, 1968: 31). Becker saw the spread of Islam in German East Africa to be a threat both to the colonial administration and the *Reich*. Becker visualized the threat to the colonial administration in the form of Muslim "troublemakers" especially from outside the colony who could use Islam to foment civil disobedience as well as mutiny among the *Schutztruppe* or Defense Force (Becker, 1968: 42). The threat to the *Reich* was, however, rather an indirect one in the form of suspected Muslim allegiance to the Ottoman Sultan in view of his universal claims to the "caliphate" (Becker, 1968: 32). Given the severity of the perceived threat presented by Islam Becker felt that "stiff punishments" were "indispensable" to the German authorities in preempting the doings of Muslim "troublemakers" (Becker, 1968: 61).

At the 1910 London meeting already alluded to, Karl Axenfeld expressed his belief that the increasing Muslim influence in German East Africa was due to two factors: "(a) the circulation of the Koran from Cairo, and, (b) the zeal of the Coastal Swahilis, whose 'high school' he had discovered to be at Mombasa, with Muscat for its fostering mother, in the provision of Islamic teachers" (CMS G3 A8/ 02, 1910: 2). A similar connection was made by Carl Becker in regard to the influence of Cairo as a publishing center and home of the world famous Azhar Mosque. However, Becker believed that the influences effective in East Africa pointed toward Somali land and the Arabs of Hadramawt (Becker, 1968: 43). However, both Axenfeld and Becker appear to have been unaware of the *Ribat al-Riyadh* (Mosque College) at Lamu, which was started by Habib Saleh in 1900.[111] The College's influence, according to Lienhardt, "spread not only the length of the Kenya coast but also into Tanganyika south of Dar es Salaam" (Lienhardt, 1959: 228).

Karl Axenfeld also impressed upon Rees the necessity for cooperation between the Berlin Mission Society and others at work in German East Africa "in mutual watchfulness over the Christians, whom the railway was attracting to the large centers along its track." In order to effectively carry such a joint endeavour, Karl Axenfeld suggested that there should be:-

(a) mutual advice whenever any natives under Christian intruction intended to leave for work at any place on the Central railway;

(b) the preparation of a short and simple address, which might be read at little Christian gatherings, and sent on by them to their brethren at the next place; and

(c) visits from Missionaries and from native teachers(CMS G3 A8/02, 1910: 3).

Furthermore, Karl Axenfeld strongly advised the CMS to send its new missionaries to Germany for a six-month course in German and another six months' course in Kiswahili. In this way missionaries would be of service soon after their arrival in German East Africa. Apparently, the importance of Kiswahili as the language of communication to spread the Gospel had been impressed on the German administration by the spread of Islam. According to Axenfeld, the rapidly increasing use of Kiswahili observed in German East Africa was second only in importance to the spread of Islam (CMS G3 A8/

02, 1910: 7). In Axenfeld's view, the growth of both at the same time was significant and if Islam's triumph was in any degree attributable to Kiswahili, then its use to spread the Gospel was self evident (CMS G3 A8/02, 1910: 8).

A CMS report for 1910 linked the spread of Islam in central Tanganyika directly to the arrival of the Central railway which, the report noted, had helped to open the region to Indian merchants:

> The biweekly train service from the Coast to the interior deposits Indian traders – zealous propagandists - on the platforms of different Stations, from whence they make their way to the remote localities pushing their religion along with their wares... All along the railway line daily pushing further West "are little Moslem mosques,[112] quite insignificant huts, but still sufficient for the scattering broadcast of the seeds of false doctrine which we know are being sent forth from each one" (CMS G3 A8/02, 1910).

Unfortunately we have no records by Indian merchants of their perceived role in the spread of Islam in this part of central Tanzania. In any case, the absence of Indian records does not detract from the fact that there is no living proof of the product of their proselytizing. Today in central Tanzania there are no Africans who are Ismailis, Ithnasheris, Bohras or Maimans which are the major Muslim denominations professed by Indian traders then as now.

While the above report gives credit where it is not due, the perception that Indians rather than Arabs spread Islam was also echoed in scholarly treatises of the time. The limited role assigned to Arab traders in the spread of Islam in the interior of East Africa is explained by T. W. Arnold as follows:

> Given up wholly to the pursuits of commerce or slave-hunting, the Arabs in Eastern Africa exhibited a lukewarmness in promoting the interests of their faith, which is in striking contrast to the missionary zeal displayed by their co-religionists in other parts of Africa (Arnold, 1913:344).

Supposedly it was not in the Arabs interest to convert Africans to Islam because that would prevent the Arabs from enslaving fellow Muslims.

Despite the missionary anxiety, the influence of Islam in Ugogo before the First World War was very superficial. The same 1910 report referred to above noted:

The Mohammedanism one meets with in native converts is of a nominal and ignorant type. They are unable to give any account of the faith they profess and as little of its founder ... With many others the profession of Islam is merely a passport to unchecked licentiousness under the garb of that *respectability* which natives are prone to associate with its adoption (emphasis added)(CMS G3 A8/ 02, 1910).

It is, however, questionable that those Gogo who converted to Islam did so "merely [as] a passport to unchecked licentiousness." Much appears to have been made of Islam's provision for polygyny as an attraction for Gogo converts.[113] The Gogo did not need to convert to Islam in order to marry more than one wife because polygyny was already a part of their culture. Moreover, the problem of licentiousness among Muslim converts also applied to Christian converts. In fact, it appears to have been a serious problem that it warranted discussion by the Ussagara-Ugogo CMS Executive Committee at its meeting held at Kiboriani, Mpwapwa in August 1911. One of the meeting's resolutions was the imposition of fines for committing adultery and fornication. The fines ranged from ten to twenty rupees (CMS G3 A8/02, 1911).

As for the nominal ignorance of Islam, it is hard to judge who between the missionaries and the Gogo was more ignorant of it. Among missionary circles the need to really understand Islam in order to combat it was recognized by the Conference of Evangelical Missionary Societies working in German East Africa, held at Dar es Salaam from 13 to 19 August 1911. The conference specifically recommended, "That each Society appoint one Missionary for the special study of Arabic, or at least of the Arabic characters, with a view to watching the Mohammedan [sic] literature being circulated in the Country"(CMS G3 A8/02, 1911). However, this recommendation was declined by the Ussagara-Ugogo Executive Committee on the grounds that they were short of staff (ibid.). How, then, could the missionaries judge Islam and its effects when they had very limited knowledge of it themselves?

It is noteworthy that the "threat" of Islamic influence was used to put pressure on the CMS headquarters in London to send more money and personnel to central Tanzania. Typical of such letters is that by E. Forsythe to Mr. Baylis, written at Mvumi on 28 November 1910:

> Truly, the door in Ugogo has never been so wide open as now and if
> we do not enter in to claim the land for Christ. The followers of the
> false Prophet will not fail to take advantage of the opportunity thus
> offered ...Which is to be triumphant in Ugogo: the Cross or the
> Crescent? The answer lies with the Christian Church at home. Oh:
> may God wake her up to a sense of her responsibility in this matter.
> 'The King's business requireth haste' ... Help us to enter while we
> may"(CMS G3 A8/02).

To the missionaries of central Tanzania, the Africans who
became Muslim were those who frequented the Arab and Indian stores.
In this regard, the missionaries at Kongwa endeavoured to open a
Mission store where, in the words of Ernest W. Doulton, "our Native
Christians would be able to buy everything they require at a reasonable
rate, and not be obliged to patronize the shops which are almost
entirely owned and run by Mahometans (sic)" (CMS G3 A8/O,
Doulton to Baxter, dated December 1, 1909). Years later a similar
concern was raised by missionaries in Uganda where Muslims, it was
said, were inclined to:

> ... help one another in burials, in marriage feasts, in trade, in agriculture
> ... If there is a Muslim *duka* (shop) a Muslim will never buy elsewhere,
> whereas a Catholic will often buy from a Muslim even if there is a
> *duka* owned by a Catholic (Kasozi, 1995: 224).

Yet, many of evangelical persuasion in England felt that the
links uniting Christianity and commerce ought to be severed, "and all
emphasis placed on direct evangelization by preachers and teachers,
both native and European" (Porter, 1977: 26).

By and large, the blame that Muslim traders were frustrating
the Christian enterprise in Ugogo was, I think, overdrawn if not
misplaced. Evidence suggests that the missionaries were contending
against deep-rooted Gogo customs and beliefs.[114] The experience of
Rev. J. C. Price speaks a lot about this dilemma. Rev. Price was stationed
at Mpwapwa from the 1880s and died there in 1895. He made three
journeys to Ugogo. However, we have on record journals of only two
of these; the one from 18 April to 19 May, 1888 and the other in
November 1888, which would be his last tour in Ugogo.

During the second journey Rev. Price conducted Sunday service
at Kikombo at which he tried to convey to "a fairly good congregation"
the idea of sin in the Scriptural sense. He used a white, red and blue
coloured flag as a visual aid. The entry in his journal explains the

intended significance of these colours: "The blue (which the Wagogo call black) representing the sinful heart, is placed at the bottom; then the red – the blood which has paid the debt we owed to God, and, is alone able to cleanse and gladden the heart of man; with the white showing the result of the application of the blood at the top" (CMS G3 A 5/O, 1888). Evidently, his congregation had a hard time comprehending what he was talking about. He notes in his journal what he thought was the problem: "I think perhaps the black needs the most explanation, for these people have no idea of sin against God in the Scriptural sense The expression 'a black heart' with them implies nothing more than sorrow or disappointment, sometimes anger, and a 'white heart' doesn't mean a clean heart but a merry heart. Of course, one has to try and show them that sin is the real cause of sorrow, and holiness the true ground of joy" (CMS G3 A 5/O, 1888). But was the Gogo's lack of understanding simply a matter of not properly relating colors to behaviour? To determine this we would need to look at the Gogo system of colour classification and determine what really the colors red, white and black meant to them; whether or not the colors black and white denoted binary opposites in the Gogo belief system as, say, expressed in their ritual practices.

On the one hand, to the Gogo the colour white neither had anything to do with "purity" nor did the colour black signify "impurity." In fact, in certain circumstances the colour white was associated with bad things. Ghosts were believed to go around dressed in white cloth. Likewise, white cloth was used for burial. However, the color black was associated with good things. A black bull was sacrificed in rituals intended to bring rain while those in attendance also dressed in black. On the other hand, had Rev. Price known the Gogo idea of sacrifice he would have been able to relate the Christian idea of the Crucification to them with different results. Jesus was the ultimate sacrifice acceptable to God for the salvation of humanity because he was without a blemish. Gogo sacrificial rituals required the killing of an animal without a blemish. Likewise, there must be a cause and effect for the sacrifice in both Christian and Gogo traditional beliefs.[115]

The next day the chief of Kikombo sent for Rev. Price wishing to know exactly what it was that Rev. Price wanted to tell him and his people about God. Rev. Price notes: "The old man (chief) sat quietly smoking his pipe without saying a word, but the others present seemed really interested, and asked questions, some of course, about the rain, and also whether I had any medicine to increase the supply of water in the river bed, where they dig holes in the sand to get the precious liquid" (CMS G3 A5/O, 1888). Rev. Price does not say what his answers to these questions were, but he notes that he had prayed that morning to God to send some rain and in the afternoon there was a storm of rain. Yet, Rev. Price and other missionaries were scornful about the Gogo religious rituals for what they erroneously called the "witchcraft" practice of "rain-making."

On 6 May, 1888, Rev. Price was able to preach to a select group of elders at Msamalo, a few miles to the south-west of Kikombo. When he was done, he asked them what they intended to do now that they had heard the Word. He notes that a good number "almost enthusiastically professed their readiness to accept Christ as their Saviour." However, Rev. Price was dismayed that the Gogo had a different idea about what it meant to be saved: "With many of them their great idea of being saved is to get plenty of food – to be saved from hunger. It is so hard to get them to see that Christ came to give us something better than mere food; but they seem to appreciate the tidings of a better land above where there will be no hunger, no poverty, no sickness, no death, although to their minds it is a land that is very far off" (CMS G3 A5/O, 1888).

Apparently the Gogo's overriding concern with their environment and the recurrent problem of famine were stumbling blocks to early Christian proselytization. If the problem was not evident to Rev. Price during his second journey, it became sharply clear during his third and last journey to the land of the Gogo. Somewhere between Chilonwa and Nayu he was unable to proselytize because he could not find anyone "particularly disposed to listen to what (he) had to say about the 'bread of life,' when they were without the 'bread that perisheth'" It was then that it dawned on Rev. Price that "To a great extent the way to these people's souls is through their bodies" (CMS G3 A5/O/30, 1889).

However, it was at Mulamba, some six miles to the west of Buigiri, that he was to encounter the only verbal objection to the Word by a Gogo man. He writes:

> One man here, the owner of the largest *tembe*, but not the chief, set
> himself against what I had to say with quite the airs of a 'free-thinker'

... There were other people, chiefly women, near enough to hear what I had to say although I did not address them. After the usual salutations and enquiries, he asked me where my gun was. I told him I had no gun with me. 'Yes, you have one in your pocket,' he said. I told him I had not, and that by saying what he did, he made me a liar; and that we regarded lying as being as bad as witchcraft, which is almost the only thing they regard as a crime. 'O no, a man who is a clever liar is fit to be a chief!' I told him that at any rate God regarded lying as very bad, and then started off to the subject of man's sinfulness and God's wonderful goodness and love in sending His son to save us from our sin and its consequences. 'O yes [the man said] I suppose it is you who have been to Msomalo [sic], and told people there about this, and they profess to believe it, but what are they the better for it? They have hunger and get sick and die just like anybody else. God is not good, He kills our children, and keeps back the rain'"(CMS, G 3 A 5/O/30, 1889)

Rev. Price countered argued that it was Satan, God's enemy, who was the cause of all the bad things that happened in the world. He went on to say:

"This world has been spoiled, and it would not make us happy to have to live here for ever, so God will take those who follow His Son to dwell with Him in a better place when they die. 'O yes [the man interjected] you mean He is going to take us up in the sky – take us away from our children and leave them orphans – very nice that. No, I don't want to go up there I don't want to hear your words, they are bad, very bad; and don't you think we Wagogo are going to listen to you, not a bit of it. Let God raise up our friends who have died, and let us all live together down here, that would be all very well, but to take us away up in the sky – No, and if you go elsewhere I will follow you and tell the people your words are bad" (CMS, G 3 A 5/O/30, 1889).

Evidently Rev. Price and the Gogo man were expressing two different dimensions of God. From a Judeo-Christian perspective we know what Rev. Price meant by "God's wonderful goodness and love" and why Satan is associated with evil. But what did the Gogo man mean by a God that was not good? Who killed children? And kept back the rain? The Gogo man in the dialogue above was expressing a simple monistic view of God: that God and Satan were one. According to Karen Blixen this dual nature of God was characteristic of African religious beliefs (Blixen, 1980). To the Gogo the occurrence of disease, natural calamities, misfortune and death was a cause of suffering which was ultimately located in God as the ultimate cause.

Ultimately, Christian missionaries came to realize that what they described as Gogo "heathenism" was a serious obstacle to the spread of Christianity.[116] In a 1910 report for the Ussagara-Ugogo Mission D. J. Rees and E. J. Baxter acknowledged the seriousness of Gogo "heathenism" missionary proselytizing. They quote a missionary as saying:

> In our Inquirers' Class we have some old Wagogo veterans who constantly remind me of the picture of St. George on the tavern sign, always on horseback but never riding on. They listen to everything in connexion (sic) with the Gospel, hear everything, criticize everything, analyse everything, believe nothing. The absurdities and moral corruptions of their heathen estate often appear to make them ashamed, yet they cling to them for the sake of old association, while the Gospel appeals to them only as a cold and abstract theory. Perhaps we should not think too unkindly of them for their tenacious adherence to their own notions and ideals, for consistency even in folly has in it something respectable (CMS G3 A8/02, 1910).

On a different note, it is important to point out that initially both Christianity and Islam only attempted to lure the Gogo away from their traditional beliefs.[117] Their competition in central Tanzania was not focused on securing converts from each other as was the case, for example, at Maneromango (Kimambo, 1999) and among the Yao (Alpers, 1972). Christian converts appear to have been attracted to the religion not for its own sake but rather "for what went with the religion" (Harries, 1954: 76), especially the access to western education and the employment opportunities such education brought (Maddox, 1999).

Missionaries in central Tanzania and elsewhere used their schools for proselytizing.[118] J. Raum, a missionary of long experience in educational work in the Territory, perceived the essence of educational pedagogy in the following terms: "The aims of the State, even in its educational activities, are political aims, and its means political means. The aims of missions, even in their educational aspects, are spiritual aims and their methods spiritual" (Raum, 1930: 574). Missionaries like Raum considered it unfair on the part of the government to require that they provide a religious-free education in their schools so that Muslims too could enrol. In Raum's view mission schools did not have to cater to the needs of Muslims:

> We admit that Government must consider the Moslem element in the population, but it would have been a better policy to give the Moslems an opportunity of setting up their own schools with Moslem teachers, than to endanger the educational and religious influence of missions upon Christian children (Raum, 1930: 565).

The provision of education by missionary agencies that disregarded the educational interests of the Muslims and Muslim complaints that the Government of Tanganyika supported the Christian element in the country in a partial manner with regard to the provision of educational facilities in Tanganyika are the subject of the following chapter. It will suffice to end this chapter with two observations. On the one hand, the case of central Tanganyika indicates that there were significant differences between Christianity and Islam in their methods of conversion. The ultimate aim of Christian missionaries was to win people to God by showing them the love of God in Christ through the medium of education and medical work. Thus missionary agencies started with a school or health center and then constructed a church.

On the other hand, Muslims did not employ *diakonia* in their proselytizing. Instead they sought to win people to God by examples of morally acceptable living styles. Due to the centrality of prayer in a Muslim's daily routine Muslims prioritized the building of mosques albeit in the form of "little huts." In most cases' mosques also served as schools or *madras* which provided religious instruction rather than secular education. Thus those who converted to Islam did so mainly because they were attracted by Islamic religious practices. Those who adopted this new way of life considered themselves *wastaarabu* or civilized, whereas those who did not came to be known as *washenzi* or uncivilized. The later were also referred to as *makafiri* or nonbelievers.

However, under the new dispensation of *Pax Britannica* those who considered themselves to be *wastaarabu* ended up being marginalized while the *makafiri* who accepted Christianity exploited the new opportunities to their advantage. Western secular education, as we will see in the following chapter, played a crucial role in advantaging Christian converts and disadvantaging Muslims. Muslim requests to have their Qur'anic schools recognized were turned down by the British administration. As a result their traditional Islamic education remained outside mainstream of educational developments which were geared to "modernization" (von Sicard, 1991: 4).

This chapter will not be complete without mention of the contribution of missionaries to literacy among the Gogo by availing with the printed word in their own language. As we noted in chapter two the history of colportage in colonial Tanzania has yet to be written. In the case of colonial central Tanganyika the selling of books was undertaken by missionaries themselves. The extent of Gogo literacy was probably reflected by the growing demand for books. Thus in 1912 John Briggs, the CMS book secretary, was anxious to obtain from the Society for Promoting Christian Knowledge in London as many books in *Cigogo* (the language of the Gogo) as were available. The Society obliged by donating 400 copies each of the Prayer and Hymn Book as well as 50 copies of the First Reading Book also in *Cigogo*. The same year two thousand copies of the *Cigogo* Book of Genesis were reprinted by the British Foreign Bible Society compared to 500 copies that had been printed in 1905(CMS G3 A8/O, Briggs to Baylis, dated 18 May, 1912).

Finally, unlike Islam the spread of Christianity in central Tanganyika was greatly aided by the missionary effort in translating the Word of God in the local vernacular. This in turn facilitated the spread of literacy among the Gogo. Efforts to translate the Bible into *Cigogo* started in 1886 when Rev. Henry Cole of the CMS translated the gospel of Matthew. The following year Rev. John C. Price translated the gospel of Luke. Later in 1889 Cole and Price collaborated to translate the gospel of John. These early efforts were crowned by the complete translation of the New Testament in 1911. After World War II The Rev. Archdeacon Oliver T. Cordell, with the assistance of Rev. Filemon Cidosa, Rev. Mika Muloli, Rev. Samwili Makanyaga (a sibling of Andereya Mwaka) and Paulo Musoloka, was able to translate the entire Old Testament into *Cigogo*. (Lusinde, n.d.).

CHAPTER SIX

CHRISTIANS VS. MUSLIMS UNDER BRITISH RULE

The advent of European colonial rule (German as well as British) in Tanganyika created a favourable political climate for the proselytization of Christianity. With the onset of European dominance the stage was set for the reorientation from the East and Islam toward the West and Christianity in the general trend of life of many Africans (Harries, 1954: 28). Consequently, as Harries has noted, "Islam in East Africa lost its position as the directive for African hopes and aspirations"(Harries, 1954: 28).

Moreover, the reorientation of African mentality away from the East and Islam and toward the West and Christianity was abated by western secular education. Physical training and moral instruction were given a great deal of consideration (Kurtz, 1972: 51). The dual system of Government and Mission schools that was introduced during the German period was inherited and maintained by the British. However, there soon emerged an inverse ratio of Government to Mission schools. In 1923 there were 4,907 public schools as opposed to 115,000 mission-funded schools; by 1935 the gap had widened even further with 8,105 public schools as opposed to 217,736 mission-funded schools (Kurtz, 1972: 51). Due to the preponderance of Mission schools the majority of school graduates were pro-Western in their mentality.

Unlike their Christian counterparts it was difficult for Muslims in Tanganyika to build and finance their own schools. In general, the few primary schools that Muslims were able to build were built and financed through fund raising. According to Sheikh K. S. Kiangi Mswia, the Muslims in Pare and Moshi (Kilimanjaro) were probably in the forefront in the effort to build their own schools after realizing their children's limited access to colonial education (*Mwongozi*, 26 October 1956). The disparity between Christian and Muslim-funded schools is evident in the following statistics of all schools in operation in Tanganyika in 1955:[119]

(a) Government and Native Authority Primary Schools   656
(b) Christian funded Primary Schools   1,692
(c) Muslim funded Primary Schools   28
(d) Government Rural Middle Schools   104
(e) Christian funded Rural Middle Schools   223

(f) Muslim Rural Middle Schools	None
(g) Government Secondary Schools	10
(h) Christian Secondary Schools	16
(i) Muslim Secondary Schools	None
(j) Government Teacher Training Centers	11
(k) Christian Teacher Training Centers	23
(l) Muslim Teacher Training Centers	None
(m) Government Technical, Medical etc.	7
(n) Christian Technical, Medical Schools	5
(o) Muslim Technical, Medical Schools	None

However, Muslims did not only lag behind in building schools for regular education. In an article in *Mwongozi* of 27 September, 1957, one A. Haider noted with concern how Muslims in Tanganyika were negligent in promoting Islamic education. He writes:

> *Moja katika jambo linalowahuzunisha wale wenye wivu juu ya dini ya Kiislamu ni kuiona hali kama Tanganyika haina maendeleo yo yote juu ya dini tukufu ya Kiislamu. Hakuna skuli yoyote ya Kiislamu ya kuwafundisha watoto wa Kiislamu elimu za juu za Kiislamu, na manufaa mengine mengi ili baadae wainyanyue nchi yao kwa mafunzo ya dini, wala hakuna hima na bidii yo yote inayofanyika ya kuwapeleka watoto nchi za nje kwa ajili ya kutafuta elimu ya Kiislamu yenye manufaa ya dunia yao na akhera yao.[120]*

Haider further blamed the East African Muslim Welfare Society and the Central Society of Tanganyika Muslims for the lack of effort to advance Islam and Islamic studies.

By the mid-1950s a more significant distinction in access to education had evolved between Christians and Muslims. Morrison offers very stark statistics which give us some idea of the nature of this disparity:

> In 1956, 711 government and native authority and twenty-seven Muslim agency institutions catered for 97,917 children; 1,846 mission schools provided 237,669 places. Even by assuming (rather generously) that Muslims comprised 75 per cent of the first figure and 20 per cent of the second, we can conclude that they were outnumbered by a factor of almost three to one (Morrison, 1976: 53).

Even more important, whereas Muslims were mostly excluded from mission-funded schools their Christian counterparts were availed unlimited access to publicly funded schools.

Muslims were not only forced to compete for fewer places in the few public schools but that competition was eschewed in favour of Christians. Such was the case at the Kitchwele Government Boys' Secondary School in Dar es Salaam.[121] Kitchwele School was closed on 28 August 1953. All students and staff were transferred to the newly built Mzumbe Secondary School in Morogoro. The teaching staff of seven consisted of six Christians (three Europeans and three Africans) and one Muslim. The student body consisted of twenty-nine students among whom 14 were Muslims and 15 were Christians. These students were being prepared to sit for the Standard X Territorial Examination Certificate and thereafter for either the Cambridge Overseas Examination Certificate, the General Education Certificate or the London Matriculation Examination Certificate.

The curriculum at Kitchwele, and later at Mzumbe, consisted of the following subjects: Kiswahili, English, Civics, Geography, History, Biology, Physics, Chemistry, Arithmetic, Algebra and Geometry. There was no option of choosing subjects but rather a student studied all subjects and had to pass all of them to receive a certificate. However, while Religion was not a part of the curriculum because Government schools were supposed to be secular, the Christian students had the option of dropping any one subject for the finals and instead sit for a special paper called "Religious Knowledge." The examination on "Religious Knowledge" was based on the Bible. Preparation for the special paper was informal. It was expected that Christian students would have learnt the basics through preparatory instructions for baptismal, confirmation and regular church attendance.

Apparently the Christian teachers did not openly proselytize in the sense that they did not teach religion in class. It is, however, possible that their behaviour and lifestyle may have influenced students in one way or another. In this regard, the ratio of Muslim vis-a-vis Christian teachers would be of significance and Christian influence stood to gain an upper hand given the preponderance of Christian teachers. Yet again whatever influence the Christian teachers may have had on Muslim students such an influence could have easily been countered by the cultural milieu outside the school, a milieu which was predominantly Islamic.

Both Dar es Salaam and Morogoro were in the Eastern Province whose population was predominantly Muslim. The predominance of Muslims in the Eastern Province bears significantly on the student enrolment by faith at Kitchwele and later at Mzumbe. We have already noted that there were twenty-nine students out of which 15 were Christian and 14 were Muslim. Since Kitchwele, and later Mzumbe, was the only Government secondary school in the Eastern Province, and since the Province was predominantly Muslim, one would have expected to see a higher percentage of Muslim rather than of Christian students. Even more significant, since Christians had additional schools they could go to Pugu, Minaki, Kwiro and Kigurunyembe there ought to have been more slots for Muslims at the only Government secondary school in the Province. The above Christian-run schools did not accept Muslim students unless they converted.

The case of Muslim student numbers at Kitchwele (and later Mzumbe) is of particular significance in other ways. A total of about 210 students in all primary schools in Uzaramo District, which were Mchikichini, Kisarawe, Kisiju, Maneromango, and Mkuranga, annually competed for placement at Kitchwele which only had three streams each for Standards Five and Six. Each stream had 30 and therefore only 90 students could be admitted to Kitchwele per year. The ninety slots were further limited by the number of so-called "repeaters." In any case, because the students in standards five and six came mostly from Uzaramo District the percentage of Muslims was quite high. This percentage would have remained higher despite that after standard six students at Kitchwele had to compete for slots with those of other schools namely Bagamoyo, Rufiji, Kilosa, Morogoro, and Mahenge Ulanga which were also in predominantly Muslim districts. All these schools had approximately a total of 240 students who competed for less than sixty slots if you exclude the number of "repeaters."

However, something strange seems to have happened in 1949 which may be related to the Muslim-Christian student ratio of those that left Kitchwele for Mzumbe on the evening of 28 August 1953. In 1949 only 24 students in the entire Eastern Province were selected to join Standard Seven at Kitchwele. The rest of the vacancies were filled by students selected from schools in the Southern Province many of whom were Christians from Peramiho. One of these students would later become the Vice Chancellor of the University of Dar es Salaam. The exception among the Christian students was one student whose parents were residents of Magogoni, Dar es Salaam. Thus it happened that a government school which previously had a majority of Muslim students came to have a majority of Christians.

Since education in colonial Tanganyika was linked to social and economic mobility, the historical distribution of educational opportunities is an important key to understanding Muslim complaints, then and now, about their marginalization. David Morrison aptly observes:

> In any society, consciousness of differences among people influences the way in which individuals and groups define goals and the means of achieving them. In other words, social structure is an important determinant of political behaviour, especially in economically underdeveloped countries . (Morrison, 1976: 50).

In Tanganyika, inequitable access to education opportunities did not only result in social and class differentiation, it also created a schism between Christians and Muslims whose effects continue to be felt today.

Due to their marginalization Tanganyika African Muslims were very vocal in their condemnation of British imperialism. The Suez Canal crisis in 1956 was an incident which Tanganyika Muslims used to criticize and condemn the British as imperialists and infidels. Newspapers like *Mwongozi*, published a number of poems that were very critical of Britain and supportive of Egypt. In the poem *Ya Allahu Ya Karima Wahiliki Makafiri*, verses 1, 3, and 5, Abu Munir (1956) asks God to protect Muslims worldwide from the infidels and to punish the enemies of Islam:

> *Kwa jina lako Manani*
> *Bismillah nasema*
> *Twakuomba Rahmani*
> *tadiriki hima hima*
> *Islamu duniani*
> *uwalinde na nakama*
> *Ya Allahu ya Karima*
> *wahiliki makafiri.*
> *Ya Allahu Ya Karima*
> *Ilahi tunalalama*
> *Wape nguvu Islamu*
> *dunia yote nzima*
> *Uwadhimili madhalimu*
> *wafikiwe na nakama*
> *Ya Allahu Ya Karima*
> *wahiliki makafiri*

111

Ya Allahu Ya Karima
Ya Ghafari Ya Rahima
Wahiliki makhasimu
kama wa siku za nyuma
Nuru ya Kiislamu[122]
Rabi isije kuzima
Ya Allahu Ya Karima
wahiliki makafiri[123]

In another poem titled *Dua* the author, Moza Ali of Malindi Zanzibar, prays that the efforts of the bullies against Egypt may come to naught:[124]

Amina itikiyeni
natumuombe Manani
Kwa jaha yake Amini
na sahaba wote piya

Baa ya hawa jeuri
ivunje ewe Jabari
Wapate kutahayari
kila walo furahiya
Rabi mpe nguvu kweli
Bwana Raisi Jamali
Atokwe na idhilali
ya adui kumoneya

Sala Ilahu Muhamadi
tuombee kwa Wadudi
Atupe sada na sudi
tushinde kwa zetu niya[125]

The author of *Dua*, like the author of *Ya Allahu Ya Karima*, strongly sympathized with the plight of Egypt against Britain. It remains unclear whether Muslims in Tanganyika sympathized with Egypt because the Egyptians were Africans or because they were Muslims. According to an anonymous contributor in *Mwongozi* of 8 February, 1957, African support was based on the principle of geographical "neighbourliness." Geographically Egypt is a part of the African continent although it is predominantly populated by Arabs. In those days of fervent nationalism "neighbourliness" was a powerful psychological force. Then, as now, because of this geographic connection, Arabs and Africans thought they had to be friends and to this end they worked hard at subduing their real differences by accentuating what they thought they had in common (Africa Today, Sept./Oct. 1975: 45-48). Yet, while Egypt and other Arab states on the African continent were considered African by geographical definition, their primary interests and aspirations then, and now, were linked with those of their Arab brethren in the Middle East.[126] If an accident of geography was too low a common denominator for genuine solidarity between Tanganyika and Egypt that of Islam was much more appealing and stronger. We have already noted how during the German period Cairo played an influential role in the spread of Islam in what was then German East Africa. The poem *Ya Allahu Ya Karima* above appeals to a sense of oneness among followers of Islam. To some Africans their faith comes first and their nationality second. Such feelings were effectively exploited by Cairo Radio during the Suez crisis as well as afterwards.

In his book *Egypt's Liberation: The Philosophy of Revolution*, Egyptian president Gamal Abdel Nasser considered Egypt's geographical position to be of particular political and religious significance. He writes:

> It is not without significance that our country is situated west of Asia, in contiguity with the Arab states with whose existence our own is interwoven. It is not without significance, too, that our country lies in northeast Africa, overlooking the Dark Continent, wherein rages a most tumultous [sic] struggle between white colonizers and black inhabitants for control of its unlimited resources. Nor is it without significance that, when the Mongols swept away the ancient capitals of Islam, Islamic civilization and Islamic heritage fell back on Egypt and took shelter there (Nasser, 1955: 86).

After taking over power, Nasser went on to fashion a foreign policy which assigned Egypt the role of champion and advocate of Africa's liberation. As Nasser put it:

> I may say without exaggeration that we cannot, under any circumstances, however much we might desire it, remain aloof from the terrible and sanguinary conflict going on there today between five million whites and 200 million Africans. We cannot do so for an important and obvious reason: we are *in* Africa. The peoples of Africa will continue to look to us, who guard their northern gate, and who constitute their link with the outside world. We will never in any

circumstances be able to relinquish our responsibility to support, with all our might, *the spread of enlightenment and civilization* to the remotest depths of the jungle (emphasis added) (Nasser, 1955: 110).

For Nasser the vehicle for the spread of enlightenment and civilization to the remotest depths of the African jungle was Islam. However, within Egypt itself Nasser's regime was intolerant to Islamic "fundamentalism" to the extent that during his rule many Muslim priests were either killed or forced to flee into exile.

Subsequently, Africa south of the Sahara in general, and East Africa in particular, became targets of a concerted Egyptian media propaganda which aimed at discrediting Western imperialism and its corollary, Christianity (Mbogoni, 1999). In July 1954, Radio Cairo started a Swahili program whose broadcasts targeted the Swahili-speaking countries in East Africa. The broadcasts stressed the racial intolerance of all European nations and exhorted Africans to rid themselves of European imperialism. The broadcasts were a reflection of an evolving Egyptian foreign policy which attempted to exploit religious sentiments for political gain.

In December 1953 the first East African Islamic Conference was held at Nairobi, Kenya. Egypt attempted to use this Conference to further its objective of using Islam as a political weapon in East Africa (Ismael, 1968: 51). In a letter read to the Conference the then Egyptian Minister of Guidance reiterated among other things that all Muslims should "wake up and fight for God" (ibid., 52). As a part of Egypt's foreign policy Islamic missions came to play a significantly important role. First, members of such missions were especially trained in the social organisation, culture, and environment of the countries where they would work. Secondly, the role of these Islamic missionaries was to create amicable religious ties between the East African nations and the Middle Eastern Islamic world with Egypt as its focal point.

It is important to note that Nasser criticized and sought to lead the struggle against imperialism, but he did not see Egypt's tutelage over Islam in black Africa as equally imperialistic. Yet the duties of the Ministry of Endowments were not confined to Egypt, but included the whole Muslim world (Ismael, 1968: 53). When Ahmed Hassan Al-Baquri, the Minister of Endowments, visited Senegal and Liberia in 1956, his intentions were to watch over Muslim affairs there and to enhance Egypt's "guardianship over the welfare of Muslims there" (ibid., 54). Egyptian attempts to create its hegemony over black Africa by using religion as an instrument were complimented by an educational policy which sought to encourage students from black Africa to enrol in Egyptian institutions of higher learning.

Thus, in 1957 at the request of Ali Muhsin Al-Barwani, Nasser offered Zanzibar forty scholarships. Al-Barwani notes in his memoirs what Nasser said to him:

> "Send the children here and we will educate them, feed them, and clothe them. At any stage they come they will receive education until they qualify ... I am also prepared to send to Zanzibar as many teachers as you need. We shall pay their salaries, provided you give them furnished quarters. Since that will depend upon your ability to meet the cost, you go and consult with your people as to how many you need and can afford to provide quarters for." (Al- Barwani, 1997: 105).

After getting Nasser's offer Al-Barwani requested if some of the scholarships could be allocated to Kenya and Tanganyika. According to Al-Barwani, the offers to Kenya and Tanganyika were not accepted due to "agitation from some elements in both Tanganyika and Kenya against sending students to Egypt" (ibid., 108). Supposedly, after the Egyptian government offered Zanzibar these scholarships the colonial governments of Kenya and Tanganyika prohibited anybody from those colonies to go to "Egypt or Greece" for education.[127]

Thus, the self-consciousness of Muslims as a marginal group in colonial society galvanized them to be in the forefront of the struggle for independence. Muslims in Dar es Salaam formed a preponderant majority of those who formed the African Association in 1929 and Jamiatul Islamiya fi Tanganyika (The Muslim Association of Tanganyika) in 1933. The secretary-general of Jamiatul was Kleist Sykes and the president was Shariff Salim Omar, the *liwali* of Dar es Salaam. Other members were Ali Jumbe Kiro, Maalim Popo Saleh, Mzee bin Sudi and Idd Tosiri. The major objective of Jamiatul was to facilitate the development of Muslims. Members of Jamiatul went from house to house collecting *sadaka* from Muslims with which Jamiatul built their first primary school on New Street (Lumumba) which opened in 1936.

According to Mohammed Said the main reason why Muslims were in the vanguard against colonial rule is because their survival and that of Islam as a religion depended on the total overthrow of the colonial state (Said, 1998). However, when the Tanganyika African National Union (TANU) was formed out of the African Association in 1954, the founders appear to have agreed to keep religion out of politics. Yet as soon as Julius K. Nyerere, a Roman Catholic, assumed leadership of TANU, he encountered factional opposition from a minority Muslim's group in TANU led by Sheikh Suleiman Takadir, chairman of the TANU Elders Council. The majority of the Muslims supported Nyerere whom they believed was in the process of building TANU into a party of national unity. The fear of the minority group was that a Christian leadership would pose a threat to Islam after independence as the colonial administration had done. Those disenchanted with the new Christian leadership in TANU split and formed the All Muslim National Union of Tanganyika (AMNUT).

The marginality of Muslims in education was evident during the 1958 parliamentary elections. The conditions for voting or standing as a candidate were that one must have an annual income of 200 sterling pounds, Standard XII education and be employed in a specific post. Some Muslims complained that these conditions excluded a great deal of potential Muslim voters and candidates who up to that time were very active in politics. Indeed, TANU was forced to field candidates who, with one exception, happened to be Christians.[128] To the politically-conscious Muslims like Sheikh Suleiman Takadir this was the beginning of Muslim marginalization which they feared would be carried over into the post independence period. In the meantime Muslims like Sheikh Takadir felt the British were being doubly unfair because they had colluded with the missionaries to deny Muslims access to western education and the job opportunities that came with such education.

Thus when AMNUT was formed in 1959 the party's leadership sought to delay the granting of a self-government until Muslims in Tanganyika were adequately educated. The leadership wrote a number of petitions to the United Nations Trusteeship Council, to the Secretary of State for Colonies and to the United Nations Visiting Mission. In a petition dated 22 November 1959 and addressed to the Chairman of the Trusteeship (Council) UN, the following assertions among others were made:

> (i)   that AMNUT represented the nine million Africans of Tanganyika;

(ii)   that TANU was not representative of the African population of the Territory and that in its campaign for self-government it was disregarding the educational interests of the Muslims in order that its own predominantly Christian leaders may ultimately monopolise political power;

(ii)   that it would be a "gross mistake" to concede a self-government until the Muslim majority of the population was in receipt of adequate higher education; and

(iii)   that the Government of Tanganyika supported the Christian element in the country in a partial manner with regard to the provision of educational facilities (CO 822/2130, AMNUT Petitions).

In response the Government of Tanganyika made the following observations:

(i)   The claim of AMNUT to represent the "nine million Africans of Tanganyika" was patently absurd. Membership of the Union was restricted by its constitution to "all adult Muslims irrespective of caste, community or colour." There were estimated to be some two to two and a half million African Muslims in Tanganyika, about one-third of the total African population. It was apparent from the results of the elections of members to the Legislative Council which took place in September 1958 and February 1959 that TANU enjoyed a very wide measure of support among the African population of the Territory;

(ii)   TANU had made the improvement of facilities for higher education a cardinal part of its programme and the party had displayed no indication in this, or in any other aspect of its policy, of any form of discrimination on grounds of religious belief;

(iii)   The attainment of a self-government would depend upon the stage of development reached by Tanganyika as a whole and not upon the stage reached by any particular section. It was the policy of the Administering Authority to give equal opportunities for advancement in all fields to all the inhabitants of the Territory, regardless of religion or race;

(iv)   There was no religious discrimination whatever in the provision of assistance to voluntary agency schools. Provided the managements of such schools fulfilled the requirements of the Education (African) Ordinance (Cap. 71) they were eligible for financial aid;

(v)   The total of grant-aided Christian mission schools in 1958 was 2,031 (not 2,800 as stated in the petition). Government and native authority schools (all of which were open to pupils of all religions) numbered 856. There were in the same year 23 grant-aided Muslim schools (CO 822/2130).

The Government went on to explain the discrepancy between Christian and Muslim grant-aided schools. According to the Government, the discrepancy which the figures in (v) above revealed indicated "a differential in efficiency and educational enthusiasm between Christian and Muslim voluntary agencies, rather than Government partiality for the former"(CO 822/2130). The Government further noted that there remained a large number of unfilled places in primary schools in the Territory - places which could well have been taken by Muslim children. This situation existed not only in Government and Christian voluntary agency schools but also, for example, in the two Muslim primary schools in Dar es Salaam where only 253 and 114 of the 360 and 180 places provided had been taken up that year. "There would, therefore, appear to be some disinclination amongst Muslim parents to send their children to school, even when places are available," the Government concluded (CO 822/2130).

Muslim antipathy to secular education was also noted by His Highness the Aga Khan during his visit to East Africa in 1958. In a letter the Aga Khan wrote to W. A. C. Mathieson, at the Colonial Office, dated 31 August 1958, he noted:

> What I find particularly disconcerting is that in the majority of Muslim schools the balance between Religious and Secular education has not been reached to the satisfaction of a very large proportion of the Muslims in East Africa. Many parents still have to decide whether they wish to send their children to Koran schools to receive a thorough religious education but to forego modern secular education, or to send them to Modern schools and try to teach Islam to their

children at home (CO 822/1584). In order to encourage a movement toward the improvement of Muslim secular education the Aga Khan pledged funds from the EAMWS to support secular schools built by Muslims on a self-help basis. In Tanganyika the Aga Khan's pledge appears to have made little impact. In any case, the pledge came a little too late. Thus Muslims entered the independence era lagging far behind their Christian compatriots in secular education and the job opportunities such education engendered.

However, even if opportunities had availed Muslims of access to secular education without the threat of Christianity, it is possible, as the Aga Khan noted, that many parents would still have opted to send their children to Qur'anic schools. Moreover, insofar as Qur'anic education defined the terms for Muslim self-understanding, making provision for it was of paramount importance compared to secular education. The centrality of the Qur'anic school was an obstacle to Muslim desire for secular education. What Lamin Sanneh says in regard to West Africa applies to colonial Tanzania:

> The Qur'anic school exists to give unrivalled preeminence to the word of God; it demonstrates the authority of the word, its scope in the education process, its role in the lives of individuals and society, and its future under Western secular pressure. Such a central place for the Qur'anic school sets it squarely on the front line of the encounter with the West...Can the child at Qur'anic school learn about moral truth and combine that at a Western school with education as objective science that is morally neutral and ethically agnostic? (Sanneh, 1996: 146)

Yet, there were Muslims in colonial Tanzania who opted for secular education. These were likely to be middle class and urban dwellers. Muslims like Abdulwahid Sykes who was in the forefront of the struggle against British colonial rule belonged to the Muslim middle class whose social and economic interests were not the same as those of the Muslim working class or the peasantry. Their lifestyle and outlook were more western oriented than Islamic. Mohamed Said observes that they had more than a good taste for good clothes by which he means western suits among other things:

> They blended the Swahili and cosmopolitan cultures. They listened to the music of Edmundo Ross, Victor Sylvester, Nat King Cole, Louis Armstrong, Alma Cogan, Bing Crosby and others; and when they felt like it, to Arab songsters, Um Kulthum, Mohamed Abdulwahab, Farid Atrash, Abdul Halim Hafidh, Feruz and Sabah.

> They also watched movies from Hollywood featuring stars like Clark
> Gable and John Wayne (Said, 1998: xxiv).

According to Mohamed Said, in Islam Tanzania Muslims had a
ready-made ideology of colonial resistance. He writes:

> Islam has always been the ideology of resistance against colonial rule
> or any other authority which tried to subjugate Muslims. Consequently,
> no government in power, either indigenous or foreign, has ever been
> king or supportive to Islam, and likewise Muslims have always been
> engaged in a continuous struggle to preserve their faith and fight for
> their rights (Said, 1998: 263).

In contrast Said observes that "Christianity became a reactionary
force siding with the colonial authority" (ibid.). Yet Sykes and other
Muslims facilitated the rise to preeminence of Julius Nyerere, a devout
Roman Catholic. This contradiction is explained away as the result of
the pre-independence Muslim politics of tolerance and conformity
(ibid., 265). Moreover, Said attributes the formation of TANU and
Nyerere's assumption of leadership to Abdulwahid Sykes' lack of
ambition. Otherwise, had Sykes wanted he would have become the
president of Tanzania (ibid., xxiv, 116). Despite Said's assertion about
a ready-made ideology of resistance which Muslims could find in
their faith, it remains difficult to identify a *jihad* tradition that could
have been evoked during the struggle for independence. This is
paradoxical given the fact that in the Dar es Salaam environment of
the 1950s politics was influenced by strong Muslim personalities
including some well learned Muslim scholars like Sheikh Suleiman
Takadir (Said, 1998: 120). The only Islamic influence in Dar es Salaam
anti establishment politics was use of *dua* during the dockworkers'
strike in 1947. The majority of the dockworkers were Ngindo, Zaramo,
Rufiji, Shomvi and Matumbi, most of them being predominantly
Muslim. According to Said, the organizing committee members that
planned the strike bounded themselves with *Ahlil Badr* "to protect
themselves against fifth columnists, treachery and black feet. Incense
was burned and the Qur'an was recited" (ibid., 63). Said further notes:
"Secured by this oath[129] and fired by invoked Muslim militancy
reminiscent of the Battle of Badr, and by reciting the names of the
martyrs who died fighting the unbelievers of Mecca alongside Prophet
Muhammad (Peace Be Upon Him), the dockworkers chose 6th
September, 1947 as the day of the strike" (ibid., 63).

Unlike the Dar es Salaam dockworkers the Muslim community in Tanganyika constituted a wide variety of interests and concerns. These varied interests had received varied representation in the form of associations like Jamiatul Islamiya fi Tanganyika. AMNUT was the only political party which claimed to represent all Muslims in Tanganyika. As we have already noted the leadership of AMNUT claimed that they were championing the interests of all Muslims including the demand for educational opportunities for Muslims to enable them to share equitably in a post colonial government. Among its detractors were some of the notable sheikhs in Dar es Salaam who categorically denied that AMNUT represented all Muslims. In fact some accused the founders of AMNUT to be nothing but self seekers (Kandoro, 1961: 184-5). The accusation was probably true of Mohamed Said Chamwenyewe, AMNUT's founder and first president.

Chamwenyewe was a founder member of TANU who resigned his membership early in 1959 for personal reasons. He had just come out of prison after serving a 12-month sentence for assaulting a Forest Guard. On his release he expected some monetary compensation from TANU for the time he had spent in jail. When nothing was offered, he considered it a snub. However, on his release he also sensed that his influence in the party had waned. In June and July he made a tour of the Central Province during which he disconcerted TANU leaders by alleging that TANU's policy deliberately intended to exclude Muslims from senior positions in the party (CO 822/1375). When he returned to Dar es Salaam, he made a formal application for the registration of AMNUT.

According to AMNUT's constitution all adult Muslims irrespective of caste, community, or colour were entitled to become members by paying a subscription fee of Sh. 1/- per annum. The objects of the party were:

(a) To present, promote and safeguard the religion, educational, political and economic interests of all Muslims in Tanganyika;

(b) To propagate, work for and promote the unity of all Muslims in political, social, cultural and economic life in Tanganyika;

(c) To promote friendly feelings and intercourse amongst all Muslims and non-Muslims in Tanganyika; and

(d)   To practice tolerance in all aspects of human activity and to practice the ideal of universal brotherhood and thereby to promote cooperation between all Muslims and non-Muslims for the political, social, cultural and economic development of the country (CO 822/1375).

In comparison, the aims and objects of TANU were the following:

(a)   To prepare the people of Tanganyika for self-government and independence;

(b)   To fight against tribalism and all isolationist tendencies amongst the Africans and to build up a nation of Tanganyika;

(c)   To fight for the removal of every form of racialism and racial discrimination;

(d)   To urge the Government to introduce compulsory and universal primary education, and

(e)   To cooperate with other nationalist and democratic organisations in Africa for the object of the emancipation of the people of Africa and the establishment of independentand self-governing African states (CO 822/859).

Evidently from their different objectives AMNUT and TANU's ideologies were qualitatively different. However, whereas AMNUT trapped itself within a narrow discursive field created by religious suspicions TANU's ideology was national and pan-African in its objects. Even before independence evidence shows that TANU endeavoured to address the concerns of Muslims including the issue of access to education. The 1955 TANU general meeting passed a resolution calling for the Government to increase the number of Government schools for Africans. At the same meeting TANU resolved to start collecting money to start its own schools (CO 822/859). Yet in spite of TANU's pledges to deal with inequities which were created by the colonial experience the party assumed power under a cloud of suspicion from certain Muslim quarters.

What concerned some Muslims the most was that the achievement of independence would not necessarily mean the end of their marginalization. They feared that a predominantly Christian government led by Nyerere,[130] a devout Catholic, would be predisposed to Church pressure to favor Christianity against Islam and its followers. Soon after independence Muslim fears were exacerbated by Church activities which appeared to position it into a favourable relation with President Nyerere. To start with, the Pope sent a delegate, Archbishop G. Del Mestri, to attend Tanganyika's independence celebrations. And His Eminence Laurean Cardinal Rugambwa (the first African cardinal) said prayers on behalf of the Catholic community at the Flag Raising ceremony in the National Stadium at midnight on 8 December, 1961. Earlier that day the cardinal had conducted a special mass for Independence Day and in his sermon he gave a religious twist to the meaning of independence. He said, *"Siku hii ya uhuru wa nchi yetu tumepewa na Mungu. Ni Mungu ametujalia siku hii, yeye aliye asili ya kila jambo lililo jema, lililo takatifu. Mwanadamu, tofauti na mnyama, amejaliwa na Muumba wake kipaji cha uhuru na uwezo wa kuwa yeye bwana wa matendo yake mwenyewe chini ya amri zilizochorwa katika roho ya kila mtu ... "[31]* (Ecclesia, January 1962).

To commemorate Tanganyika's independence, the T. M. P. Bookshop in Dar es-Salaam, which was owned by the Catholic Church, ordered medallions which were to be worn by Catholics on independence day and other important festivals afterwards. The medallions had the imprint of the Virgin Mary on one side and on the other a message that read *"Bikira Maria Ulinde Uhuru wa Tanganyika,"* which was a plea to the Virgin Mary to protect Tanganyika's independence. Despite disclaimers that the medallions did not represent any form of religious discrimination some of those who wore them were assaulted in the streets of Dar es Salaam (*Ecclesia*, January 1962).

The St. Joseph Cathedral intended to cater to the spiritual needs of Julius Nyerere. A clergy meeting on 20 November 1962 was informed that a permanent seat for the President-Elect and his wife would be reserved within the Sanctuary. In another meeting on 18 December 1962 the clergy voted in favour of creating a private chapel in the State House which Nyerere had requested. However, it was decided that the services of the private chaplain would have to be paid for by the President himself. The decision was intended to preempt Muslim criticism: "They would then consider the Catholic Faith of the President to be his private affair and not identify him with any religious community" (*Ecclesia*, December 1962).

A year after Tanganyika was given independence, it became a Republic. This momentous event was celebrated by a High Mass conducted by His Eminence Laurean Cardinal Rugambwa on 9 December, which happened to be a Sunday. It is reported that more than 3,000 people attended the Mass in St. Joseph's Cathedral. In the sanctuary sat the President and Mrs. Maria Nyerere together with the Minister of Commerce and Industry and Mrs. Kahama. Catholic Members of Parliament, representatives of TANU and Trade Unions, Catholic members of the Foreign Embassies and senior civil servants had reserved seats in the nave of the Church. The Cathedral was decorated with the National and Papal Flags and the sanctuary looked very impressive with a big 'canopy' in the national colors. In the words of the editor of *Ecclesia*, "It showed that the Church was not unaware of such an historic event that was close at hand" (*Ecclesia*, January 1963).

Twenty two years later the Church would again show that it was not unaware of another historic event namely the retirement of President Nyerere in 1985. On 3 November 1985 a farewell mass was conducted at St. Joseph's Cathedral for the retiring Nyerere. Six people prayed and read select verses from the Bible. Gabriel Sieta, praying on behalf of the Catholic youth, thanked God for Nyerere's leadership. He prayed also that God would enable Catholic youths to become future leaders in the likeness of Nyerere. Sister Astrida, praying on behalf of other nuns, thanked God for enabling Nyerere to understand and encourage the work of nuns in Tanzanian society. She prayed also that God would provide new leaders who would understand and support the work of nuns in the country. A priest prayed that there continues to be a good relationship between the Church and Government in order to facilitate evangelical work and cooperation in safeguarding the rights and honor of all citizens of Tanzania (St. Joseph's Cathedral Archives, File for 1983-1985).

At the above farewell mass a total of Shillings 23,070 was collected and donated for the building of a church at Butiama, Nyerere's birthplace and retirement home. Another Shillings 22,000 was collected from the four Dar es Salaam parishes and donated for the same purpose. St. Joseph's parish added another Shillings 10,000 for the project (*Daily News*, 4 November 1985). Behind this "generosity" was a spirit of appreciation for what was perceived to be Nyerere's contribution to the Church. This was clearly expressed in the *Risala* which was read to Nyerere during the farewell mass. A part of that *Risala* noted: *"Sifa unazostahili kupewa za kuleta maendeleo ya Siasa, Uchumi na Ustawi wa Jamii kwa Taifa letu, tunawaachia Wananchi na Viongozi wengine. Sisi tunataka kukushukuru na kukusifu kwa kazi zako za Kitume. Katika mazungumzo na hotuba zako ukiwa Mwenyekiti wa Chama na Rais ... mara nyingi uliwakumbusha wasikilizaji au wasomaji juu ya Maandiko Matakatifu ... "* [132] Thus, for instance, after announcing the Arusha Declaration in February 1967 Nyerere sent Christmas cards to all Party and Government leaders with a message from The Acts of the Apostles, Chapter 4:32, 34 and 35. [133]

The relationship between the Catholic Church and Julius Nyerere is further explored in the next chapter. It will suffice to mention here that although Nyerere was a devout Catholic neither all Roman Catholic missionaries supported him during the struggle for independence nor were all Catholic priests supportive of his policy of Ujamaa after independence. Yet as we will see in the next chapter Muslim criticism was that Nyerere ruled at the behest of the Catholic Church or that his Ujamaa ideology was unduly influenced by Christian ideals. The impression one gets from such criticism is that Nyerere was a Christian/Catholic first and everything else second. What led these critics to that position is that they have applied to Christianity in Tanzania what they have applied to Islam in the Middle East. Christianity, however, does not demand such loyalty as Islam does by insisting on the inseparability of religion from politics.

Despite Muslim criticism it can be argued that Nyerere was a nationalist (and pan Africanist) first and everything else second. Following independence Nyerere was confronted with the problem of how the newly independent state was to develop. Tanganyika was a huge country, sparsely populated in most parts, and with poor communications. Of particular difficulty was the problem of continuing to supply the dynamic which was needed to raise living standards and to create a nation once the impetus of the struggle for independence had lost its urgency - "and yet to ensure that the dynamic [would] continue to manifest itself with moderation and restraint, with no breakdown of law and order ..., with no lapse into strife on tribal, communal and religious lines" (British Council of Churches, "The Political Situation in Tanganyika, May 1961," MSS. Afr. s. 1604).

Even more important than the matter of development was the problem of creating a nation out of more than 120 ethnic identities. If a nation is an imagined community, as Benedict Anderson argues

(1991), Nyerere and his Muslim and other critics had different visions of Tanganyika as a new nation. While his critics aspired to use ethnic and religious institutions for sectarian interests, Nyerere imagined a nation in which institutions such as labour unions would function as modes of representing the collective good. For instance, whereas strikes organized by the Tanganyika Federation of Labour (TFL) against the colonial regime were accepted as legitimate, after independence striking against the government was made illegal. Labour unions were forced to become collaborators of the government and abandon their sectarian claims. Thus TFL was replaced by the National Union of Tanganyika workers (NUTA). In the political arena the introduction of single party rule de-legitimized political contestation by other interest groups. The introduction of Ujamaa socialism in 1967 reduced entire categories of people to class enemies.

CHAPTER SEVEN

RELIGION AND POLITICS AFTER INDEPENDENCE

In the previous chapter we noted how some Muslims were suspicious that TANU and Nyerere would not care for their interests after independence. Of particular concern was whether after independence the Government would cater to the educational needs of Muslims. Evidence indicates that soon after independence Nyerere was concerned about improving Muslim access to secular education. Nyerere's concern was articulated in a confidential memorandum that he wrote to the Catholic Secretariat of the Tanganyika Episcopal Conference in December 1963. The memorandum titled "The Problem of Education in Tanganyika" was actually a personal appeal by Nyerere to the Churches to take an active part in helping the nation solve one of its pressing problems[134] (MSS. Afr. s. 1471). The memorandum is attached as Appendix III.

As the leader of independent Tanganyika Nyerere was not only concerned about solving the basic problem of educating the masses of his people but also redressing the educational imbalance between Christians and Muslims brought about by their different colonial experiences. "The only possible answer,' Nyerere wrote, 'indeed the only just answer, is to give priority to the provision of schools at which Moslems can be educated without offence to their religious scruples" (MSS. Afr. s. 1471). Nyerere exhorted the Churches to take the challenge as a moral obligation. He wrote:

> I know the Church has always been reluctant to associate itself with education which is not directly Christian and under its own control. I am saying that it is urgently necessary for the Church to think again. Where the sincere religious beliefs of a Moslem, or other non-Christian, people make it impossible for them to use Christian schools, I cannot believe Christians are justified in doing nothing. On the contrary, I believe Christians in particular have a positive duty to go out of their way to give all the help they can - and to give it in a way which can be accepted (MSS. Afr. s. 1471).

He informed the Churches that failure to help would leave the Muslims with no alternative but to seek help from other sources which could be injurious to their faith. He had in mind "those who talk glibly of 'brotherhood' while denying the very source of brotherhood

- the Fatherhood of God." As far as he was concerned, if this were to happen because Christians were prepared to turn their backs rather than give help in a way which the Muslim conscience could accept, who would be to blame?

Evidently Nyerere respected Muslim conscience and was concerned about Muslim lack of access to an education system dominated by missionary agencies. He thought it was wrong and could be politically divisive. He may have learnt from AMNUT's political agitation that on the political level the educational gap between Christians and Muslims in Tanganyika was potentially explosive. In AMNUT's leaders he must have seen people who were ready to make political capital out of it. Yet for Nyerere the problem of Muslim education was not truly a political problem at all. In "The Problem of Education in Tanganyika" he writes:

> Those who are trying to make it a political issue are an insignificant handful and, thank God, the vast majority of our people are not misled by the hypocrisy of the few who try to cloakpolitical self-seeking under a mantle of pseudo-religious fervour. No; the problem as I have stated it is a moral one. And it is on the moral plane that I must seek the understanding and assistance of the Christian Church, and indeed of all those who are in a position to help (MSS. Afr. s. 1471).

Nyerere explained the reason for his appeal for help from the Church. He believed that the response to his Government's own appeals for funding from charitable organisations would be limited if not hostile. He writes:

> One of the reasons for the almost hostile reaction to a government's appeal for help with its educational programme is the question of who is to benefit by that help. Even sincere Christians very often seem to feel that it is not enough to give help just because it is needed.

They want to be sure their giving helps only their fellow Christians, or potential fellow Christians. So that many charitable individuals and organisations, who would be ready and eager to respond generously to appeals from the Christian churches are decidedly less ready to do so when a similar appeal is made to them directly by a government. Those sources the Church can, and I believe should, approach on our behalf (MSS. Afr. s. 1471).

Obviously Nyerere appealed to the Churches because he himself was a Christian and he believed they would listen. Did the Churches seek to benefit from this association? Recent Muslim and Christian scholarship suggests that the Churches had undue influence over Nyerere and his politics (Said, 1998; Njozi, 2000; Sivalon, 2001). First, there is the well-known friendship between Nyerere and Father Richard Walsh. The two first met at Tabora where Nyerere taught after returning from Makerere, and was later reunited at St. Andrew's College, Pugu. According to Sivalon, Father Walsh may have been instrumental in encouraging Nyerere to engage full time in the struggle for independence (Sivalon, 2001: 17).

Second, there was his relationship with the Maryknoll Fathers who in 1956 financed Nyerere's London to New York trip where he spoke at the United Nations. Throughout his seven-week stay in the United States Nyerere stayed with the Maryknoll Fathers and Sisters. Following an enquiry from the Vatican, Father William Collins justified the expenses as follows: "The Maryknoll agreed to pay for the round trip ticket from England to New York, the USA. His round trip from Tanganyika to England was paid for by his Party. The Maryknoll agreed to finance him because he is a Catholic leader from Musoma District and we thought it would give him the opportunity to witness the condition of Catholicism in the United States of America and perhaps to get scholarships for Tanganyikans" (Quoted and translated from Sivalon, 2001: 18).

Father Collins went on to say that the Maryknoll's support of Nyerere was in line with British colonial policy of encouraging the natives to prepare for self rule. Moreover, as Nyerere was a Catholic leader, Father Collins observed that it was in the interest of the Church to help him: "This is a good Catholic, a person of wisdom whose ambition is to lead his people toward full independence. He knows that there are radicals in his Party, but he is striving to guide it toward an acceptable direction. His Party has been registered officially and it is not a clandestine party" (ibid., p. 18).

Since Father Collins says that what the Maryknoll Fathers did was for the good of the Church, he must have expected Nyerere to reciprocate in the future. Indeed, Father Collins came to consider Nyerere as a vital link between the Church and the government. But in what ways was Nyerere, as President, beneficial to the Church? Sivalon tells us that Nyerere's close relationship with the Church was reflected by his close working relationship with important officials of the Church who helped him in his political endeavours and in leading TANU (Sivalon, 2001: 19). Sivalon does not tell us how the Church concretely benefitted from this relationship.

However, we are made to understand that from the mid-1950s till about 1966 the Catholic Church in Tanzania made a conscientious effort to prepare its followers to assume positions of authority after independence. The Nyegezi Institute in Mwanza was built by the White Fathers for the purpose of training such future leaders. Once in such positions of authority Catholic followers were expected to pre-empt what the Church considered to be the two major undesirable tendencies namely Marxism and Islam.

In an Apostolic letter titled "African and the Christian Way of Life," written in 1953, the Bishops of Tanganyika outlined the Church's desired socioeconomic system after independence. The letter extolled the virtues of the traditional African way of life especially the emphasis on a sense of community, respect for traditional leaders, respect of law, of tradition and of governance as well as wisdom and faith in God. The Bishops also suggested that it ought to be the government's responsibility to ensure that there was equal access to basic necessities such as food, clothing and shelter as well as to prevent the enrichment of a few at the expense of the majority (Sivalon, 2001: 24-25).

Needless to say, some of the above suggestions constituted the basis of Nyerere's policy of Ujamaa as promulgated by the Arusha Declaration in 1967. However, it is difficult to say that Nyerere's ideas of Ujamaa were mainly influenced by the above Apostolic letter. It is well known that he was open to other influences. His attitude toward capitalism and private property was perhaps more influenced by his reading Shakespeare's *The Merchant of Venice*, which he translated into Kiswahili. Nyerere also acknowledges the influence of the American author Henry George. The basic ideas of Ujamaa, especially regarding land ownership and use, are very close to those expounded by Henry George (See Appendixes I and II).

Moreover, there were things that the Bishops suggested which Nyerere was opposed to. Thus, whereas the Bishops favoured traditional authority, Nyerere was disinclined to use the authority of chiefs after independence. He in fact abolished chiefdoms in 1963! On their part the Bishops, as we will later see, held back their support for the Ujamaa policy with which Nyerere intended to transform Tanzanian society.

In another Apostolic letter issued in 1960 the Bishops instructed their Catholic followers to maintain peace and to respect elected leaders and accept them as legitimately chosen even if they had encountered no opposition. In this letter the Bishops of Tanganyika also exhorted Catholic followers to respect the family, to respect other faiths, and to understand that all parents had the right to educate their children according to the teachings of their faith. In the same year another Apostolic letter titled *Unity and Freedom in the New Tanganyika* was intended to show Catholic followers how they could live in a pluralistic society. First, it explained the pluralistic nature of Tanganyika society according to tribes, customs, politics and religion (Sivalon, 2001: 27). The letter exhorted Catholics to respect these differences. According to Sivalon, this particular letter very much pleased Nyerere because it helped to ease Muslim anxiety over a post independence government led by a Christian.

Although the Bishops asked their congregations to be tolerant of other religions, they harboured suspicions that some Muslims were intent on establishing an Islamic state while others were intent on causing chaos (Sivalon, 2001: 28). Father Schildknecht, the Director of the Religious Affairs Department of the Council of Bishops from 1959 to 1966, wrote a number of memoranda exhorting Catholic priests to be vigilant against Islam and communism. A 1963 report of the Religious Affairs Department had this to say about Islam:

> *Uislamu unazidi kuleta matatizo. Waislamu wamefaulu sana katika vyombo vya juu wakijaribu kuleta mang'amuzi yao huku wakifaidika na huduma zetu za kijamii, bila kukubaliana na masharti ya ushirikiano katika mfumo wa wengi jinsi ilivyotajwa kwenye "Unity and Freedom"* [35] (Quoted by Sivalon, 2001: 34).

The report went on to express concerns about an impending conference of the leaders of the Bohora, Ismaili, Ithnasheri, and Sunni congregations; the transfer of the headquarters of the EAMWS to Dar es Salaam in 1961; and the visit of a group of sheikhs from Egypt under the sponsorship of Mortamar (Pan Islamic Congress).

The Church's concerns above may have been further reinforced in 1962 when a pan-territorial congress of Muslim organisations was called in Dar es Salaam to discuss the future role of Islam in independent Tanganyika. The following organisations attended: EAMWS, Dawat al-Islamia, Jamiatul Islamiya fi Tanganyika, Jamiatul

Islamiya fi Tanganyika "A" and the Muslim Education Union (Said, 1999). Items of the agenda included the teaching of Islam and the role of tabligh in Tanzania. The congress determined that although there were many Muslims in Tanzania, many of them did not understand Islam well. In this regard it was decided to establish immediately a department of tabligh that would facilitate the work of calling others to Allah (Tewa, unpublished manuscript, not dated, 28).[136] On the matter of secular education many delegates deplored the poor standard of many Muslims in Tanzania and agreed, as a matter of priority, that a department of education must be set up immediately and charged with organizing the funding of Muslim schools.

The 1962 congress elected Tewa Said Tewa, a Cabinet Minister and founder member of TANU, Chairman of the Territorial Council of EAMWS and Alhaj Aziz Khaki, an Indian, the secretary-general. Members of the executive committee were Bibi Titi Mohamed, Alhaj Saleh Masasi, Sheikh Amir bin Juma (who headed the department of tabligh), Sheikh Abdallah Jambia, Sheikh Khamis Kyeyamba, and Sheikh Bilali Rehani (Tewa manuscript, 29). Under Tewa's leadership the EAMWS embarked on a territorial campaign to promote Islam and Muslim welfare services especially the building of schools.[137] According to Tewa, within a year success was noticeable in the number of new Koranic schools opened and new mosques built. What was more important to the EAMWS leadership was the appreciation by many Muslims that EAMWS was their own Society, "which (would) help them in their Tabligh work and for the development of their religious and secular education" (Tewa manuscript, p. 31).

Apparently the efforts by EAMWS to mobilise Muslims all over the country were misinterpreted as "mixing religion and politics." Similarly, when the TANU Elders Council, whose members were all Muslims, increasingly acted as a religious lobby group it was perceived to be "mixing religion and politics." In March, 1963, the national executive committee (NEC) of TANU dissolved the eleven-man Elders Council. At the same time a select committee of NEC was formed and was mandated to campaign throughout the country against the tendency to "mix religion and politics." Among the members of this select committee was Sheikh Abdallah Chaurembo (who was the Chairperson), Omar Londo, M. Kihere (MP and Area Commissioner for Same), Edward Barongo (Parliamentary Secretary, Ministry of Agriculture), and Sheikh Musa Rehani.

Their campaign was closely followed by the local press which reported on some of their condemnations. Sometimes their condemnations went to the extreme. Thus, at a public rally in Mwanza a member of the committee, Mwalimu Kihere, said that people who tried to stir up religious dissension in Tanganyika should not only be rusticated but caned periodically. "In stubborn cases I would suggest such people be shot," he said (*Tanganyika Standard*, October 14, 1963, p. 3). At the same rally another member, Barongo, castigated the Catholic Church for fanning religious fears by suggesting that more Muslims than Christians occupied important positions in TANU and Government. Barongo refuted this by saying that out of 17 Ministers only five were Muslims, four out of 20 Parliamentary Secretaries were Muslims, 19 out of 62 Area Commissioners were Muslims and only four out of 15 Regional Commissioners were Muslims (ibid.). Ironically it did not occur to Barongo that the very statistics he was offering substantiated the Muslim claims about their apparent discrimination and marginalization. The same irony was missed by his counterpart, Omar Londo, who strongly attacked local Muslim sheikhs for indulging in political activities. Londo said the Government was aware of a "master plan" backed by some outside powers to enable Muslims to gain political power (ibid.).

At another meeting at Moshi Sheikh Abdallah Chaurembo reminded his listeners that Tanganyika's struggle against colonialism had been fought and won by people of all religions. Likewise, the struggle to build the nation called for close cooperation. He warned that any kind of obstruction aimed at destroying harmonious relations would not be tolerated (*Tanganyika Standard*, October 16, 1963, p. 5). It is important to note that Muslims were especially being called upon to realize the importance of thinking in national rather than religious terms. Muslims who saw themselves as Muslims first and Tanganyikan second were the ones accused of stirring religious dissension and "mixing religion with politics." The reason why such Muslims considered their religion rather than national identity as their most important frame of reference had something to do with the Islamic concept of *Dar-al-Islam*. Believing, as they did, that Muslims constituted a majority of Tanganyikan population they considered Tanganyika to be *Dar-al-Islam* or a Muslim country. They therefore aspired to see the country governed and led by Muslims.

Meanwhile, as the above campaign was going on, Nyerere issued an order to deport from Dar es Salaam two leaders of Dawat al Islamia. The men, Abdillah Shneider Plantan, president of Dawat al Islamia, and Hamisi Jumanne Hamisi Abedi, general secretary, were accused of exploiting religious differences for political purposes. An official statement stated that the Government had been aware for some time of certain activities by these two men. As a result of investigations and of evidence supposedly produced on an oath, the President was satisfied that they had been exploiting religious differences for political purposes in a manner which was dangerous to peace and good order in Dar es Salaam. Plantan was deported to Mbulu, in the Arusha Region, and Abedi to the Chunya district of the Mbeya Region (*Tanganyika Standard*, October 12, 1963, p. 1). The significance of these deportations is that they happened mid-October, 1963, when the Territorial EAMWS was holding its congress in Dar es Salaam.

Perhaps to assuage Muslims fears following the above deportations, Tewa Said Tewa, the president of EAMWS, invited President Nyerere to address the congress. Nyerere assured the delegates that Government was committed that people in Tanganyika enjoyed the right to worship where they wish and in the way they like. He said the Government would not choose a religion for the people to follow and it did not matter to it which religion people observed (*Tanganyika Standard*, October 15, 1963, p. 3). On his part, Tewa assured the President that EAMWS had no intention of meddling in politics. Tewa said those Muslims who were fomenting trouble were doing so on their own behalf and did not represent EAMWS (ibid.). Tewa further reiterated that EAMWS was only interested in mobilizing Muslims in matters related with their education.

However, besides mobilizing Muslims locally the EAMWS leadership also endeavoured to cultivate ties with Muslims elsewhere, especially in the Middle East. Thus in April 1964 a high-powered delegation comprising of Alhaj Tewa Said Tewa, Sheikh Hassan bin Amir, Sheikh Omar Abdallah, Alhaj Aziz Khaki, Mwinjuma Mwinyikambi, Alhaj Max Mbwana, Alhaj Saleh Masasi, Alhaj Issa Mtambo and Alhaj Omar Muhaji left Tanzania for a tour of the Middle East. They subsequently visited Egypt, Jordan, Kuwait, Iraq and

Lebanon. The objectives of the tour included a solicitation for funds to support Muslim educational projects. The delegation succeeded to raise a considerable amount of money in cash and in pledges.

Since the main objective of the EAMWS according to its 1957 constitution was to propagate the expansion of Islam in East Africa the above tour of Islamic countries may have been interpreted by the Nyerere government as an attempt to open Tanzania to increased contact and influence from the Islamic world. In this regard, what happened to Tewa Said Tewa can be interpreted as a pre-emptive strike against such endeavours. Upon the return of the delegation Tewa was dropped from the cabinet and appointed ambassador to the Peoples Republic of China.

However, the loss of Tewa's leadership was not the main cause of the demise of the EAMWS. Rather, separatist tendencies within EAMWS were exploited by the government to encourage the formation of BAKWATA. Factionalism within EAMWS became evident during the 1966 EAMWS conference held in Arusha. Some Tanzania Muslims not only demanded the formation of autonomous regional entities out of EAMWS but also the revision of the Society's constitution. Although these separatist efforts were not successful in 1966, they did succeed in 1968. On 17 October 1968 Adam Nasibu declared that the Bukoba branch of EAMWS was henceforth independent. Bukoba's withdrawal from EAMWS was followed by the Tanga and Iringa branches. By mid-November nine regions had withdrawn from EAMWS. Among the reasons given for splitting from EAMWS was the Aga Khan's patronage of the Society and the fact that the EAMWS's secretary-general was not an African.

By and large, what sealed the demise of EAMWS in Tanzania was its ambivalence if not hostility to TANU's new policy of Ujamaa socialism as enunciated by the Arusha Declaration of 1967. Among other things the Arusha Declaration stipulated the nationalization of banks, factories, plantations and real estate worth more than Shs. 100,000. The objective was to undermine capitalist interests in favour of Ujamaa socialism. Those affected included Indian Muslims who were in control of lucrative businesses in commerce and industry. Since the Indian sponsors of the EAMWS stood to lose their properties, they became staunch opponents of the Arusha Declaration.

Needless to say, ordinary Tanzanian Muslims who had nothing

to lose supported the introduction of Ujamaa socialism. They did not see it being contrary to the teachings of Qur'an. Adam Nasibu, the regional secretary of EAMWS in Bukoba, organized demonstrations in Bukoba in support of the Ujamaa. Nasibu's enthusiasm for Ujamaa was not favourably received by the leaders of the EAMWS who went on to orchestrate his ostracism but to no avail. It appears that some of the leaders or influential patrons of EAMWS whose properties had been nationalized were behind the campaign to vilify Adam Nasibu.[138]

In the meantime, Nasibu and others who had withdrawn from EAMWS organized the Iringa National Islamic Congress, which was held from 12-15 December 1968, in Iringa. It is estimated that about 200 delegates from all over the country attended. According to Tewa, among the delegates almost all Muslims in positions of leadership such as Ministers, Regional Commissioners, Party Regional Chairmen and TANU National Executive Members attended (Tewa manuscript, 81). Some delegates from Zanzibar also attended including Sheikh Abeid A. Karume, the first Vice-President of Tanzania, who opened the Congress. In his opening speech, Karume accused the EAMWS of having pursued policies which were antagonistic to TANU and Afro-Shirazi Party (ASP). He warned against religious "pretenders from outside," and called for Muslim leadership to be placed in the hands of the people themselves (Tewa manuscript, 82). The Second vice-president, Rashid Kawawa, in a closing speech spoke of the need to remain loyal to the ruling party (Chande, 1998: 138).

The main outcome of the Iringa Congress was the drafting and adoption of a constitution for a Supreme Council for Tanzanian Muslims, popularly known by its acronym BAKWATA. The Congress also called upon the Government and ruling Party to grant immediate recognition to the new body, and declare EAMWS unlawful and to freeze its funds. On 20 December, 1968, the Minister for Home Affairs, Said Ali Maswanya, issued an order declaring both the Tanzania branch of EAMWS and the Tanzania Council of EAMWS to be unlawful under the provision of section 6 (1) of the Societies Ordinance (Tewa manuscript, 83). Such was the ultimate demise of the EAMWS and the birth of BAKWATA, both of which are believed by many Muslims to have been orchestrated behind the scene by Nyerere for his own political gain.

However, whatever influence Nyerere may have brought to bear on the demise of the EAMWS and the formation of BAKWATA, Tewa unlike other Muslims had the insight to understand that Nyerere only succeeded because Tanzania Muslims were divided in the first place.[139] According to Tewa, the demise of the EAMWS was engineered by Muslims who had failed to gain its leadership: "They formed BAKWATA and all those Muslim politicians who took part in breaking East African Muslim Welfare Society were elected on the national leadership of BAKWATA" (Tewa manuscript, 86).[140] Alhaj Saleh Masasi, a TANU central committee member, was elected as the national Chairman and Sheikh Abdallah Chaurembo, another party faithful, was elected as the Deputy Chairman (Chande, 1998: 138). As a result of these ties to TANU, BAKWATA was received in some Muslim circles with suspicion. Also BAKWATA was accused of being a sectarian society only catering to the interests of mainland African Sunni Muslims (ibid., 139).

By and large, whereas Muslims like Nassibu and organisations like BAKWATA supported Nyerere's policy of Ujamaa, his own Catholic Church did not, at least initially. The Church's ambivalence or unspoken hostility toward Ujamaa was based on what it considered to be the danger of secularism and of totalitarian state control (Robinson, 1963). In regard to secularism there were concerns in certain circles about statements made by some public figures that in Tanzania religion was to be a purely private matter restricted to worship in churches and other places of worship. On the danger of secularism Robinson, a Maryknoll missionary based in Tanzania during the sixties, writes:

> ...there is a growing feeling that religion has no place in the political and social fields of society where it may become a divisive factor ... The theory seems to be that the state is quite capable in itself to bring about the better life, and where the fields of Church and State impinge on each other, as in education and correction, the Church will in time appear superfluous. Where they are different, the Church will be quietly ignored and dropped as irrelevant (Robinson, 1963: 261).

In regard to secularism Robinson was reiterating a long held Church belief that no practical solution to the alleviation of the condition of the poor masses will ever be found without the assistance of religion and the church (Pope Leo XII). In his encyclical letter of 1891 Pope Leo XIII writes:

> Doubtless this most serious question (of land ownership) demands the attention and the efforts of others besides Ourselves – of the rulers of States, of employers of labour, of the wealthy, and of the working population themselves for whom we plead. But We affirm without hesitation, that all the striving of men will be vain if they leave out the Church. It is the Church that proclaims from the Gospel those teachings by which the conflict can be put an end to, or at least made far less bitter.. (Reproduced in Henry George, 1965).

In 1937, Leo's successor Pope Pius XI reiterated in an encyclical letter the same position about the Church's contribution in human affairs. Pope Pius also voiced concern over the increasing tide of secularism especially in Europe. He hoped that "the fanaticism with which the sons of darkness work day and night at their materialistic and atheistic propaganda will at least serve the holy purpose of stimulating the sons of light to a like and even greater zeal for the honor of the Divine Majesty."

By the early 1970s there also was growing concern at the Vatican about secularism in Tanzania and other eastern African countries. It was in this regard that the Secretariat for Non-Believers organized a colloquium at Gaba Seminary, Uganda, to discuss the problem. The colloquium determined that there was a serious problem of "indifferentism and unbelief" among the African educated elite and recommended religious education at third-level institutions (Shorter, 1997: 1). The academic atmosphere at the University of Dar es Salaam (hereafter UDSM), indeed, reflected a state of unbelief especially among members of the faculty. In the early 1970s Marxism was in vogue and religion was discredited as "the opium of the people." Ideological classes were organized and took place on Sunday mornings to offer students an alternative to Sunday mass. These classes, conducted by Walter Rodney, Kassim Guruli and Grant Kamenju among others, turned out to be very popular.[141]

Subsequently Marxism at the University of Dar es Salaam found its way into the curricula especially in courses developed and taught using a historical materialist approach, for example Development Studies and East African Societies and Economies. The former was mandatory to all freshmen and the later was mandatory for the general degree of Bachelor of Arts. In these courses students were taught that the course of human history has nothing to do with the will of

God but rather depends on human agencies, i.e., it is in the course of living their lives that human beings make their history. In this regard historical materialism suggests that humans, and not God, have the ability to change their own history toward a happy conclusion, viz. a world of abundance and complete equality otherwise known as socialism. In the context of Tanzanian history Nyerere's Ujamaa policy was supposed to facilitate the achievement of socialism in Tanzania. Ideally, an Ujamaa society was envisaged to be a friendly, fraternal (calling each other *ndugu*), communally organized society in which the collective good would triumph over individualism (Nyerere, 1968).

To the ideologues at the Hill, as UDSM was popularly known, religion had nothing to contribute toward the creation of a socialist society in Tanzania. If anything religion, believed by Marxists to be false consciousness, was likely to fetter the realization of socialism. As far as Marxists are concerned, because religion places salvation from bondage and misery in the after life it does not solve the problem of exploitation here and now. And by offering hope in supernatural intervention to solve problems on earth religion denies human agencies and in doing so serves to prolong inequality and injustice. Yet as the upsurge of liberation theology in Latin America during the 1970s would show, religion has not always been a conservative force. However, the declaration of Ujamaa and its implementation in the early 1970s compounded the Church's fears about secularism. The policy was suspected of tendencies that were deemed to be potentially anti Christian and authoritarian. The evidence for the later included the formation of national organisations and services from the top by imposition rather than from the bottom through the democratic process (Robinson, 1963: 162). But in general, the Church in Tanzania appears to have drawn its suspicions about Ujamaa socialism from the encyclical letter of Pope Pius XI on communism which voiced similar concerns raised in the encyclical letter of Pope Leo XIII already referred to above. The Church in Tanzania was very reluctant to accept Ujamaa.

By 1974, seven years after the declaration of the Ujamaa policy, Nyerere was on the verge of being very disillusioned with the Catholic Church because of its continued lack of support of Ujamaa. On 3 August 1974 Nyerere called Father Robert Rweyemamu, who was then the Secretary-General of the Tanzania Episcopal Conference, to his

Msasani residence for an interview.[139] The president told Father Rweyemamu that he wanted to explain to him the philosophy of Ujamaa. Nyerere expressed his desire that hopefully Father Rweyemamu would convey the meaning to higher Church authorities especially to the Pro-Nuncio (Mgr. Cerrano was there) and the Episcopal Conference of the Tanzania Bishops.

Nyerere started the interview by expressing to Father Rweyemamu an idea that he had first expressed to a delegation of Bishops who had gone to see him at State House in March 1974. He had told the Bishops that he wished they could explore the possibility of recruiting priests from Latin America or find ways of developing some forms of exchange or visitation programmes with that continent. Nyerere explained to the Bishops that priests from Latin America would be better able to understand and appreciate what was being attempted in Tanzania in the form of Ujamaa policies; that they would see that TANU and the government were trying to find solutions to problems of social justice similar to those in Latin America. Nyerere was expressing his admiration of Latin American liberation theology.[142]

Nyerere then went on to tell Father Rweyemamu that in 1970 he had been asked by Archbishop Mihayo if the government could help conduct a seminar on Ujamaa for the benefit of Church staff who needed to be better acquainted with the ideas of Ujamaa. The seminar was held at Tabora and was not only attended by Catholic priests and nuns, but also by non-Catholic and Muslim leaders. Nyerere attended the seminar and gave the opening speech. In his opening address, Nyerere first explained the relationship between the ruling party, TANU, and religion. He categorically said that neither was TANU religiously influenced the way Christian Democratic Parties in Europe were[143] nor did Tanzania have an official religion like England, Italy or Pakistan did (Nyerere, 1970: 3-4). Tanzania was neither a Christian nor an Islamic state.

Secondly, he reiterated that TANU's concerns were entirely of this world (ibid., 33). He noted that TANU's ideology of *ujamaa* socialism made the party the champion of the oppressed and the exploited in Tanzania. Furthermore, he explained that Tanzania's *ujamaa* socialism was not to be confused with European (read Marxian) socialism. Unlike European socialism, *ujamaa* socialism was not anti religion rather it was against exploitation based on private ownership of the means of production such as land and factories (ibid., 12-13). In any case, Nyerere pointed out, the reason European socialists were against religion was because the Church in Europe had a history of countenancing exploitation and the misery of the masses arising from it (ibid., 21). Nyerere appealed to the Bishops, priests and sheikhs to judge *ujamaa* socialism by the merits he had delineated; to say if living together or working together for the common good was a bad thing (ibid., 32). He challenged them to point out if the *ujamaa* ideology was against the teachings of the Muslim or Christian Scriptures. But, as he said, he did not think it did:

> *Hatudhani kwamba inapingana na lolote Maimamu mlilotumwa katika Kuruani...Kama lipo mtalisema wakati wa Semina hii. Mtawajulisha viongozi wetu mahala ambapo haya tunayoyaeleza, haya yanapingana na Kuruani...Kama haya tunayoyasema yanapingana na Injili, Wakubwa msione haya, msione haya katika mazungumzo mtuambie kwamba Injili inakataa: kwamba "mafunzo ya Bwana Yesu yanakataza haya mnayoyasema, haya ya kuzuia unyonyaji, maana Bwana Yesu anapenda sana unyonyaji!"[44]* (Nyerere, 1970: 38)

However, Nyerere left Tabora a disappointed man. He told Father Rweyemamu:

> I stayed three days. The first day, I noted that the priests were very reserved, they did not speak out if they followed the main points in the lectures. On the second day, they started.

> Actually it was Father Otto who started and he has been a member of TANU for many days. Then a few others followed. The questions they put betrayed that they had worries ... our Catholic priests were really worried, and still many did not speak up. I was unhappy about the Seminar. It was only the Catholic priests who seemed not to be clearly convinced of programmes. At Dodoma where Protestants had their one-day Meeting on Ujamaa, it was the contrary; they had no worries. So I still asked myself why our own religious leaders were not getting the idea.[145]

Before Nyerere left Tabora he was shown a booklet titled *Huu ndio uhuru*. Nyerere noted that it was a translation of *Divini Redemptoris*, the encyclical of Pius XI on Communism.[146] According to Nyerere the booklet was published by the Church in Tanzania in 1970 for propaganda reasons. Apparently the publishers likened Communism to Ujamaa by using TANU's symbol of Mwenge, the Uhuru torch, on the booklet's cover. Nyerere wondered why the Church chose to publish this rather than, say, *Populorum Progressio*. He was convinced that the

Catholic church in Tanzania could not apply *Divini Redemptoris* without opposing Ujamaa.[147] In this regard it is instructive to take a closer look at the encyclical *Divini Redemptoris*.

In the first instance, the Pope called Communism "the satanic scourge" (Pius XI, 1937: 6). The Communist ideals of justice, equality and fraternity were declared to be delusive promises (ibid., 6). The encyclical scoffed at the idea of absolute equality as a rejection of hierarchy and divinely-constituted authority, including the authority of parents. It considered the Communist emancipation of the woman a threat to the juridical-moral bond of matrimony. Pope Pius wrote: "She is withdrawn from the family and the care of her children, to be thrust instead into public life and collective production under the same conditions as man" (ibid., 7). What would be the condition of a human society based on such materialistic tenets, asked Pope Pius XI. His answer was that it would be a humanity without God, a society opposed reasoning and to Divine Revelation. Pope Pius was concerned that such a society devoid of the fear of God in the hearts of men would be susceptible to passions capable of the most atrocious barbarity.

Furthermore, Pope Pius XI also noted that "The preachers of Communism are also proficient in exploiting racial antagonisms and political divisions and oppositions. They take advantage of the lack of orientation characteristic of modern agnostic science in order to burrow into the universities, where they bolster up the principles of their doctrine with pseudo-scientific arguments" (op. cit., 9). As for the rapid diffusion of the Communistic ideas seeping into every nation, great and small, advanced and backward, Pope Pius blamed such diffusion on "propaganda so truly diabolical that the world has perhaps never witnessed its like before" (op. cit., 10). Moreover, one of the sorry effects of this propaganda was said to be the destruction of Christian civilization and the Christian religion by banishing every remembrance of them from the hearts of men, especially of the young.

Pope Pius further noted that although Communism was antireligious by its nature, "the law of nature and its Author cannot be flouted with impunity. Communism has not been able, and will not be able, to achieve its objectives even in the merely economic sphere...After all, even the sphere of economics needs some morality, some moral sense of responsibility, which can find no place in a system so thoroughly materialistic as Communism"(op. cit., 12). After indicting Communism Pope Pius explained how *civitas humana* was its opposite. He emphasized the belief that not only has man a spiritual and immortal soul but is marvelously endowed by his Creator with gifts of body and mind. He wrote:

> He is a true "microcosm," as the ancients said, a world in miniature, with a value far surpassing that of the vast inanimate cosmos. God alone is his last end, in this life and the next. By sanctifying grace he is raised to the dignity of a son of God, and incorporated into the Kingdom of God in the Mystical Body of Christ. In consequence he has been endowed by God with many and varied prerogatives: the right to life, to bodily integrity, to the necessary means of existence; the right to tend toward his ultimate goal in the path marked out for him by God; the right of association and the right to possess and use property"(op. cit. 13).

Thus according to the Catholic Church the above God-granted rights constitute true freedom and are the basis of human happiness. In this regard it is easy to understand why the Kiswahili translation of *Divini Redmptoris* was titled *Huu ndio uhuru*

In Nyerere's view the publishers of *Huu ndio uhuru* were trying to make him appear as though he was a communist agent, the secret vehicle of philosophical materialism. He told Father Rweyemamu that what he was trying to do was in fact to prevent communism:

> We know what social order means better than Bishops, we know how to effectively prevent communism. And, believe me, communism will never come to Tanzania if our efforts succeed. Recently I intervened to stop University Students who were creating a "Cheche" Movement, like that in Russia.[148]

Nyerere wanted Father Rweyemamu to know this so he could well advise the Church authorities. What he said next is worth quoting in full:

> I am a layman, but I try to do what I can and will not come against my own Church. We want to liberate the Church from the "matope" [i.e., mud] which she has accumulated over the centuries by being identified with world situations in Europe. If in other countries Catholicism has tampered on progress, human justice and prosperity, in Tanzania we can make her succeed better than elsewhere. I want to give the Church a better chance here so that she will not be blamed, as in the Catholic countries. Tanzania is not a Catholic country, but Catholicism is strong. Tell the Bishops I have established in TANU a department

of political education and I put a Lutheran Minister in charge. He was not a great politician, but I selected him because of his balance, gentleness and strong solid faith so that political education will not grow out of hand into extreme tendencies. In the TANU National Executive Committee, two of the Members are ordained ministers of religion. Their Bishops may have a problem with that, but I trust it is a good way to assure the Party of sound people. I would like my own Church to have no worries and misunderstandings.[149]

In response Father Rweyemamu reassured Nyerere that the booklet *Huu ndio uhuru* had been reprinted at Tabora for commercial rather than propaganda purposes. Father Rweyemamu went on to express his reservations about particular aspects of Ujamaa. Of particular gravity was Ujamaa's tendency to elevate the human person on the basis of his material individuality. He said that on this score the difference between Ujamaa and dialectical materialism was virtually negligible. He further noted that although TANU professed no religious affiliation, it needed to create a climate in which human progress and human society would not lose sight of the spiritual and religious values. In Father Rweyemamu's view the basis of cooperation between Church and State required the recognition by both parties of the necessity of spiritual as well as temporal values in human development.[150]

As we have already noted, besides the Church's concerns about the dangers of secularism and Ujamaa's potential for authoritarianism, during the sixties and seventies the Church was concerned also about what it perceived to be the danger of Islam. According to Robinson, "whereas the Christian Churches (had) been making every effort to live in harmony and cooperation in a pluralistic society, respecting freedom of conscience, and the separation of Church and State, the Muslims seem(ed) to be taking advantage of this situation to further their own interests both religiously and politically, using political pressures to weaken the Christian position" (Robinson, 1963: 263). Muslim political clout was supposedly enhanced by their numerical preponderance in TANU as well as in the government. Their ultimate objective, according to Robinson, was the realization of a Muslim State.

In regard to perceived Muslim discrimination after independence, especially in education, Robinson thinks it was more of an excuse. He writes:

African Muslims are not interested in building up their social services such as schools, as both Government and Christian Churches encourage them to do; their policy seems to be to exert their influence to de-Christianise the Christian institutions, and eventually, if possible, make them Muslim, at least in Muslim areas (ibid., 263).

We do not know for certain that Muslims indeed intended to de-Christianise the Christian institutions and make them their own. What we know is that in 1970 the state made all private schools public as a precondition for its policy of compulsory education for all children of school age (Nyerere, 1963).

In 1968 when the Catholic Church was celebrating the first centenary of its evangelical mission in Tanzania, it was running 1,378 primary schools, 44 secondary schools, eight teacher training colleges, 15 trade schools and 48 home craft centers. The Church then had also 25 hospitals, 75 dispensaries, 74 maternity clinics and 11 medical training schools. All of them were nationalized in 1970. When privatization became possible again in the early 1990s, the Church started again building schools. In 1991 the Church had 413 kindergarten schools, 82 secondary schools including 23 junior seminaries, 73 technical and vocational schools, 48 home craft centers for girls, two teachers training colleges, and six schools for the disabled. In the medical sector, the Church operated 223 health centers and dispensaries and 36 hospitals including the 850 bed referral hospital at Bugando, Mwanza.[151]

In 1992 the Catholic and Protestant Churches, assisted by German partner Churches, negotiated a memorandum of understanding with the Tanzania government. In this memorandum the government recognized the important role played by the Churches in the social services sector. The government pledged to assist the Churches financially and promised never to nationalize Church institutions again. At present the Churches together run more than 50 per cent of all medical services and secondary schools in Tanzania. These services are open to all people regardless of religious affiliation.[152]

After a relatively quiet decade of the seventies concerted Islamic proselytization in Tanzania as elsewhere in East Africa came to the fore starting in the early 1980s into the1990s. What was happening in Tanzania was a part of a global phenomenon. Like other religions, Islam was reasserting itself globally as well as influencing global politics. On the one hand, with the assassination of Anwar Sadat, the specter of the Iranian Revolution, the taking of American hostages and Ayatollah Khomeini calling for a global *intifada* the 1980s came to be known as the decade of Islamic "fundamentalism." On the other, the decade of the 1990s not only saw the fall of the Soviet Union but also the coming to power of the Talibans in Afghanistan and the introduction of electoral politics in some Middle Eastern countries. In this regard, political Islam was both violent as well as subtle with a tendency toward becoming an increasingly visible force in civil society.

A number of local Muslim organisations were in the vanguard of Islamic radicalism in Tanzania. These included Ansar Sunna, the Union of Muslim Preachers in Tanzania, the Tanzanian Council for Qur'an Reading, the Islamic Writers' Workshop known as Warsha, the Youth Muslim Association and the Ahmadiya Muslim Mission. Some of these organisations had close connections with Islamic organisations centered in the Arab world. Arye Oded has amply documented the influence and reach of some of these organisations in black Africa (1987). A look at some of the Islamic organisations based in the Middle East which have influenced Tanzania's religious climate is pertinent.

The Organisation of the Islamic Conference (O.I.C.), with head offices in Jeddah, Saudi Arabia, was founded in 1970. It dealt with Inter-Islamic relations at state level. Its mandate was to coordinate Arab aid to African member states for development programme and the construction of mosques as well as organizing courses for Muslim religious leaders in Arab and African states. In 1983 the O.I.C. invited Tanzania's vice-president, Aboud Jumbe Mwinyi,[153] to tour Saudi Arabia. It also paid his expenses for the pilgrimage to Mecca which was a part of the tour. At the time Aboud Jumbe Mwinyi was one of the Muslim African leaders most active in strengthening African-Arab relations. During his tour he met with the heads of the O.I.C., and requested aid for Tanzania in the form of teachers and preachers (Oded, 1987: 287). Agreement was reached during his visit on the opening of a branch of the World Muslim League in Dar es Salaam (ibid.).[154]

Aboud Jumbe Mwinyi's public role in promoting Islam in Tanzania is probably one of the things that cost him the Vice-Presidency.[155] Evidently he did not realize what it meant to Nyerere, for instance, for Zanzibar to have strong ties with the Arab world. In a conversation with Fletcher-Cooke way back in 1957 Nyerere referred to Zanzibar as "a historical and geographical anachronism." He saw it as "a projection southwards of the Middle East and, in addition, a projection backwards into the Middle Ages" because of the presence of "the Sultan and his Arab henchmen and supporters" (MSS. Brit. Emp. S. 526/2, Fletcher-Cooke Interview with John Tawney, 9 February, 1970). When they met again in Dar es Salaam in 1968 Nyerere told Fletcher-Cooke that Zanzibar was still one of his biggest headaches. Had Aboud Jumbe known Nyerere's sentiments he probably would not have used Islam to promote close ties with the Arab world.

Unfortunately it was late in his life that Aboud Jumbe realized he had to follow his religious conscience in whatever he did. In his book *Safarini* he writes: *"Kila mmoja lazima ajihadhari jinsi anavyotumia uhuru aliokirimiwa wa kuchagua, hiyari aliyobarikiwa ya kuamua na madaraka na dhamana aliyokabidhiwa ya kutenda, akikumbuka kuwajibika kwake, binafsi ataposimama mbele ya Mola wake katika marejeo yake Siku ya Mwisho"*[56] *(Mwinyi, 1988: 15).* More specifically he knew the dire consequences for those who mistrust the Qur'an and fight Islam overtly or covertly (ibid., 24-25). To the obscurantist and critic of the Qur'an Aboud Jumbe Mwinyi has this to say: *"Hakuna amezaye kudosarisha, kugeuza wala kubatilisha Ukweli, Usahihi, Uhakika na Usafi wa Uongozi huo, pamoja na mabadiliko yote yaliyotokea na yatakayotokea katika ujuzi wa walimwengu, kutokana na maendeleo yo yote na uvumbuzi wo wote wa sayansi!"*[57] *(Mwinyi, 1988: 31).*

More pertinent to this study is that Aboud Jumbe Mwinyi believed, as other Muslims do, that there is a fundamental difference between Christianity and Islam. In *Safarini* he writes: *"Kuwachukua wanadamu, viumbe vya Mwenyezi-Mungu, na kuwafanya kuwa miungu au watoto wa miungu sio jambo jipya...(W)atu kufanya kufru ya kuamini visa na hikaya hizo ni dhambi isiyosameheka."*[58] This statement is made after he quotes from Chapter 9 verse 31 of the Qur'an: "They have taken as lords beside Allah their rabbis and their monks and the Messiah son of Mary, when they were bidden to worship only One God. There is no God save Him. Be He Glorified from all that they ascribe as partner (unto Him)!"

In another book that Aboud Jumbe Mwinyi published in 1994 titled *The Partner-Ship*, he devotes an entire chapter to a discussion of religion and politics in Tanzania. Jumbe reiterates the belief that there is an ongoing conspiracy between the Church and "the seemingly Christian oriented government" to marginalize Muslims. He offers

John C. Sivalon's book as evidence of such conspiracy. He writes:

> A careful study of Dr. John C. Sivalon's book, *Kanisa Katoliki na Siasa ya Tanzania Bara 1953 hadi 1985* gives a rare insight of a calculated campaign against Islam. In other words the book itself is a voluntary confession on the part of the author, of Roman Catholic activities in Tanzanian politics; a Church which is inseparable from the Vatican, whose embassy is among the earliest to be established in Tanzania...That its contents have never been challenged or repudiated by the Union or Tanganyika Government(s) or by CCM, is a living testimony to the authenticity of those confessions (Jumbe 1994: 116).

Other than the allegation of a conspiracy to marginalize Muslims, Jumbe accuses those leaders, be they of the Church, of CCM, or the Union Government, who advocate for a separation of religion from politics of applying double standards. For example, Jumbe queries why the presence of the Vatican Embassy in Tanzania has never been questioned but Zanzibar's decision to join the O.I.C.[159] was vehemently opposed with threats being made to impeach President Ali H. Mwinyi; demands made for President Salmin Amour of Zanzibar and some of his ministers to be dismissed; and Muslim Ministers in the Union Government being called to resign for allegedly wanting to "Islamize" Tanzania (Jumbe 1994: 115).

Apparently, Jumbe did not know the difference between subscribing to an organisation like the O.I.C. and having diplomatic relations with a sovereign state which the Vatican is. Tanzania's membership in the O.I.C. would entail her to subscribe to its objectives. And what are the objectives of the O.I.C.? Article two of the Charter of the O.I.C. states that its first objective is "to promote Islamic solidarity among member states." Other objectives include efforts "to strengthen the struggle of all Muslim peoples with a view to safeguarding their dignity, independence and national rights." By signing the Charter member-countries commit themselves financially and politically to the aims and objectives of the O.I.C. In this regard, as Joseph Kenny notes, "It is clear...that any country that joins the OIC, even though it may profess to be secular by its constitution, is actually committing itself directly to the advancement of Islam."[160]

The African Islamic Center (hereafter A.I.C.) in Khartoum, Sudan, was also alleged to be involved in revitalizing Islam in Tanzania. The A.I.C. was jointly founded by Arab states. Its stated major objective was that of spreading Islam in Africa. In the late 1970s and early 1980s the Center organized a number of international conferences. As vice-president, Aboud Jumbe, was a participant of the 1982 conference which discussed strategy and planning for the spreading of Islam in Tanzania. It appears that Sudan subsequently developed a closer relationship with Muslim organisations in Tanzania which facilitated the reception of Sudanese preachers. On 25 April, 1993 the government announced that it had expelled three Sudanese Muslim teachers for promoting Islamic "fundamentalism."[161]

Another Sudan-based organisation that was involved with advancing the Islamic cause in Tanzania was Munadhamat al-Dawat al-Islamia. In 1988 Munadhamat organized a three-day conference that was held at Dar es Salaam. About one hundred and fifty delegates from Arab and East African countries attended the conference, which was chaired by former Sudanese Head of State, General Abdul-Rahman Muhammad Hassan Wuwaru Ddhahab (*Daily News*, 26 March, 1988, p. 1). In his opening speech, read on his behalf by the minister of education Kighoma Ali Malima, President Ali Hassan Mwinyi hailed Munadhamat's contribution to the welfare of Tanzanians by initiating water supply projects in Zanzibar and mainland Tanzania (*Daily News*, 24 March, 1988, p. 1). The conference approved the proposed expenditure of 1.2 million dollars for various projects in Tanzania for the year 1988.

Besides the Sudan, a number of Arab countries were also involved during the 1980s and 1990s in an extensive Islamic propagation campaign mostly through their embassies. Arab ambassadors participated in religious ceremonies on Muslim holidays, made presents of Islamic and Arabic literature, and offered charitable donations to the needy. Most Arab embassies had cultural centers which facilitated the propagation of Islam. As early as 1971, Egypt founded an Islamic cultural center in Dar es Salaam, "with the aim of introducing Islamic consciousness among Tanzania's Muslims and of teaching Arabic" (Oded, 1987: 288). Ten years later, in 1981, "the Egyptian minister of Religious Trusts decided to step up the center's activity, and sent four religious officials there 'in order to strengthen cooperation with Tanzania's Muslims" (ibid.).

Some Arab countries such as Libya not only funded activities intended to promote Islam but also openly encouraged anti-Christian sentiments. At the Pan-African Youth Conference, held in Benghazi in March 1974, Muammar Gaddafi proclaimed that Christianity 'was in Africa, a means of destroying the African essence,' and he called upon the Muslims to set out on a holy war to expel Christianity from the continent (Quoted by Oded, 1987: 301). Today Christian fears are intensified by declarations that are accompanied by acts or attempts to convert African Christians to Islam.

Muslim radicalism in Tanzania and elsewhere in East Africa at the end of the twentieth century was also the result of the growing influence of radical organisations centered in the Middle East. The merger of Al Qaeda led by Osama Bin Laden[162] and Islamic Jihad led by Dr. Ayman Al-Zawahiri was completed in 1998. The merger resulted in the formation of the World Islamic Front for Jihad Against Jews and Crusaders (*The New York Times*, 21 November 2001, B5, 1). That same year there were bombings of American embassies in Nairobi, Kenya, and Dar es Salaam, Tanzania. Subsequently, among the 22 most wanted for questioning by the United States of America, one was a Tanzanian Muslim who was suspected to have been recruited by Al Qaeda.

External funding fueled intense and acrimonious competition between Muslim organisations as their leaders got embroiled in accusations and counter-accusations against one another. For instance, Sheikh Yahya Hussein alleged that Ansar Sunna was being funded by foreign benefactors whom he named to be the International and Relief Agencies of Saudi Arabia, the African Muslim Agencies of Kuwait, the Islamic World Review and Islamic World League both of Saudi Arabia. Others that he named were Munadhamat Al-dawa Al-Islam of Sudan, the Islamic Call Society of Libya and the Union of Muslim Council for Eastern, Central and Southern Africa based in Saudi Arabia (*Majira*, 13 March 1998).[163]

Sheikh Yahya attributed the then ongoing rivalry between Islamic groups to foreign donors whose intention, he alleged, was to foment hostilities that went against Islamic values. Secondly, Sheikh Yahya alleged that among the practices opposed by Ansar Sunna was the celebration of the Prophet Muhammad's birthday, respect for the five daily prayers, meeting to read the Qur'an and offering non ritual prayers (*dua*) for the dead. He reiterated that by opposing these practices Ansar Sunna was a worse enemy of Islam than any other religion.

In response to Sheikh Yahya's allegations, Ansar Sunna's Sheikh

Salum Rajab Sima said the real problem with BAKWATA's leadership was their ignorance of the teachings of the Qur'an. He accused BAKWATA sheikhs of being unable to read, understand and interpret the Qur'an (*Majira*, 13 March 1998). Sheikh Sima also acknowledged that his organisation received funding from abroad. However, he reiterated that the money was used to spread Islam rather than to foment religious hostilities.

Despite the above hostilities and disagreements during the presidency of Ali Hassan Mwinyi the centrality of the Qur'an in political life was given official approval. One of his ministers of state, Professor Kighoma Ali Malima, formerly a minister of education, was known for his leaning toward a greater participation of Muslims in education and politics (Lacunza-Balda, 1997: 119). As minister of education Malima visited Iran from 6 - 14 March, 1988 at the head of an official delegation. Lacunza-Balda writes: "Iranian officials did not miss the opportunity to suggest to K. A. Malima that the ministry of education in Tanzania should introduce the teaching of the Qur'an to its school programme and follow the educational programme of Iran" (ibid., 119).

We do not know how Prof. Malima reacted to this advice, but what we know is that he did not last long at the Ministry of Education before he was transferred to the President's Office in a cabinet reshuffle. This chapter cannot be complete without mentioning the case of the formation of the Dar es Salaam Islamic Club (hereafter D.I.C.) in 1998, under the leadership of former President Ali Hassan Mwinyi. According to an article that appeared in the *Sunday Observer* (Dar es Salaam) of 5 July, 1998, the formation of the D.I.C was part of a strategy by the O.I.C. to further the Islamic influence in Tanzania.[164] It was alleged that the offices of the D.I.C. were intended as temporary headquarters of the O.I.C. in Tanzania. The author of the *Sunday Observer* article questioned the manner in which Ali Ameir, the minister for home affairs, allowed the registration of the D.I.C. when his ministry was at the same time campaigning to de-register some churches, including the popular Full Gospel Bible Ministry of Rev. Kakobe.

Moreover, the author of the *Sunday Observer* article questioned the involvement of former President Mwinyi and noted that Mwinyi did not appear to understand what should come first: "*kufanya kazi kwa manufaa ya taifa na kuendekeza matashi ya Uarabu wa Kiislamu. Hili la Uarabu wa Kiislamu ndio lililomchukua zaidi, kwa mujibu wa wachunguzi wa mambo, ambalo linapelekea katika maangamizo ya taifa."* Mwinyi was blamed for letting himself be used by Arab nations whose intention was to control Tanzania politically and economically. The *Observer* article reminded readers that the consequences of Arab involvement in Tanzania and elsewhere in sub-Saharan coountries have always been negative, including the enslavement of blacks by the Arabs. Tanzanians were cautioned to beware of religious fanatics who were bound to open doors to Arab neo-slavery.

In conclusion, during the early years of independence not many Muslims were appointed to high-level Government jobs because few were qualified for such jobs. The Nyerere administration addressed the problem of Muslim education by nationalizing schools that were run by Christian agencies, making education compulsory and free. Yet, by the time he retired in 1985 there were feelings in some Muslim circles that Muslims continued to be discriminated against in regard to access to higher education and high-level administrative jobs. Thus, when Ali H. Mwinyi succeeded Nyerere as president many Muslims believed their discrimination would come to an end. But it appears that even the Mwinyi administration was not able to satisfy Muslim expectations.

However, the ten years of Mwinyi's presidency saw an unprecedented involvement by outside Islamic agencies in Muslim affairs in Tanzania. The availability of external funding appears to have encouraged the formation of local organisations whose agenda included the revitalisation of Islam. Organisations such as Ansar Sunna and Warsha called upon Muslims to live their lives according to the teachings of the Qur'an and the Sunna. It was under such a climate of Islamic revivalism that some Muslims protested against the rearing of pigs and the selling of pork in their neighborhoods. Others demanded that female students be permitted to wear the *hijab*. These two issues are the subject of the following chapter.

CHAPTER EIGHT

THE PORK AND *HIJAB* CONTROVERSIES OF THE 1990s

In 1993 some Muslims in Dar es Salaam attacked and demolished butcheries which specifically sold pork. Why did such butcheries become the target of Muslim anger? Before we consider what led those Muslims to do what they did, there is need to familiarize the reader with Islamic dietary laws and practices. To begin with, what is permissible to eat is called *halal*,[165] and what is prohibited is called *haram*.[166] Even though the purpose of eating is to sustain the body, Islamic dietary laws and practices recognize that one may not indulge in everything that could possibly be edible. It is, therefore, recommended that one eat only those things that Allah has deemed good to eat. In the Qur'an, Chapter 7 verse 160 we read: "...Eat of the good things wherewith We have provided you." Thus, Muslims are required to abide by what Allah prescribes in the Qur'an as good to eat and drink. And to abstain from what has been prescribed as unfit for consumption.

According to the Qur'an and Hadith, all marine life forms are *halal* regardless of how they are procured or whether they are caught by Muslims or non-Muslims.[167] In Chapter 16 verse 14 it says: "And He it is Who hath constrained the sea to be of service that ye eat fresh meat from thence. . ." Moreover, Muslims can eat marine products without the requirement of bleeding or slaughtering. However, unlike fish and other marine products not all land animals are *halal* to eat. The Qur'an, as we will see, prohibits the eating of carrion, blood and the flesh of swine. And unlike marine animals, land animals must be slaughtered according to Islamic specifications. The animal to be eaten must be slaughtered by a sharp object, that is capable of making the animal bleed by severing the two jugular veins. The person doing the slaughtering must at the same time mention the name of Allah over the animal he is slaughtering (Chapter 6 verse 118).

Muslims are prohibited from eating meat from an animal slaughtered without the mention of Allah's name or strangled. Thus, Chapter 6 verse 121 says: "And do not eat of that which the name of Allah has not been mentioned, for truly that is impiety." Restrictive dietary laws and practices are not only characteristic of Islamic cultures. Non-Muslim peoples in Tanzania and elsewhere have restrictions over the consumption of certain animals which are considered to be taboo.[168] How do we account for both the universality of taboos and the paradox of prohibiting the consumption of certain otherwise desirable foods? Various theories, as we will see, have been propounded to explain the origin and rationale of such taboos. Some of these theories have emphasized religious, political, economic, ecological and cultural influences. The prohibition of pork among Jews and Muslims is normally attributed to their Scriptures (the Mosaic Law for Jews and the Qur'an for Muslims) and is sanctioned by resort to their command: "Eat not this flesh". In the case of Christianity, despite its close affinity to Judaism, it did not adopt the Jewish view that the pig is an unclean animal whose flesh should not be eaten (Simoons, 1961: 23).

In some parts of Africa south of the Sahara Christianity was responsible for the spread and domestication of pigs as well as their consumption. To the contrary, in other parts Islam was responsible for discouraging both the keeping of pigs and their consumption. In the islands of Pemba and Zanzibar current evidence suggests that domesticated pigs were first introduced by the Portuguese in the sixteenth century (Walsh, 1999). In Pemba local people subsequently took to rearing pigs for sale to the Portuguese. As Walsh has noted.

If these pig-breeders were indeed local Muslims, then their desire to profit from the Portuguese must have overridden any religious qualms they or their neighbours might have had about keeping these 'unclean' animals. It is possible, of course, that the actual labour involved was left to slaves or other workers of mainland origin, though we have no evidence of this.

In the mainland of Tanzania sources indicate that the domestication of pigs was introduced by Christian missionaries. Early Lutheran and Catholic missionaries in Dar es Salaam kept pigs as part of their endeavour to be self sufficient in food. Later on other mission stations elsewhere also practised animal husbandry which included pig keeping. There appears to be no evidence that these early practices embroiled the missionaries into conflict with their Muslim neighbours.

It remains unclear when exactly Tanzanians who are non-Muslims developed a taste for pork. It is possible that early converts were the first to be exposed to the consumption of pork by missionaries. But it is also likely that from times immemorial people in some parts of Tanzania may have eaten the flesh of wild swine which they either hunted for the pot or as a pest. Whatever the case may be, it appears that by the early 1990s pork had become a very popular delicacy in Dar es Salaam and other towns to the extent of being nicknamed *kiti moto*, after a popular local TV programme.

The popularity of pork did not augur well particularly with a group of radical Muslims who were members of the Tanzania Council for Promoting the Qur'an, otherwise known by its Kiswahili acronym BALUKTA.[169] In 1993 they attacked and demolished several pork butcheries in Dar es Salaam. According to *An-Nuur*, a Muslim newspaper, prior to the attacks Muslim residents of several Dar es Salaam suburbs namely Ubungo Kibangu, Tabata, Segerea, Kisukuru and Kibamba had complained to City Council about the rearing of pigs and the selling of pork in their areas to no avail (*An-Nuur*, September 17-24, 1998).[170] One resident of Tabata was quoted as saying: *"Kwetu sasa nyama ya nguruwe inachomwa mishikaki na kuuzwa kwa wapita njia, tumewaandikia wahusika mpaka sasa hawajachukua hatua zo zote."*[171] Another resident of Ubungo Kibangu, who gave his name as Abu Malik, said in his neighborhood pork was being sold right in front of residential houses. Mr. Malik not only called the selling of pork "haramu" but complained that pigsties were a nuisance due to their bad odor. Mr. Malik wondered, *"Wahusika wanafanya nini wakati mazingira na afya za wananchi ziko hatarini kiasi hiki?"*[172] (An-Nuur, September 17-24, 1998).

According to *An-Nuur*, the Muslims who demolished the butcheries were opposed to the rearing of pigs and the selling of pork for religious as well as sanitary reasons. Athough the Qur'an prohibits the consumption of swine flesh it also makes it permissible by necessity. Thus, in Chapter 2 verse 173 it is written: "He hath forbidden you carrion, and blood, and swine flesh, and that which hath been immolated to (the name of) any other than Allah. But he who is driven by necessity, neither craving nor transgressing, it is no sin for him. Lo! Allah is Forgiving, Merciful."[173]

However, the Qur'an does not explain why swine flesh should not be eaten.[174] Because of this lack of explanation Muslims have had to extrapolate the possible reasons for the prohibition of pork from scientific knowledge and other sources. Muslim scholars cite findings from medical research that suggest the possibility of pork causing health risks such as the transmission of germs and parasites like trichina worms which cause trichinosis. Besides trichina there are supposedly many other worms, germs and bacteria which are commonly found in pigs, many of which are specific to the pig, or found in greater frequency in pigs.

Despite the health risks of microbial and parasitic infections which have been used to validate the Qur'anic prohibition of pork these infections can be controlled. Infection from cysticerci, the larvae of the pork tapeworm, can only result from the consumption of raw or insufficiently cooked pork. *Trichinellosis* is one of the more serious parasitic zoonosises transmitted through pork. But only pigs that are fed with infected tissues of pigs or other animals can be the source of infection. In the United States *trichinellosis* has been brought under control through boiling of pig feed. Moreover, wild pigs are probably more likely to be infected than domesticated pigs whose diet can be controlled.

Sanitary hazards of pig breeding and handling include exposure to certain bacterial infections like leptospirosis, brucellosis and anthrax. It is claimed that people who work in piggeries or handle live pigs or after slaughter may come into contact with pig balantidial dysentery (*Balantidium* coli) which they can then transmit to other people. However, fear of bacterial infection is not restricted to pigs alone. Other animals such as cattle and sheep have also been known to be sources of infectious diseases to humans. As Abdussalam notes, the brucellosis contracted from sheep and goats (Malta fever, *Br. melitensis* infection) is much more serious and more widespread than swine brucellosis.[175] Likewise, *leptospirosis* can also be transmitted from sheep and goats as well as from cattle. So why is it that the pig was singled out for prohibition as a carrier of deadly germs and bacteria? The reasons have less to do with health risks posed by pig breeding and pork consumption (Farb and Armelagos, 1980: 113-117).

According to Farb and Armelagos, the Judaic and Islamic prohibition of pork had more to do with ideology than with health reasons. They argue that the danger of *trichinosis* can hardly have been the rationale for the Mosaic or Islamic prohibition of pork "since the parasite, which was not even observed by scientists until 1821, was considered harmless to humans until 1860" (Farb and Armelagos:

113). They also note that the assertion that the pig was tabooed because it is a filthy animal is not convincing: "In the wild state, the pig is not filthy; it wallows in mud and excrement only when confined in the barnyard, as a way of keeping its skin cool through evaporation, since it lacks sweat glands" (ibid., 114).

Farb and Armelagos also point out that the prohibition against pork does not appear in the Bible until after the Exodus from Egypt. Before that Noah had been told in Genesis 9: 3 that "every moving thing that liveth shall be meat for you." It was after the Flood that God prescribed the consumption of complete, whole and perfect animals, especially those with cloven hoofs and that chew curd (or ruminants). Since the pig has cloven hoofs but does not chew curd its ambivalent state dictated that it be considered unfit for consumption. Moreover, the pig was singled out for prohibition because when the Jews were under the rule of Antiochus IV of Syria this ruler symbolised the subjugation and humiliation of the Jews by sacrificing pigs in the Temple of Solomon. Antiochus IV also forced Jews to eat pork as an act of submission to Syria (ibid., 117).

Thus when the Jews liberated themselves under Judas Maccabeus the first thing the Maccabees did was to enforce more rigorously the prohibition of the consumption of pork over other taboos.

Likewise, ideology and ecology more than anything else are said to have influenced Islamic prohibition of pork. The Qur'an's forceful condemnation of pork is supposed to have been a "tactical decision on the part of Mohamed, it gave Islam a point of clear distinction from the Christians, who were its major adversary and who had no objection to pork" (op. cit., 117). Farb and Armelagos also suggest that pork consumption in Arabia may have been permitted had ecological conditions been favourable for the raising of swine. As it were, pigs could not be reared because they competed with humans for the same foods -grains and nuts- and for water, the most scarce resource in Arabia, without providing secondary benefits. They provided no wool or milk, they could not carry loads or be ridden like the camel.

We have noted above how Antiochus IV forced Jews to eat pork as an act of submission to Syria. When the Muslims conquered Christian Nubia they demonstrated their victory by two acts: they jailed the priests and slaughtered the pigs of the Nubians. European colonialists did not force Muslims in Tanzania to eat pork as an act of submission. However, the rearing of pigs was contemplated by the German administration as a snub to Islamic faith. Similarly, those who kept pigs in Dar es Salaam during the 1990s may have deliberately intended it as a snub; more so where pigs were left to fend for themselves by roaming about the neighborhoods where Muslims lived.

The "radicalism" exhibited by those who demolished the pork butcheries was similar to that of the Taliban in Afghanistan. There in early 2001 the Taliban leader Mullah Mohamed Omar issued an edict against all "un-Islamic" graven images, whether human or animal, which were considered idolatrous. The edict led to the demolition of the largest statues of the Buddha at Bamiyan as well as smaller Buddhist sculptures elsewhere in Afghanistan. The demolition of the statues at Bamiyan may also have been politically motivated because Bamiyan was a base of Taliban's opposition, the Northern Alliance's "rebel" forces led by ousted Afghani President Burhanuddin Rabbani. Similar vandalism aimed at foci of community identity also happened in Zanzibar where a number of churches were reported burnt in the last decade of the twentieth century. In Wete, Pemba, the Roman Catholic Church was frequently stoned by local youths because of keeping pigs.

Besides the controversy involving the rearing of pigs and the selling of pork the 1990s also witnessed another controversy which was about the wearing of the *hijab*, a scarf used to cover a female's head, neck and bosom. In 1995, apparently due to demand, the Ministry of Education had to acquiesce to the wearing of the *hijab* by Muslim students. The Ministry sent a letter, EDC/10/60/VOL.1/4/7 dated 28 August, 1995, to all heads of institutions of learning to inform them of the decision to allow the wearing of the *hijab*. Soon, however, there were complaints from Iringa, Dar es Salaam, Zanzibar and other places that the Ministry's directive was either being disregarded and/or students who wore the *hijab* were being harassed (*An-Nuur*, Sept. 4 -10, 1998; Oct. 23 -29, 1998; Nov. 27 - Dec. 3, 1998).

The demand to wear the *hijab* was made on religious and moral grounds. Chapter 24 verse 31 says: "And tell the believing women to lower their gaze and be modest, and to display of their adornment only that which is apparent, and draw their veils[176] over their bosoms, and not to reveal their adornment save to their husbands or their fathers or husbands' fathers, or their sons or their husbands' sons, or their brothers or their brothers' sons or sisters' sons, or their women, or their slaves, or male attendants who lack vigour, or children who know naught of women's nakedness. And let them not stamp their feet so as to reveal what they hide of their adornment. And turn unto Allah together, O believers, in order that ye may succeed."[177]

Therefore, female students who were prevented from wearing the *hijab* felt as though their religious rights were being infringed upon. In 1998 one medical student at Bweni, Zanzibar, preferred to drop out of school because she was not allowed to wear the *hijab* (*An-Nuur*, Oct. 23 - 29, 1998). She is quoted to have said that the *hijab* was not only an important aspect of her Islamic faith, but the act of wearing it made her feel respectable. What did she mean by feeling respectable? We will come back to this matter in greater detail later. In the meantime it is imperative to ask, what caused opposition against the *hijab*?

First, it is presumed that the heads of the schools on the mainland who opposed the wearing of the *hijab* at their schools were Christian. Yet, their opposition was not framed in religious terms but rather in secular terms. Tanzania inherited a western secular school culture that requires students to wear uniforms. Headmasters and headmistresses opposed to the wearing of the *hijab* considered it to be an aberration. A similar argument was recently made by the New York Police Department (NYPD) concerning whether or not to allow a Sikh police officer to wear his turban. The NYPD argued that a turban is not a part of its police uniform and would not allow an officer to wear one for religious or other reasons. Likewise, there was recently an interesting case in Florida, USA, where a Muslim woman requested not to take off her *hijab* to have her driver's licence photograph taken. When the authorities insisted she sued but the judge ruled against her.

Outside of Tanzania opposition against the *hijab* has been a part of the feminist movement which sees the *hijab* to be a symbol of the oppression of women. According to Azam Kamguian:

> For us, the veil is not just another kind of clothing; and opposing it is not just defending the right to freedom of clothing even though it is put forward as such. Veiling internalises the Islamic notion in women that they belong to an inferior sex, and that they are sex objects. It teaches them to limit their physical movements and their

> free behaviour. Veiling is a powerful tool to instutionalise women's
> segregation and to implement a system of sexual apartheid. It signifies
> the subjugation and servitude of women based on Islamic doctrine
> and Koranic teachings.

Much more than a way of clothing, hijab is the manifestation of an outright Islamic misogynism and an antiquated view on women's status. It is designed to control women's sexuality much more effectively than any other religion or ideological system.[178]

Yet there are Muslim women who consider themselves to be feminists who wear the *hijab* and find the experience liberating. Such is the case of Naheed Mustafa, a young Canadian-born and raised, university graduate who says young women are reclaiming the *hijab*, reinterpreting it in light of its original purpose – "to give back to women ultimate control of their bodies."[179] Naheed Mustafa further notes: "Wearing the hijab has given me freedom from constant attention to my physical self. Because my appearance is not subjected to public scrutiny, my beauty, or perhaps lack of it, has been removed from the realm of what can legitimately be discussed. No one knows whether my hair looks as if I just stepped out of a salon, whether or not I can pinch an inch, or even if I have unsightly stretch marks. And because no one knows, no one cares." However, according to El-Guindi such feminist language trivializes the essence of *hijab* (El-Guindi, 1999: 161).

Whatever view about the veil one may find appealing, we are basically dealing with cultural as well as religious notions of the female body and sexuality. The question, however, is why Islam unlike other religions is so uncompromising about female bodily modesty, their seclusion, their chastity, their sexuality, their protection, and their control. It is because women are considered to be the source of *fitna* or discord.[180] According to Hekmat the Qur'an's injunctions, for both men and women (Chapter 24 verses 30 and 31) are evidence that Muslim men at the time of Muhammad could not be trusted to control their sexual urges upon seeing unveiled women except perhaps those who were close of kin (Hekmat, 1997: 192 - 194). He notes that Muhammad himself was one of the men who were unable to control their lust upon looking at unveiled women (ibid., 193). The pertinence of this explanation is questionable. In fact, Hekmat himself notes that Muslim men who travel and study in western countries have no problems interacting with unveiled women there.

Islam's concern with veiling partly has something to do with honor which is conceptualized in terms of its women's modesty (Antoun, 1968: 688). However, Islam did not invent or introduce the custom of veiling. It has been ascertained that ancient Greeks, Jews, Romans, and Assyrians practiced veiling to some degree whereas Hellenic and Byzantine cultures are also known to have practiced the seclusion of women. Some scholars suggest that influences from these cultures may partly explain the adoption of these practices by Arabs before the advent of Islam and afterward. Therefore, Islam's concerns with the separation of the sexes and emphasis on the modest of women has to be seen and understood within a broader context of human sexual relations.

In the physical world of Hinduism the male and female genders symbolise a dichotomy that has its equivalent in the divine world with its male and female deities such as Rama and Sita, Siva and Sakti, Krishna and Radha, and Buddha and Tava (Walker, 1968: 391). Although the power of lust sustains the Hindu cosmic order, sexual intercourse is not without serious dangers. It is believed that the emission of semen causes loss of vital energy. To obviate this hazard men are advised to abstain from sex. Triumph over sex represents a conquest of the lower self by the higher which is the desired religious goal of Jains and Buddhists (ibid., 392). Otherwise, sex is encouraged and the female is the target of male seduction because much as women have desires they cannot proceed further than mere wishing (ibid., 381). Yet a woman can endeavor to be indirectly seductive by the way she dresses: "If she dresses to expose herself, she desires to be further exposed" (ibid., 382).

It is generally accepted that seclusion and veiling were existent in India since ancient Aryan times. Sanscrit literature mentions the abundant use of veils by Aryan Hindu women, especially those of high status such as Brahmins. Even goddesses practiced veiling. It is said, for instance, that when Rama saw Parasurama approach he directed his consort Sita to turn aside and veil herself. Besides evidence from Sanskrit literature, numismatic studies have also confirmed that veiling was a common practice amongst Aryan women. Coins from the Lohara dynasty depict a half cross-legged goddess with a veil on her head. Later on, European travelers made references to the veil worn by Indo-Aryan women and the severe restrictions placed upon them.

In traditional or so-called animistic religions male and female genders also symbolise a dichotomy that is animated by sex. In some belief systems because sex was identified so closely with the power of life, "the sexual organs were often objects of veneration, if not outright worship" (Meagher, et. al., 1979: 959). But the power of sex was also visualized in negative terms. Among the Gogo of Tanzania it was traditionally believed that a hunter's wife must abstain from sex. If she did not her husband would be at risk of being killed while away on the hunt. In other societies sexual intercourse before going to battle was considered ill-advised. Abstaining from sex was intended for the retention of strength.

Likewise, in the Judeo-Christian world sex became a generating point for customs, traditions, moral codes, and religious beliefs. In 1Timothy, 2: 9-10, the Apostle Paul suggests that "the women should dress themselves modestly and decently in suitable clothing, not with their hair braided, or with gold, pearls, or expensive clothes, but with good works, as is proper for women who profess reverence for God." What Paul says was later expounded in greater detail by Tertullian, in a treatise entitled *On the Apparel of Women*. According to Tertullian a married woman is not supposed to preoccupy herself with self-decoration because what matters is her chastity and not her beauty. Tertullian's counsel encourages women away from the idea that they exist as attractive objects for men (Mortley, 1981: 82).

Tertullian was also concerned with the problem of lustful desires which cause men and women to commit adultery and fornication. In his treatise entitled *On Purity* he notes how during his time (he lived from ca. 160 - ca. 230 AD) the condition of human virtuousness was declining. And it was in this regard that he vehemently condemned a Papal Edict which promised to forgive adulterers. For Tertullian adultery, and its twin fornication, is the enemy of the purity of the flesh which is symbolic of man's fidelity to God (Tertullian, trans. by Le Saint, 1956: 59). The sweet seduction of lust, says Tertullian, is one of the things which withdraw men from the things of God. He therefore recommends as a safeguard of chastity the cultivation of the virtue of self-restraint.

Evidently the problem of lust vexed the Church as well during the Middle Ages. According to the *Encyclopedic Dictionary of Religion*, seduction in medieval moral theology consisted of unjustly injuring the physical and moral integrity of a woman, especially an unmarried virgin. It is likely that at this time veiling was adopted as one of the safeguards or signs of chastity. The veil came to be seen as a traditional symbol of constancy and conjugal fidelity or symbolised, as with Christian nuns, the rejection of marriage itself. Widows also took the veil to signify their intention of remaining without the consolation of sexual union after the death of their husbands (Meagher, et. al., 1979: 3649).

In Islam, as we have already noted, the protection and control of women has something to do with honor. There are other reasons, however. Muhammad is said to have said, "The woman is exposed to shame, for if she leaves her house, Satan seeks her out and gains possession of her honor. And the woman who remains closest to God, the exalted, is the woman remaining in her home." Muhammad also said, "There are three who will never enter the Garden: the *dayyuth*, the *rajulatu* among women, and the drunkard." Muhammad's Companions asked: "Of the drinker of wine, we know him, but what is the *dayyuth*?" Muhammad said: "It is he who does not grow angry when strangers enter upon his woman." They asked, "And who is the *rajulatu* among women?" Muhammad said, "It is the woman who seeks to dress and act like men" (Quoted by Antoun, 1968: 686). This particular *hadith* calls upon Muslim men to be vigilant against the possible sexual transgressions of Muslim women because if they do not they risk becoming *dayyuth* who will not enter Paradise.

Moreover, it is of particular interest to note that the Qur'an devotes an entire chapter to women and none to men. According to Mortley, one is tempted to think that Allah is more preoccupied with regulating the lives of women than men (Mortley, 1981: 102). Certainly one of the Qur'an's greatest contributions to the world's manner of being are its rules of behavior. Yet, its mixture of recommendations, rules, and prohibitions do point to serious Arabic social and moral problems at the time of the advent of Islam. One of these problems is said to be the debauchery men engaged in. The Qur'an addressed the problem by permitting and legalizing polygyny as well as access to the favors of female slaves (Chapter 4 verse 3).

By and large, while the permission for men to marry up to four wives may have diminished the urgency of adultery and fornication on the part of men, it may have tended to make women more susceptible to lustful desires if such marriages lessened their chances of obtaining sexual satisfaction (Mortley, 1981: 105). Indeed, the problem appears to be anticipated in Chapter 4 verse 129 which reads: "Ye will not be able to deal equally between (your) wives, however much ye wish (to do so). But turn not altogether away (from one), leaving her as in suspense. If ye do good and keep from evil, lo! Allah is ever Forgiving, Merciful." One of the safeguards against adultery was the severe punishment of death by stoning. Less severe safeguards included seclusion and veiling.

Furthermore, the protection and control of female sexuality is said to be done for the benefit of women as the weaker of the two sexes. Chapter 4 verse 34 says: "Men are in charge of women, because Allah hath made the one of them to excel the other, and because they spend of their property (for the support of women). So good women are the obedient, guarding in secret that which Allah hath guarded. As for those from whom ye fear rebellion, admonish them and banish them to beds apart, and scourge them. Then if they obey, seek not a way against them. Lo! Allah is ever High, Exalted, Great." Thus, according to the Qur'an women are physically weak and economically dependent on men. Because of their vulnerability their honor, their property, and their lives are susceptible to exploitation by the arbitrary whims of men. Therefore, women must be protected and the purpose of veiling is to offer this protection (Antoun, 1968: 690).

It is not known when the practice of veiling was introduced in Tanzania. It might be as old as Islam itself. In his book entitled *Zanzibar: City, Island, and Coast* Richard Burton describes elite Arab women in Zanzibar town dressed in layers of cotton garments with Muscat veils exposing only their unrecognizable eyeballs (Burton, 1872: 114). Unlike the Arab women, half-caste girls were not veiled and wore single loose pieces of red silk or checkered cotton. Their frizzly hair was twisted into pigtails; their eyelids were stained black and their eyebrows lengthened with paint. Zanzibar slave girls not only went about unveiled but also shaved their heads (ibid., 115). Arab men used a type of head-dress called kilemba or wore kofia (red fez) and skull-caps (ibid., 382).

It appears that indoor separation of the sexes was practiced by Arabs. Burton says he did not see any higher classes of Arab women at home. He therefore describes their domestic attire from hearsay: "In the house they wear tight Mezar, Sarwal, or pantaloons of Oman silk or cotton fastened at the waist...Abroad they appear masqued with the hideous black 'Burka' - veil of Oman." He also notes that they preferred strong and heady perfumes of musk, ambergris, ottar of roses, and the large Indian jasmine (ibid., 388). In contrast, the Swahili women went around unveiled and freely mixed with men in the bazar (ibid., 436). Moreover, the latter's morals are said to have been loose: "Chastity is unknown...the (Swahili) man places paradise in the pleasures of the sixth sense, and the woman yields herself to the first advances" (ibid., 419). Conversely, Arab women of status resisted the advances of foreigners for fear of scandal but availed their favors to their African male servants due in part to the neglect of their husbands - who preferred African concubines!

Things changed significantly following the abolition of slavery. In her excellent study, *Pastimes and Politics* published in 2001, Laura Fair notes that one way that the freed slaves demonstrated their changed status was to dress like their former masters and mistresses. The *baibui* was widely adopted as a symbol of African women's equality with Arab women. Moreover, wearing the *baibui* became synonymous with being feminine and chaste. To be out in public without it was tantamount to being *uchi* or naked (Fair, 2001: 18).

Following its introduction in the early 1900s, the *baibui* was first adopted by elite Arab women. However, the *baibui* was especially adopted as a hallmark of respectability by the Arab concubines, *masuria*, and the so-called half castes. Their example was soon followed by ordinary African Muslim women. For the freed slaves wearing a *baibui* was a repudiation of earlier cultural practices, as noted by Burton and others, that attempted to distinguish "respectable" women from not so respectable ones. Which brings us back to what the medical student mentioned earlier may have meant by feeling "respectable" when she wore the *hijab*. How does clothing make one respectable?

According to Fair, first and second generation Zanzibari freed slaves associated veiling with respectability. This association had to do with their newly acquired status as well as their growing understanding of Islamic prescriptions for modesty in dress and behavior (Fair, 2001: 89). Also veiling was associated with affluence which in turn made one appear upwardly mobile. Fair writes: "Women often saved over considerable periods of time in order to purchase a higher-grade fabric for their baibuis, as one's public presentation of self-worth was literally wrapped in the choice of baibui cloth" (ibid., 91). Yet, a good quality *baibui* does not make a lower class wearer wealthier. All the wearer is doing is present an image which is far from reality. Such physical deception can also encourage moral deception, as many of Fair's respondents noted. The relative anonymity of a *baibui* allowed women the freedom to engage in immoral behavior that contradicted the very images of respectability they were seeking to portray.

The above discussion takes us back to the problem of female modesty which Christianity, Islam, and other religions are concerned with. Both the Bible and the Qur'an portray women as full of guile and as temptresses or easily tempted. In the Bible Adam's wife, Eve, is tempted by the serpent and in turn tempts Adam to eat the forbidden fruit (Genesis 3: 1 - 7). In the Qur'an the story of the temptation of Joseph by Potiphar's wife (Genesis 39: 7 - 12) underlines the guile of women (Qur'an 12: 23 - 28). More importantly, in both Scriptures temptation is also portrayed as a test of character. Both the Bible and the Qur'an together with the Hadith provide evidence of women's limited capacity for right conduct. Women are supposedly driven by inordinate sexuality as they are informed by evil forces. As we noted above, they are believed to be the cause of *fitna* or discord. In the Muslim world this view of women's limited capacity for modest behavior has found official affirmation in the legal opinions of *ulama* who have argued for the seclusion and veiling of women to minimize the moral damage they can cause to society (Antoun, 1968: 674).

The problem, however, is that forms of dress such as the *hijab* are only intended to obviate the physiological causes of men's attraction to women. The emphasis on how Muslim women should dress to appear "respectable" obscures the reality of their dis-empowerment. As Patricia Jeffery notes in regard to Indian women in *purdah*, the devaluation of women has something to do with their economic dependency on men (Jeffery, 1982: 195). In the village where Jeffery conducted her research women's movements and demeanor were partly constrained by fear of punishment or worries about being deprived of their subsistence (ibid., 195). However, despite the active endorsement and perpetuation of the veil, Muslim women have also complained and protested about their lives behind the veil and other Islamic doctrines which undermine gender equality.

In Tanzania the problematic nature of some of the norms enjoined by Islam was first aired, as far as I know, in 1988 at a conference on Women and Development which was organized by the Chama cha Mapinduzi (CCM). In a paper presented by Judge Hamis Msumi it was noted that the presence and application of parliamentary, customary and Islamic laws in Tanzania's legal system was the cause of problems militating against the provision of justice to women. Contributing to the discussion of Judge Msumi's paper the late Sophia Kawawa, formerly the chairperson of the Umoja wa Wanawake Tanzania (UWT), singled out the Islamic law of marriage for criticism. She said that Muslim leaders and lawmakers should sit together to see how the Islamic law of marriage could best be applied in Tanzania. She suggested that polygyny, which is sanctioned by the Qur'an, made most women suffer and that it was just fair if it would be reviewed (*Daily News* [Dar es Salaam], 9 May, 1988, p. 3).

When Sophia Kawawa's remarks were reported by the mass media they immediately provoked hostility in some Muslim circles. In Zanzibar Sheikhs Ali Hemedi Jadir of Mchangani mosque, Nassor Abdallah Pachu (Kikwajuni) and Saleh Juma (Forodhani) denounced Mrs. Kawawa in their Friday sermons on 13 May, 1988. It is not clear whether the sheikhs accused Mrs. Kawawa of apostasy. According to the classical legal definitions of apostasy in relation to the Qur'an a Muslim commits apostasy if he or she repudiates or criticizes some of the Scriptures (Peters and De Vries, 1976-77: 4). Thus Mrs. Kawawa's opinion about the practice of polygyny was tantamount to committing apostasy because it was contrary to what she must have known to be sanctioned by the Qur'an. In other words, she could have been declared a *murtadd* (apostate), on the ground that she questioned an incontestably established Islamic doctrine.

Following the Friday prayers on 13 May, a mass of demonstrators took to the streets of Zanzibar to dramatize their anger against Mrs. Kawawa's comments about polygyny and the need to change it. The demonstrators clashed with the police, leaving one dead and several injured (*Daily News*, 16 May, 1988, p. 1). In the aftermath, President Mwinyi reiterated that Tanzania was a democratic country, adding that citizens had a right to air their views freely in seminars and other legitimate meetings. He asked the Muslim community in the country to exercise restraint, stressing that the Government had no mandate to enforce amendments of the holy scriptures like the Qur'an (*Daily*

167

News, 16 May, 1988, p. 1). It is worthy of note that while Kawawa's comments were roundly condemned the issues she raised were not publicly addressed, engaged with or argued against by her Muslim detractors.

Of particular importance is that the Kawawa controversy also involved her freedom of opinion and expression, not as a Tanzanian (as expressed by President Mwinyi) but as a Muslim woman. Apparently what the sheikhs and demonstrators in Zanzibar were saying is that Mrs. Kawawa had exceeded Islamic bounds of freedom of opinion and expression. But what are these bounds? The Qur'an calls on Muslims to contemplate the dominion of the heavens and the earth, and what Allah has created (Chapter 7 verse 185). Also one *hadith* has it that Muhammad advised some people not to fecundate their palm trees; but when it appeared that non-fecundation of the palm trees prevented them from bearing fruit, he declared that this was his personal opinion, that his personal opinion in such matters was liable to be right or wrong, that his opinions pertaining to all worldly matter should be taken in this light, and that the people had the right to discuss their worldly affairs and to treat them as directed by their experience and knowledge (Quoted by Wafi, 1967: 66).

However, Muslims are not permitted to discuss or give opinion on religious matters. In the *hadith* referred to above Muhammad is said to have said: "I am but a human being. Whenever I order you about some religious matters, then obey it. But whenever I tell you from my own opinion then I am only a human being, and you may know better your worldly affairs" (ibid., 66). Most Muslims presume that polygamous marriage and veiling are religious matters enjoined by the Qur'an and are not permissible for discussion. It is, therefore, understandable that most Muslims did not support Mrs. Kawawa and certainly offered no opinion about polygyny, or for that matter the *hijab* and the consumption of pork, that was contrary to Islamic teaching.

To conclude, the scope of the Muslim obligation to command right and forbid wrong during the 1990s in Tanzania included enjoining belief in the unity of God (*tawhid*), forbidding polytheism (*shirk*), demolishing pork butcheries, and demanding the right for Muslim school girls to wear *hijab* scarves. However, the performance of the duty was mostly verbal in the form of *mihadhara* or public rallies. In doing so Muslim preachers were following a tradition passed down from the Prophet Muhammad himself. A tradition attributed to him says, "Whoever sees wrong and is able to put it right with his hand, let him do so; if he can't, then with his tongue; if he can't, then with [or in] his heart" (Quoted by Cook, 2000: 33). The Muslim *mihadhara* of the 1990s are the subject of the following chapter.

CHAPTER NINE

MUSLIM *MIHADHARA* AGAINST CHRISTIANITY IN THE 1990s

The presidency of Ali Hassan Mwinyi from 1985 to 1995 provided a conducive political climate for the establishment of several radical Muslim organisations whose agenda was Islamic revivalism. Speakers from some of these groups engaged in public preaching or *mihadhara* whose objective was to discredit Christianity in favor of Islam. However, it must be noted that Islamic revivalism since the early 1980s was a response to Christian "crusades" led by "born again" Christian preachers. Needless to say, the ensuing competition inflamed grassroots tensions between Christians and Muslims. By 1989 the Christian clergy was becoming wary about the Muslim *mihadhara*. That year the Christian Council of Tanzania (CCT) issued a warning that if the Muslims did not desist from their endeavors to publicly discredit Christianity there would be violence and bloodshed. On 28 February 1993 another Christian body, the Tanzania Episcopal Conference (TEC), issued a similar warning. Yet the Muslims persisted. Indeed, bloodshed did finally occur following the riots at the Mwembechai Mosque on 13 February 1998.

The Christian clergy and the Government blamed the 1998 Mwembechai disturbances and the general atmosphere of tension in the 1990s on the *mihadhara*. Father Camillius Lwambano, whom Njozi blames for instigating Government intervention in the Mwembechai mosque affairs, is said to have complained that he had heard Muslim preachers at the mosque ridicule Jesus Christ (Njozi, 2000: 5). Another Christian complaint was that Muslim preachers were preaching Islam using the Bible to pour scorn on Christians and their religion (Njozi, 2000: 10).

But why were Muslim preachers in the 1990s portraying Christianity in a bad light? I guess for the same reasons that missionaries had for ages portrayed Islam negatively. However, as far as the Muslims were concerned, they were not offending Christian religious sensibilities. Njozi poses a pertinent question: What did Muslims stand to gain by ridiculing Christians? Although Njozi alludes to psychological satisfaction as a possible motive he does not follow through with a sustained analysis of this motive. Rather he offers a superficial argument that the *mihadhara* were attracting many Christians some of whom actually converted. Njozi takes the few conversions as evidence that those who converted did not feel as though their Christian sensibilities had been offended. Otherwise, Njozi asks, why would an insulted Christian accept Islam? (Njozi, 2000: 11).

Besides the possibility of deriving some psychological satisfaction, the ridiculing of Christianity by Muslim *mihadhara* preachers was intended to discredit Christianity in order to gain converts. For them to have said they respected the legitimacy or validity of Christian doctrines would not have gained them converts. The endeavor to discredit Christianity was a matter of strategy aimed at supplanting it. It may, therefore, not be farfetched to think that the "success" of the 1990s *mihadhara* in Tanzania was because the preachers used the Bible to point out what was "wrong" with its message. However, some of the Muslim preachers demonstrated a limited knowledge of the Bible. The author had a chance of listening to one such preacher exhorting his listeners that should they encounter any Christians they should ask them which of the five Jesus mentioned in the Bible they believe in! Besides the ridicule it probably did not occur to this preacher to question what the Qur'an says about Jesus whom the Muslims call Isa. As a prophet Jesus is said to have been given a Book, the *Injil*. The suggestion that Jesus, like Muhammad, was entrusted with a Book has been disputed by Christian commentators. Jesus, they point out, brought no Book: he himself was the living Word of God.

Mihadhara preachers claimed that their criticism of the Bible was based upon what the Qur'an says. Indeed, as we have already noted, the Qur'an contains verses which repudiate some of the basic teachings of Christianity. However, according to Dr. Mark Durie the Qur'an may not be a credible source for Biblical history. He writes, "The Qur'an, written in the 7th century CE, cannot be regarded as having any authority whatsoever to inform us about Jesus of Nazareth. It offers no evidence for its claims about biblical history. Its numerous historical errors reflect a garbled understanding of the Bible." Regardless, *mihadhara* preachers maintained that according to the Qur'an the Bible had been corrupted and as such cannot be believed to be the Word of God. The claim of Biblical corruption was further reinforced by the teachings of none other than Sheikh Ahmed Deedat of South Africa.

During his tour of Tanzania in 1981 Sheikh Ahmed Deedat, a well known Muslim critic of the Bible, used the Bible in order to discredit it on its own basis. He had been invited by The Muslim Students Association of the University of Dar es Salaam (MSAUD). The MSAUD could not have invited a more fervent opponent of Christianity than Sheikh Ahmed H. Deedat. His lifelong career and ambition, derived from the Qur'anic principle, "Produce your Proof if ye are Truthful," has been to provide proof about the deep-rooted "misconceptions" of Christianity. He has even come up with a "Combat Kit" intended to "turn the tables" against Christianity (Deedat, 1994: 11). This "Combat Kit" has been offered to Muslims as their "lethal weapon against Bible-thumpers" (Deedat, 1994: 33).

The so-called "Bible thumpers" are none other than born-again Christian revivalists otherwise known in Tanzania as *walokole*. It is noteworthy that the Muslim *mihadhara* became popular at a time when the Christian revivalist movement in Tanzania was at its apogee. Contending for the faith, as Mulahagwa calls it, started in the 1940s. Mulahagwa notes that.

> By 1970 the revival movement was a force to reckon with in the country. It had been started by lay Christians taking the initiative in its promotion and sustenance, but gradually the mantle of leadership passed to the clergy or lay preachers turned pastors. This transformation had a dual effect on the movement. First, it brought a qualitative change in the way people related to their Christian faith. They became more committed believers under born-again charismatic pastors and leaders. Bible studies and Christian fellowships raised their level of understanding of the scriptures and testimonies edified by them (Mlahagwa, 1999: 299).

Muslim *mihadhara* preachers, however, were out to debunk the theological basis of this revivalism. Both crusade evangelists and Muslims invited renowned international preachers in their endeavor to expand their influence. As we have noted, one of those invited by the Muslims was the renown Sheikh Ahmed Deedat.

Because crusade evangelism drew strength from the Bible as "the inspired Word of God and God's revelation to man," *mihadhara* preachers endeavored to show that the Bible is not the Word of God. According to Deedat the Bible is full of contradictions and its numerous "errors" are "proof" that it cannot be the Word of God. Deedat's assertions about the Bible have been addressed by Christian preachers and scholars. In his book titled *Peace with God* (1984: 26) Billy Graham suggests that "apparent contradictions were caused by incorrect translations rather than divine inconsistencies." According to Jacques Dupuis the Bible is the word of God in human words but those who wrote it were inspired by God (Quoted by Mohammed, 1999: 54). By making use of the concept of inspiration Dupuis and others acknowledge that the word of God expressed in human words "does not suppress, in those who transmit the revelation, the limitations nor the imperfections that are the lot of the human condition" (ibid.).

Perhaps no one else has responded in depth to Deedat's criticism of the Bible than John Gilchrist, who is a compatriot of Deedat. One of the allegations that Gilchrist addresses concerns the issue of the virgin birth of Jesus. Deedat notes that in the King James Version (hereafter KJV), Isaiah 7:14 reads: "Therefore the Lord himself shall give you a sign: Behold, a virgin shall conceive, and bear a son, and shall call his name Immanuel." However, in the Revised Standard Version (RSV) the word virgin has been substituted by the phrase "a young woman." According to Deedat, this is supposed to be one of the foremost errors in the Bible. However, Gilchrist points out that whereas the Hebrew word for virgin is *bethulah*, Isaiah uses instead the word *almah*, which is rendered as virgin in the KJV translation. He further notes:

> Isaiah uses the word almah rather than bethulah because the latter word not only means a virgin but also a chaste widow (as in Joel 1.8). Those who translate it as a young woman (so the RSV) give a literal rendering of the word whereas those who translate it as virgin (so the KJV) give its meaning in its context. Either way the young woman was a virgin as Mary duly was when Jesus was conceived.

Moreover, modern Christian theologians and scholars have emphasized the personal character of God's revelations. They point out that those who wrote the Gospels, for instance, witnessed God's revelations as personal encounters. For them the revelations were not some verbatim messages from God but rather a matter of how they experienced God and how they responded to their experiences. They differed in communicating their revelations mainly because of differences in modes of speech and limitations of culture. Thus the contradictions alluded to by Deedat do not mean that it is God who is self-contradictory, but rather those who speak in God's name (Mohammed, 1999: 54).

To the contrary, Muslims believe that Muhammad received the word of God verbatim and recited it verbatim. In other words, Muslims do not believe that any human influence intruded in the transmission of that verbatim message from God through the angel Gabriel. Yet, as we noted in chapter four, the fact that some parts of the Qur'an were abrogated indicates that its transmission was also conditioned by history and other influences. In this regard neither the Bible nor the Qur'an is divine scripture in the pure sense. For theologians like Gilchrist, however, at issue is the Muslim allegation about the corruption of the Bible. Gilchrist's protest is worth quoting at length:

> We have never ceased to be amazed, however, at the general Muslim claim that the Qur'an has never been changed whereas the Bible has allegedly been so corrupted that it is no longer what it was and therefore cannot be regarded as the Word of God. All the evidence history has bequeathed to us in respect of the textual history of the Qur'an and the Bible suggests, rather, that both books are remarkably intact in the form in which they were originally written but that neither has escaped the presence, here and there, of variant readings in the text. We can only presume that the fond illusion of Qur'anic inerrancy and Biblical corruption is the figment of pure expediency, a convenient way - indeed, as the evidence shows, a desperate and drastic way - of explaining away the fact that the Taurat and Injil are actually Christian rather than Islamic in content and teaching.

In Tanzania the *mihadhara* of the 1980s and 1990s were a reflection and evidence of a resurgence of Islam. They also represented a continuation of an age-old Islamic tradition, namely the quest to prove the authenticity of Islam. Among the Muslim *mihadhara* preachers there were those who outright dismissed, disparaged or scorned anything Christian. It appears that this category of preachers was composed mainly of unlettered preachers. Then there were those whose interest was to find connections between Islam and Christianity. This second category of preachers did not only seek to affirm the authenticity of Islam but also attempted to use the Bible to validate and support the authenticity of the Islamic faith. Thus they could neither ignore the Bible nor could they render conclusive judgement against it.

To Christians in Tanzania the use of the Bible by enemies of their faith was reminiscent of how Satan himself quoted from the Bible to lure Jesus into doing what he was not supposed to do (Tumaini, 2000). But there has to be other reasons why Christians found what Muslim preachers were saying about the Bible to be unacceptable. As believers, Christians read the Bible through what Mollenkott calls the "inerrancy grid" which prevents them from seeing evidence that the Bible contains contradictions, a variety of perspectives, and approaches (Mollenkott, 1999: 229). Muslim scholars of the Bible, however, apply to the Bible the hermeneutic or interpretive principles with different results.

How many Christians, asks Mollenkott, know that there are two different versions of creation in the Book of Genesis chapters one and two? "In one, Adam and Eve were created simultaneously and given a mandate together, while in the other, Adam was created first, then all the animals and other phenomena, and finally, Eve" (Mollenkott: 1999: 229). Such a discovery, Mollenkott suggests, would cause some Christians considerable shock and dismay as it did to her. What is revealing about the example above is that either Christians pay no attention to what they read in the Bible or use some interpretive grid which screens out anything that might interfere with their belief that the Bible is the Word of God. As Mollenkott says, when someone creates any doubt or ambiguity in the Bible's message(s) it is liable to make believers feel as though "all along they have submitted to delusion, possibly Satanic delusion" (Mollenkott, 1999: 230). It is, therefore, probable that Tanzania Christians who converted to Islam after attending *mihadhara* did so not because they were gullible but because their beliefs in the Bible were profoundly shaken.

However, the same argument can be applied to Muslims. Believing, as Muslims do, that the source of everything in the Qur'an is Allah Himself, who would not be profoundly shocked were they to know that some of the verses have awkward parallels in pre-Islamic Jewish books of fables and fairy-tales? Yet this is the case regarding how Cain came to bury his murdered brother Abel as explained in the Qur'an (Chapter 5 verses 27-31, quoted by Gilchrist). Chapter 5 verse 31 reads: "Then Allah sent a raven scratching up the ground, to show him how to hide his brother's naked corpse." But according to Pirke Rabbi Eliezer, a Jewish book of fables and folklore has a story that

Adam wept for Abel and did not know what to do with his body until he saw a raven scratch in the ground and bury its dead companion. At this Adam decided to do as the raven had done. In the Qur'an it is Cain who sees the raven but in the Jewish book it is Adam. Gilchrist notes, "As the Jewish book predates the Qur'an it appears that Muhammad plagiarized the story and, with convenient adjustments, wrote it down in the Qur'an as part of the divine revelation!"

Until recently Islam in Tanzania was not a missionary propagated faith. The Muslim *mihadhara* of the 1980s and 1990s were therefore a departure from the traditional way of "witnessing" Islam in Tanzania. What worried the Christian clergy the most about these *mihadhara* were the alleged insults against Christianity.[194] However, Njozi notes that "when in 1993 President Ali H. Mwinyi invited Muslim and Christian leaders to the State House, the church leaders could neither substantiate nor define the insults" (Njozi, 2000: 12). Instead of trying to find a theological justification which would convince Christians not to convert to Islam, the Christian clergy pressured the government to restrict Muslim preaching inside the mosques.[195]

Another issue of contention was whether or not Muslim preachers were blaspheming Christianity by saying Jesus is not the son of God.[196] Section 129 of the Tanzania Penal Code imposes a criminal restraint on the freedom of religion provided for in Article 19 of the Constitution of the United Republic of Tanzania. Article 19 of the Constitution provides that "any person who, with deliberate intention of wounding the religious feelings of any person, utters any word, or makes any sound in the hearing of that person, or makes any gesture in the sight of that person, is guilty of an offence." To be guilty of blasphemy, therefore, depends on the determination that the uttered words were intended to wound religious feelings and that, in fact, the uttered words were injurious to religious feelings.

Evidently, whatever priests like Lwambano and lay Christians heard in these *mihadhara* was considered by them to be injurious to their religious feelings. However, as far as the Muslims were concerned what they said about Christianity was not blasphemous. In fact, according to Njozi, they were exercising their freedom of expression. "Everyone,' says Njozi, 'has the right to freedom of thought, conscience and religion...so long as criticism, however disconcerting it may be to prevailing orthodoxy, is a search for the truth. . ."(Njozi, 2000: 154).

Yet, we know that truth, especially religious truth, cannot be objective. Whereas Muslim preachers and scholars insist on revealing the "truth" about Jesus they are extremely sensitive to any criticism of Muhammad. However, as Harries noted long ago:

> Since Muhammad founded a religion...He must submit to be judged by ethical and religious standards. The comparison between Muhammad and Jesus must inevitably present itself. Since Islam claims to be a universal religion, and even to supercede Christianity, Muslims themselves must submit to having their Prophet judged by the highest moral and religious standards known to men (Harries, 1954: 58-59) After all, Muhammad himself emphasized that he was merely a messenger of God; that he was a man among men and had no power to work miracles.

Moreover, it is arguable whether Muslim preachers and scholars in Tanzania really understand the qualitative differences between the two religions much as they emphasize freedom to pursue the "truth." Again, what Harries said long ago remains pertinent to the dialogue between the two faiths. As Harries noted:

> Sin in Islam is simply that which Allah forbids. There are certain things permitted (*halal*) and others forbidden (*haram*)...There is nothing in Islam which resembles the Christian conception of sin as a fall from grace, an alienation from God. In the absence of any feeling of estrangement between God and man, there is no need for reconciliation, no need for redemption, nor for a Saviour from sin, nor for being born again in the likeness of the Spirit. This reveals the great gulf separating Christianity from Islam (Harries, 1954: 65)

However, since the unforgivable sin in Islam is to conceive another God besides Allah, it is understandable why Muslims have great difficulty to accept the Christian doctrine of the Trinity. What Muslims preachers in Tanzania appear not to understand is the importance of the doctrine of the Trinity in explaining the role of Jesus. Again, the contrast between Muhammad and Jesus drawn by Harries is worth quoting at length:

> In Islam revelation was not in Muhammad but in the message disclosed to him and (later gathered into a book), the Qur'an. It has always been what he taught as revealed truth that matters because he is thought to be the instrument of revelation, not the incarnation of God and redeemer of the world.
>
> In the Christian religion, on the other hand, it is not so much what Jesus said as what He was and is and did that makes Him the unique

disclosure of God, entirely different from all other religious founders, prophets, teachers and mystics (Harries, 1954: 58).

The futility of engaging Muslims in a theological debate may not have been lost on the Christian clergy in Tanzania. Islam, says Sheikh Deedat, is not a competitor among religions (Deedat, 1987: 23). Insofar as Muslims like Sheikh Deedat do not accept the plurality of religions there is no basis for any meaningful dialogue. But the Christian clergy's refusal to discuss what they considered to be Muslim blasphemies did not help their cause either. They were caught in a dilemma succinctly expressed by H. Kraemer as follows:

> Islam itself is creedal and doctrinal to the core. To present Christianity as a set of doctrines is to rouse the militantly intellectualist spirit of Islam (and of all creedalism), and to move entirely outside the religious sphere. Its wilful rejection of Christianity is directed against some definite Christian doctrines and is crystallized in some of its own doctrines. Moreover, even if the missionary avoids presenting Christianity in a doctrinal way, the Moslem will often force him by his attacks to pronounce upon doctrinal matters. The missionary approach, in so far as it is dependent on its own initiative, must abjure all doctrinal approach...(Kraemer, 1969: 356-357). Kraemer's book was originally published in the 1930s in preparation for the Tambaram Mission Conference in India. But what he observed then remains relevant to this day.

Every garment has a seamy side, however. The Qur'an, like the Bible, has a history too. The Christian clergy in Tanzania could have raised serious issues regarding its authenticity and whether or not it is the Word of God. According to Toby Lester, the discovery in 1972 of some of the oldest fragments of the Qur'an at the Great Mosque of Sanaa, in Yemen, "revealed aberrations troublingly at odds with the orthodox Muslim belief that the Koran as it has reached us today is quite simply the perfect, timeless, and unchangingly Word of God" (Lester, 1999: 44). In light of such evidence Lester writes:

> The mainly secular effort to reinterpret the Koran - in part based on textual evidence such as that provided by the Yemeni fragments - is disturbing and offensive to many Muslims, just as attempts to reinterpret the Bible and the life of Jesus are disturbing and offensive to many conservative Christians.

Lester further suggests that the Yemeni fragments indicate that the early history of the Qur'anic text is uncertain. Even more important, "the text was less stable, and therefore had less authority, than has always been claimed".

The first installments of the Qur'an are said to have been revealed to Muhammad in 610. Muhammad, who could neither read nor write, received and reported the revelations verbatim to his followers. These in turn either memorized them or wrote them down. According to the Islamic tradition when Muhammad died, in 632, the Qur'anic revelations had not been gathered into a single book. Rather until then they were recorded only "on palm leaves and flat stones and the hearts of men." The first edition of the Qur'an was put together during the Caliphate of Uthman (644-656) from various gathered pieces of scripture that had been memorized or written down by the Prophet's companions.

Likewise, the same can be said about a lot of Muslims who do not understand the Qur'an although the Qur'an itself says it is for people who understand. As Lester notes:

> Despite its repeated assertions to the contrary, however, the Koran is often extremely difficult for contemporary readers-even highly educated speakers of Arabic-to understand. It sometimes makes dramatic shifts in style, voice, and subject matter from verse to verse, and assumes a familiarity with language, stories, and events that seem to have been lost even to the earliest of Muslim exegetes (typical of a text that initially evolved in an oral tradition) (Lester, 1999: 54).

The result has been that Muslims less knowledgeable in the Qur'an often shift the responsibility for doctrinal exposition to the *ulama*. With such Muslims there is no argument, but only explicit belief that the theologians (in Cairo or Mecca) know all the answers.

Besides the use of public platforms religious dialogue was also conducted through the pages of newspapers such as *Msemakweli* and *An-Nuur*. The latter newspaper, as we have noted, is owned and operated by Muslims. *An-Nuur*'s Muslim correspondents more or less raised the same objections against Christianity that were raised by Muslim *mihadhara* preachers. Thus in the July 17 - 23, 1998 issue of *An-Nuur* one Masoud Mohammed endeavored to show that the Bible is seriously flawed as exemplified by the "contradictory" genealogies of Jesus in Matthew and Luke. Mohammed notes that in the Gospel of Matthew the genealogy of Jesus starts with Solomon through Jacob, the father of Joseph. On the other hand, Mohammed says, in the Gospel of Luke one sees completely different names except that of Joseph whose father is Heli and not Jacob. Therefore, concludes Mohammed, the Jesus in Matthew is not the same Jesus in Luke!

The question about the genealogy of Jesus in the Gospels has been addressed by John Gilchrist. Gilchrist points out that the Hebrew line of Jesus' descent indeed appears in both Matthew 1: 2 - 16 and Luke 3: 23 - 38; that there is difference between these two records from Abraham to David but thereafter they diverge considerably (Gilchrist, 1999: 50). Matthew traces the line of Jesus' genealogy through David's son Solomon while Luke traces it through David's son Nathan. It is this divergence that Muslims suggest the genealogies are contradictory and cannot be reconciled. However, as Gilchrist notes, every child has two genealogies, one through his father and another through his mother. In both Matthew and Luke, Joseph, the legal guardian and registered (not biological) father of Jesus, was descended from David through Solomon while Jesus' mother Mary was descended from the same ancestor through Nathan. Thus there is no contradiction between them (ibid., 51).

Moreover, Gilchrist explains, in Matthew the focus of revelation about the birth of Jesus is Joseph to whom the Angel Gabriel appears. In Luke's Gospel, however, Mary is the center of attention and only the appearance of Gabriel to her is mentioned. In regard to Luke, Gilchrist writes: Unlike Matthew he mentions no women in Jesus' ancestry and, to maintain the general practice of outlining the masculine order only, Luke records Joseph as the *supposed* father of Jesus. He very carefully qualified Joseph's role so that it would be clear that he was not recording the genealogy of Jesus through his representative father but rather his *actual* genealogy through his real mother Mary (op. cit., 51).

Speaking of genealogical controversies, it is surprising that *Msemakweli* and *An-Nuur*'s correspondents did not query the genealogical connection between Abraham and the Arabs or Abraham and the Christians. As is well known, Judaism traces its spiritual lineage to Abraham through Jacob who is descended from Isaac, Abraham's second born son to Sarah, his legally wedded wife. Christianity traces its spiritual lineage to Abraham through Jesus who is descended from David the son of Solomon. Islam likewise traces its spiritual lineage to Abraham through Ishmael, Abraham's first born son by his Egyptian concubine Hagar.

In other words, the claims of Judaism and Islam are based on direct ancestral connections: the Jews and the Arabs are sort of "distant cousins" by virtue of being biologically descended from the brothers Isaac and Ishmael respectively. Thus in the Judeo-Christian and Muslim traditions, the terms "Arab(s)" and "Ishmael(ites) generally have been associated and even regarded as interchangeable. But are they? We will return to this issue shortly. Meanwhile, unlike the claims of Judaism and Islam, Christianity claims spiritual rather than biological connections with Abraham. In Romans 9: 6 - 8 we read: "It is not as though the word of God had failed. For not all Israelites truly belong to Israel, and not all of Abraham's children are his true descendants; but "It is through Isaac that descendants shall be named for you. This means that it is not the children of the flesh who are the children of God, but the children of the promise are counted as descendants."

It is a paradox that the Qur'an neither mentions Hagar by name nor does it give details about the birth of Ishmael. The Book of Genesis, however, provides greater detail about the plight of Hagar and Ishmael. Abraham banished Hagar twice, first when she was pregnant with Ishmael and later when he was thirteen years old. Following the second banishment Genesis says Hagar and Ishmael wondered about in the wilderness of Beer-sheba. More importantly, Genesis 21: 20 says, "God was with the boy, and he grew up; he lived in the wilderness, and became an expert with the bow. He lived in the wilderness of Paran; and his mother got a wife for him from the land of Egypt." Thus, the Bible does not place Ishmael anywhere near Mecca as the Qur'an claims (Chapter 14 verse 37)

Moreover, according to the Bible, Ishmael was the ancestor of certain nomadic peoples who lived in the deserts between Palestine and Egypt and North Arabia (Ephal, 1976: 225). This is in line with what the Bible says that Hagar got him an Egyptian wife and they lived in the wilderness of Paran. Ishmael's progeny includes twelve names: Nebaioth, Kedar, Adbeel, Mibsam, Mishma, Dumah, Massa, Hadad, Tema, Jetur, Naphish, and Kedemah. Ephal notes that the "Arabs" mentioned in the Assyrian documents in the second half of the eighth century B.C. refer to nomadic tribes and tribal confederations in the Syro-Arabian desert and northern Sinai whose names are similar to the names of the "Sons of Ishmael" mentioned above. However, as Ephal points out, the area associated with the "Sons of Ishmael," "from Havilah to Shur, which is opposite Egypt in the direction of Assyria" (Gen. 25: 18), is much smaller than the area associated with the "Arabs" in Assyrian documents. The area mentioned in Genesis 25: 18 corresponds with that formerly inhabited by the Ishmaelites in the days of the Patriarchs (Ephal, 1976: 228).

So when and how did the confusion between Ishmaelite and Arab begin? According to Ephal, the term Ishmaelite was used prior to the mid-tenth century B.C. and referred to the main tribal confederation south of Palestine. It then fell into disuse only to reappear in Jewish sources from the fourth century B.C., as well as in Arabic sources of the early Islamic period (ibid., 227). The term "Arab", says Ephal, was used to refer to nomadic peoples as in Isaiah 13: 20, which is the earliest datable biblical reference to the Arabs in about the eighth century B.C.

In other words, its usage denoted a particular mode of life rather than the name of an ethnic group. If there was no traditional *pater eponymous* as Arab who fitted in the genealogical-tribal system going back to the Patriarchs, how can the Qur'an's claim that Ishmael is the ancestor of modern Arabs and Islam be explained? Ephal solves the puzzle by pointing out that the classical Arab genealogies of the early Islamic period are a combination of two genealogical systems: "the 'actual' Arab genealogies of the pre-Islamic period (developed over generations in the peninusula [sic] as an indispensable means of protecting the existence and status of every individual and tribal unit in a society lacking a central authority), and biblical genealogies, introduced from purely ethnological and cultural interest. This incorporation of biblical sources in Arabic genealogical concepts is part of the broader process of absorbing Jewish elements into early Islamic culture" (Ephal, 1976: 235). Another hotly debated issue on the pages of *An-Nuur* was the divinity of Jesus. In the issue of July 24 - 30, 1998, one Paskal Msemakweli had this to say:

> *Ninyi mliokazana kusema Yesu siyo Mungu mnatarajia msaada gani kwa rais hata muombe kuonana naye? Kama dini yenu inasema Allah ndiye Mungu mimi dini yangu haisemi hivyo bali inasema Yahwe ndiye mungu pekee. Sasa nitakapoandika kwenye baskeli yangu Allah siyo Mungu, au Muhammad siyo Mtume Je, huo si uchokozi? Katika dini yangu kuna amri kumi kutoka kwa Mungu wangu, amri ya kwanza inanikataza kuabudu miungu wengine miongoni mwa hao miungu wengine ni Allah. Je kwa kuwa kitabu changu kinasema hivyo, nidiriki kuwaambia Waislamu waache kumkiri Allah bali wamkiri Mungu Yahwe*

*ninayemtambua mimi kwa kuwa tu kitabu changu kinasema hivyo? Eleweni wazi
kwamba kusema Yesu siyo Mungu huo ni uchokozi wala siyo uhubiri.*

Msemakweli is asking Muslims if they would accept as valid his
claim that since his scriptures say there is no God except Yahweh
therefore Allah is no God, or Muhammad is no prophet?

In conclusion, it can be said that it is customary of religionists
to claim that everything is wrong and unacceptable except the tenets
of their own faith. The religious claims that characterized the *mihadhara*
and correspondence in the newspapers in Tanzania during the 1990s
almost resembled a dialogue of the deaf. Each side believed it was
right. As the Swahili say, "kila mwamba ngoma huvutia kwake." The
Government did not make matters any better either in the way it
intervened in the Mwembechai crisis or in banning the importation
of Hamza Njozi's book on the same subject. The banning of Njozi's
book and the refusal to create a commission of inquiry to investigate
the Mwembechai killings suggest that either the Government had
something to hide or Njozi was telling some truths it would prefer to
remain secret.

CHAPTER TEN

CONCLUSION: COEXIST OR CO-EXTINCT

As the twentieth century came to a close religious tension in Tanzania flared up and threatened the peace that Tanzanians had enjoyed for thirty years since independence. On the one hand, religious revivalism which had started in the early eighties encouraged both Christian and Muslim preachers to attempt to convert each other's followers. However, as they endeavored to convert each other Christians and Muslims reasserted their unyielding commitment to their own beliefs while discrediting those of the others. On the other, the last decade of the twentieth century witnessed increased Muslim political activism. They used public fora and civic as well as religious organisations to criticize the Government, which they believed was not only Christian-dominated but since independence had deliberately marginalized Muslims especially in the public sector. Former President Nyerere was particularly singled out for the problems Muslims faced since independence.

Nyerere was criticized for deliberately not appointing Muslims to positions of authority in the Government as well as for ruling Tanzania as though it was a Christian country. Nyerere's Ujamaa ideology was said to be informed by Christian doctrine. These critics do not say whether or how the ideals of Ujamaa were repugnant to Islam, however. In any case, such criticism does not take into consideration the fact that Nyerere tried to draw lessons from Islamic scriptures as well. On the question of slavery, for instance, Nyerere pointed out that the Qur'an did not sanction it; that whatever is said in the Qur'an about slavery predates its revelation: "*Kama limo jambo la utumwa katika Kuruani, linaeleza utumwa ulivyokutwa; lakini sivyo ulivyoanzishwa na Kuruani*" (Nyerere, 1970: 45-46).

Moreover, Nyerere's belief in racial equality is closer to what the Qur'an teaches than what can be found in the Bible. In the Qur'an, Chapter 49 verse 13 we read, "O mankind! Lo! We have created you male and female, and have made you nations and tribes that ye may know one another. Lo! the noblest of you, in the sight of Allah, is the best in conduct." Equally important, Islam sees racial equality as an antidote to human conflicts. As Iqbal notes:

> The student of history knows very well that Islam was born at a time when the old principles of human unification, such as blood relationship and throne-culture, were failing. It, therefore, finds the principle of human unification not in the blood and bones but in the mind of man. Indeed, its social message to mankind is: "Deracialize yourself or perish by internecine war" (Iqbal in Tariq, 1973: 134-5).

However, Nyerere as is well known endeavored to create a deracialized society after Tanganyika's independence. In 1952 while he was a student at the University of Edinburgh Nyerere wrote a paper on the racial problem in colonial East Africa. What he said is worth quoting at length:

> The Africans and all the Non-Africans who have chosen to make East Africa their home are the people of East Africa and frankly we do not want to see the Non-Africans treated differently either to our advantage or disadvantage ... We must build up a society in which we shall belong to East Africa and not to our racial groups. And I appeal to my fellow Africans to take the initiative in this building up of a really harmonious society. The Europeans have had the initiative and all the opportunities for over two hundred years and everywhere they have succeeded in producing an inter-racial chaos.

> We appeal to all thinking Europeans and Indians to regard themselves as ordinary citizens of Tanganyika; to preach no Divine Right of Europeans, no Divine Right of Indians and no Divine Right of Africans either. We are all Tanganyikans and we are all East Africans. The race quarrel is a stupid quarrel, it can be a very tragic quarrel. If we all make up our minds to live like 'ordinary sort of fellows' and not think that we were specially designed by the Creator to be masters and others specially designed to be hewers and drawers of water we will make East Africa a very happy country for everybody (Nyerere, 1967: 28-29).

When the Government presented its Citizenship Bill to the Legislative Council in October 1961, considerable opposition was expressed to clauses which enabled non-Africans to acquire citizenship by right if they and one of their parents had been born in Tanganyika, and by registration in certain other circumstances (Nyerere, 1967: 126). Arguing in favor of the motion, Nyerere accused those opposed to it as "potential Verwoerds" and "know-nothings" who believed in equality not only on the basis of a person's color but on the basis of one's ethnicity (Nyerere, 1967: 128). To those who demanded a free Tanganyika for Africans only, Nyerere had this to say:

> Discrimination against human beings because of their colour, is exactly what we have been fighting against. This is what we have formed TANU for ... and so soon sir, so soon before even 9 December some of my friends have forgotten it. Now they are preaching discrimination, colour discrimination as a religion to us. And they stand like Hitlers and begin to glorify the race. We glorify human beings, sir, not colour (ibid., 128).

In 1967, after Nyerere had declared that Tanzania was going to build socialism he hastened to say that socialism was not racialism. In an article that he published in *The Nationalist* of 14 February 1967, Nyerere cautioned that there had been one or two signs that some individuals wished to use Ujamaa policies as a means of fostering racial hatred. He explained the essence of socialism to be the "belief in the oneness of man and the common historical destiny of mankind. Its basis, in other words, is human equality" (Nyerere, 1968: 257). He further emphasized that:

> Socialism is not for the benefit of black men, nor brown men, nor white men, nor yellow men. The purpose of socialism is the service of man, regardless of colour, size, shape, skill, ability, or something else. And the economic institutions of socialism, such as those we are now creating in accordance with the Arusha Declaration, are intended to serve man in our society. Where the majority of the people in a particular society are black, then most of those who benefit from socialism there will be black. But it has nothing to do with their blackness; only with their humanity (Nyerere, 1968: 258).

Nyerere's idea of racial equality was opposed by both African Christians and Muslims prior to independence as well as afterward. Unlike Christian opposition, however, Muslim opposition went further in that race was used as a political platform in the formation of the Tanganyika African National Congress (ANC.) and the All-Muslim National Union of Tanganyika (AMNUT). Members of the ANC. under the leadership of Zuberi Mwinyisheikh Manga Mtemvu turned out to be a "small, violent racialist group" (Listowel, 1965). Why did the Muslim Mtemvu turn out to be a racialist whereas the Christian Nyerere appeared to do what Islam commended? Only the late Mtemvu would have known the answer.

Christian-Muslim tensions in Tanzania that culminated in open hostilities during the 1990s – which were triggered off by Muslim *mihadhara* – were symptomatic of fundamental differences between Christianity and Islam. Their entanglement in misunderstanding and disagreement does not mean that Tanzanians were the first to have passed this way. Rather they were re-enacting a confrontation whose contours had already been outlined by the polemics of the early twentieth century. The Muslim *mihadhara* resurrected an age-old dialogue concerning fundamental differences between Islam and Christianity. One overriding difference is that Christianity is theologically at variance with Islam although both profess to believe in the same Almighty, Omniscient and Omnipotent God.

On the one hand, the main reason Jesus cannot be accepted by Muslims as more than a prophet (the Son of God) is that he does not fit into the Islamic understanding of how God has revealed Himself to the world. For Muslims the Qur'an is not only God's revelation but the very source of salvation. The following excerpt from a sermon by one Ahmad ibn Abdullah on the first day of Al-Muharram, the Muslim new year's day, is revealing:

> The greatest thing to which men of good heart are exhorted and the noblest thing to which a wise penitent is guided is the word of God, whereunto whosoever clings, as to a rope, he will not be destitute. For God the most high says: By his word shall the guided be guided. When the Qur'an is read listen to it, listen to it in silence, it may be you will find mercy. I take refuge with God from the accursed Satan ...In the mighty Qur'an God has greatly blessed both you and me. H e has granted us the favour of His signs, the recollection whereof is prudent. He accepts from me and from you the recital of it, for He both knows and hears (Quoted by Cragg, 1959: 30-31).

However, for Christians Jesus the Christ is the revelation of God. Colin Chapman aptly notes: "Islam rules out the possibility of God revealing himself through an incarnation. For Muslims, therefore, however exalted Jesus may be, he cannot possibly be anything more than a person of 'surpassing greatness'" (Chapman, 1995: 243). Thus whereas Islamic Theology teaches that God Himself cannot be known, Christian Theology teaches that God can be known because He revealed Himself through Jesus the Christ.

On the other hand, Christians feel compelled to point out to Muslims that the Jesus of the Qur'an is a very pale reflection of the Jesus of the New Testament (Chapman, 1995: 243). In fact, some Muslim scholars acknowledge that the Qur'an does not cover the life of Jesus in any great detail as regards specific events. The miracles he performed and the powers which he was given are referred to, but mostly in general terms (Ata ur-Rahim, 1979: 206). Thus, Christians have argued, there is something about the Jesus of the New Testament that Muslims do not understand. This is Jesus the Word who became flesh and made his dwelling among us (John 1: 14). It took a long time for his disciples Peter and Thomas to acknowledge Jesus as more than a prophet of God (Mark 8: 29; John 20: 28). So it is not surprising to Christians that Muslims have a hard time dealing with Jesus who to them is a very enigmatic prophet. Yet, in professing their faith Muslims reiterate a very special and intimate relation between God and His apostle Muhammad. Muhammad has a special place in the Divine economy of revelation. Muslims believe that God through the Prophet Muhammad brought His revelation to mankind to its climax and His favor to its crowning purpose:

> In Muhammad prophesy comes not only to its ultimate term but to its universal range. In the Qur'an, though admittedly an Arabic document (with its Arabic quality an inalienable part of its status as the Divine word), and therefore not readily accessible to all, is the revelation to end revelation (Cragg, 1959: 35).

However, Islam does not only claim universality, but it also claims inclusive finality "in the totalitarian sense of being hostile to partialities and opposites, demanding from all a submissive integration into itself"(ibid. 36). It is the obligation of each and every Muslim to further the cause of Islam until, as the Qur'an proclaims, it becomes the religion of the whole world.

By and large, the cause of Christian-Muslim hostilities in the 1990s was the concerted Muslim effort to discredit Christianity in order to convert Christians to Islam. Hitherto both faiths had proselytized and competed to convert those Africans who continued to adhere to traditional religious beliefs. But was the drive for converts worth the risk of plunging Tanzanian society into the abyss of interfaith conflicts and bloodshed? To me the answer is a definite no!

Furthermore, is there any valid reason for Muslims and Christians to fight to convert one another and the so called "nonbelievers" who actually happen to worship the same God? Regardless of how long Christianity and Islam have been in Africa, they remain alien to the continent. Before they came into contact with either religion, African people had their own religious beliefs and concepts of a Supreme Being or Great Spirit. The only difference is that (a) what Africans traditionally knew about God was revealed to them in different ways, and (b) they acquired their awareness of God primarily experientially and also cognitively (Muzorewa, 2001: 24). Therefore, to deny that Africans knew God before the introduction of Christianity and Islam is to deny the universality of God.

As Muzorewa aptly notes, when an African converts from traditional religion to Christianity (or Islam for that matter), the conversion is merely ecclesiological, i.e., to worship God in the Christian fellowship (Muzorewa, 2001: 15). In other words, conversion simply means changing one's method of worshiping God rather than changing one God for another. In this context it is pertinent to ask: is it right for Christians and Muslims to preach to each other or to those who do not subscribe to either of the monotheistic religions? Moreover, must such preaching be acrimonious? These are certainly hard questions and their answers cannot be easy. Whereas each faith acknowledges the importance of spreading the Word of God to each other and among "unbelievers," differences between them in theology, worship, divinity and other matters cannot be amicably resolved. And certainly, as the Qur'an says, only God knows best and will judge worshipers, be they Christian, Muslim or other, in those matters about which they have differed (Chapter 39 verse 46).

It appears, therefore, that the solution to the religious enmity between Christians and Muslims must be complete and unqualified religious freedom and tolerance. However, this is to assume that Muslims and Christians have the same understanding of religious freedom and tolerance. But do they? I do not think they share the same understanding. It is the difference in the understanding, interpreting and application of religious freedom and tolerance between Christians and Muslims which historically have constituted the basis for misunderstanding between the two faiths in Tanzania. It is therefore important to examine how these concepts are understood and interpreted in Christianity and Islam in order to shed light on the fundamental cause of present-day religious conflicts and confrontations between Christians and Muslims. Before we do so it is necessary to consider what the Tanzanian Constitution says about religious freedom.

The Constitution of Tanzania recognizes freedom of religion (viz. Article 19) which includes the right to manifest religious beliefs by worship and practice or by teaching and dissemination in other forms. But Tanzania's criminal law (Penal Code, Section 129) puts restraint on practices which may jeopardize public safety and other civil rights and freedoms. Section 129 provides that "any person who, with the deliberate intention of wounding the religious feelings of any person, utters any word, or makes any sound in the hearing of that person, or makes any gesture in the sight of that person, is guilty of an offence." However, some Muslims (see Abu Aziz's long open letter to the Attorney General which appears as an Appendix in Njozi's *Mwembechai Killings*) argue that the above provision is inapplicable if what is said about one religion by followers of another is considered to be true (Njozi, 2000: 154-5). Aziz writes:

> Therefore, cognizant of the multi-religious heritage of Tanzanian society, it is not an offence for a Christian to say that Jesus is God or is the Son of God this being the basis of Christian faith. Neither is it an offence for a Muslim to say that Jesus is not God or God's son this being an article of Islamic faith that God is one and does not have equals, partners, or sons. It is also not an offence for a Christian to state that Jesus was crucified and resurrected this being the foundation of Christianity. And neither is it an offence for a Muslim to state that Jesus was not crucified or resurrected this being part of Islamic faith that there is no vicarious atonement of sins. The bottom line is that what is blasphemy in Christianity is not blasphemy in Islam and vice versa (Njozi, 2000: 155-6).

However, the problem is that while Aziz sees no problem for any Muslim to criticize the basic beliefs of Christianity, he and most Muslims are neither amenable nor tolerant of any criticism of the beliefs of Islam. What is more important, as Muslims they are not free to criticize the teachings of Islam even if such criticism could be an honest pursuit for religious truth. For instance, it has never occurred to Muslims to ask why Muhammad (or the Qur'an) could not have possibly accepted the divinity of Jesus. To do so would have seriously undermined Muhammad's own claim to prophethood let alone to be the seal of prophets! Moreover, Muslims who have dared to criticize the teachings of the Qur'an or to convert to other religions have faced harrowing experiences. The celebrated case of Salman Rushdie is well known. What is not widely known is the threatening stance of Ayatollah Ruhollah Khomeini's *fatwa* that he issued on 14 February, 1989. The *fatwa* read as follows:

In the name of God Almighty; there is only one God, to whom we shall all return; I would like to inform all intrepid Muslims in the world that the author of the book entitled *The Satanic Verses* which has been compiled, printed and published in opposition to Islam, the Prophet and the Koran, as well as those publishers who were aware of its contents, have been sentenced to death. I call on all zealous Muslims to execute them quickly, wherever they find them, *so that no one will dare to insult the Islamic sanctions.* Whoever is killed on this path will be regarded as a martyr, God willing (Quoted in *The Oxford Encyclopedia of the Modern Muslim World*, vol. 3, 1995: 443; emphasis added).

The Ayatollah's threat was intended to intimidate and instil fear in any Muslim (or non-Muslim) who dares to question the teachings of Islam.

While the Rushdie affair was still raging, another critic claimed the spotlight. It was none other than the celebrated Egyptian feminist and professor Dr. Nawal al-Saadawi. In 2001 a lawyer by the name Nabih al-Wahsh took her to court, accusing her of being an apostate. According to al-Wahsh:

"What she said about the pilgrimage and the laws of inheritance is atrocious. She has offended the feelings of Muslims ... These opinions are poison for Muslims." In her own defense al-Saadawi posed the issue as follows: "I said we have to rethink about the inheritance law because we have 30% of families in Egypt where the mother is working and paying for the family and the husband is not working ... It is the mother who is the provider for the family, so why women inherit only half?" Al-Saadawi was indirectly questioning the validity of Chapter 4 verse 34 under circumstances where gender roles are reversed. Chapter 4 verse 34 reads in part as follows: "Men are in charge of women, because Allah hath made the one of them to excel the other, and because they spend of their property (for the support of women). So good women are the obedient ..."

Her court case was intended to intimidate al-Saadawi as a woman not to question her perceived inferiority or to demand for equality between the sexes.

Apart from competition for converts and religious intolerance, what has stoked the fires of a religious animosity in Tanzania since independence has been the elevation of religious identity over other identities. In this regard there is a lot of sense in what Nawal al-Saadawi says in opposing the elevation of religious identity above all else.

Identities built on religion have been closely linked with the history of religion that is written in endless rivers of blood flowing in the name of God (Saadawi, 1999: 17). One of the causes of the shedding of blood has been religious intolerance. It was against religious intolerance that former President Ali Hassan Mwinyi warned in 1986. He said: "Peace and cooperation are essential for the welfare of all citizens. It can be built and maintained on the basis of human equality, and respect for each other and each other's beliefs. Racial and tribal origin is a matter of God's will, and beyond human control. And religion is a personal matter. It is a question of faith, and therefore cannot be forced upon anyone; *yet if it is sincerely held it will be defended at all costs, regardless even of martydom* [sic]," (Daily News, 2 May 1986, quoted by von Sicard, 1991: 6, emphasis added). However, when all is said and done Christians and Muslims in Tanzania, as People of the Book, need to acknowledge each other's humanity and equality before God. The Qur'an offers the best solution to the enmity caused by scriptural and theological disputes: "God is your Lord and our Lord: Unto us our works and unto you your works; let there be no dispute between you and us. God will bring us together and to Him we shall return"(Chapter 2 verse 139, Chapter 42 verse 15). Equally important would be the understanding that virtue is not the monopoly of one faith, nor vice the monopoly of the other.

END NOTES

1. Religion is defined here as a system of beliefs and practices that refer to a sacred, divine domain, deities, or God(s).
2. All biblical references are from the New Revised Standard Version, Cokesbury, 1990.
3. Initially what is today mainland Tanzania was known as German East Africa. The colony was renamed "Tanganyika Territory" when the British took over after World War I. The new name was officially announced in the British press on 31 January, 1920. In 1964 following the union between Tanganyika and Zanzibar the new political entity was named Tanzania.
4. In general, despite these periods of conflict, Christian-Muslim relations have been harmonious. On the level of ordinary people it is common that believers from the two faiths have participated in each other's festivals, funerals, and have even inter-married.
5. The other cracks were ethnic, racial and class differences.
6. This was caused by the disobedience of Adam and Eve by partaking of the forbidden fruit. This brought the separation between God and human beings when the two were expelled from the Garden of Eden. Christians believe that this separation can only be overcome by reconciliation which Jesus the Christ has brought about in order to make human beings heirs again to God's inheritance, only this time in the perfection of creation in the hereafter.
7. I am grateful to Alamin Mazrui for this anecdote.
8. The people of Byzantium (Constantinople) used to have a myth that Constantinople had been founded by Keroesa, the daughter of the moon-goddess, Io-Hera (see Mallouhi, 2000: 7).
9. In the case of the Gogo of Central Tanzania "rain-stones" which were used in what Europeans dubbed as "rain making" rituals were ridiculed by missionaries. They later exalted in their destruction which they considered to be symbolic of the failure of the power of Satan.
10. To the missionaries African divinities were nothing but devices of the Devil to keep humans away from God and in a state of darkness and superstition. Both monotheistic faiths considered African traditional religion worshipers as people who had no idea of heaven and hell.
11. For this and the next paragraph: Hodge, "Training of Missionaries," pp. 84-91. For similar training for Muslims in East Africa see p. 19.
12. The curriculum for the short-term course included Bible lectures (1) on the Old Testament history from the beginning of the Jewish Monarchy to the close of the Old Testament Canon with introductions to the Prophetic Books, (2) on the Life of Christ and the harmony of the four Gospels, (3) on one of the Gospels in Greek, (4) on introductions to a few of the New Testament Epistles; some analytical exposition of the doctrine as well as the history and contents of the Prayer Book; and Christian Evidences and Logic.
13. While the training undertaken at Islington may not have deliberately been intended to turn out missionaries who could not hold out on their own in intellectual discourses about world religions such missionaries turned out to be uncritical and intolerant of any criticism against Christianity. As Hodge notes, it would be of very great interest to be able to examine the correspondence of these men with the CMS before they were accepted as missionaries, or for training as missionaries, in order to paint a fuller picture of the type of men they were and to know why it was that they offered themselves for missionary service. Unfortunately, no such correspondence exists.
14. "Those who believe, and have left their homes and striven with their wealth and their lives in Allah's way are of much greater worth in Allah's sight. These are they who are triumphant."

15. "Insofar as Mwembechai Muslims wishing to Islamize all those who are not Muslim that I have no knowledge of but I do not think they have the ability to do so. A person does not become a Muslim except by believing in Islamic faith. And faith is in the heart such that there is no way of forcing a person to have it."

16. All references are from The Glorious Koran, by Marmaduke Pickthall (1976).

17. Besides the problem of abrogation, scholars of Qur'an ic studies have also had to deal with the problem of whole chapters (surahs) missing from the Qur'an. According to John Gilchrist (2002), Abu Musa al-Ashari, a close companion of Muhammad and one of the earliest authorities of the Qur'an, is recorded to have told Qur'an-reciters in Basra: "We used to recite a surah which resembled in length and severity to (Surah) Bara'at. I have, however, forgotten it with the exception of this which I remember out of it: 'If there were two valleys full of riches, for the son of Adam, he would long for a third valley, and nothing would fill the stomach of the son of Adam but dust.'" (Sahih Muslim, vol. 2, p. 501). Gilchrist also quotes another close companion of Muhammad, Abu Musa, as saying, "And we used to recite a surah which resembled one of the surahs of Musabbihat, and I have forgotten it, but remember (this much) out of it: 'O people who believe, why do you say that which you do not practise' (61.2) and 'that is recorded in your necks as a witness (against you) and you would be asked about it on the Day of Resurrection'" (17.13). (Sahih Muslim, vol. 2, p. 501). Gilchrist concludes that these records of at least two lost chapters are proof that the Qur'an is not perfect and complete as Muslims claim.

18. See the Qur'an, chapter 2, verses 6 - 28.

19. See, for example, Chapter 9 verses 5 and 29; and Chapter 4 verse 34.

20. The main thesis of Mahmoud Taha regarding the evolution of Islamic law is summarized by his translator, Abdullahi An-Na'im, in the introduction to The Second Message of Islam (Syracuse University Press, Syracuse, 1987), 21-24.

21. The Sudan Government executed Taha for suggesting what he felt were needed reforms within Islam.

22. The militarization of Christianity in the middle ages represented a break from a long tradition of refraining from bloodshed in Christ's name. However, when Christianity was eventually adopted as a state religion by the Roman Emperor Constantin the church became a consenting party to warfare even if it persisted in disavowing bloodshed.

23. The literature on Muslim-Christian relations is enormous. One of the latest contributions which is relevant to the Tanzanian case is the monograph by Ovey N. Mohammed, Muslim-Christian Relations: Past, Present, Future (Maryknoll, N. Y.: Orbis Books, 1999).

24. During the scramble and partition of East Africa the Germans and British conceded a ten-mile wide strip of coastal land stretching from Kenya to the mouth of the River Ruvuma bordering Mozambique.

25. To the contrary, African Muslims were exhorted to memorize the Qur'an regardless of whether they understood what they memorized or not. This is because at the time it was popularly believed that the Qur'an ought not to be translated but rather read in Arabic which was the language of its revelation.

26. Von Sicard notes that Johannes Kupfernagel knew some Hindi and was well versed in Arabic. These qualifications enabled him to reach the Indians and Arabs in Dar es Salaam. Unfortunately due to ill health the Kupfernagels left in 1907 to return to Germany. The promising work Kupfernagel had started among the Indians and Muslims was discontinued and would not be taken up for fifty years.

27. In the case of the Swahili their language and culture were coterminous. As Nyerere once put it, the people of Bagamoyo are linguistically and culturally

closer to the people of Unguja than to the people of Bunda while the people of Tanga or Mafia are culturally more compatible with the people of Pemba than with the people of Tunduma. In this regard poetry which was critical of Christianity and German rule was probably more effective and better received along the coast than further in the interior.

28. The poem has 4,584 verses and is said to be one of the longest in an African language. The name Rasi 'lGhuli is not the real name of the Yemeni ruler who was defeated by the Muslims. Rather it is a derogatory term which means "serpent's head." The real name of the ruler was Mukhariq bin Shahab.

29. Quoted and translated by Charles Pike, "History and Imagination: Swahili literature and resistance to German language imperialism in Tanzania, 1885-1910," The International Journal of African Historical Studies, vol. 19, no. 2, 206. However, I replaced Pagans with Infidels in the first verse being in agreement with Ann Biersteker's definition of majahili, as infidels.

30. The mention of dogs in the third verse is of significance considering that the dog is considered to be najis or filth which a Muslim ought to avoid. It is tempting to think that al-Buhriy could possibly have been alluding to the Nubian and Shaangan mercenaries employed by the Germans.

31. The poem, in the author's possession, is a 1957 reproduction, by W. H. Whiteley, of that collected by A. Lorenz in Lindi in 1912 and published by him in the Mitteilungen des Seminars fur Orientalische Sprachen, vol. xxxvi/3, 1933.

32. Whiteley translates the verses (7-9) as follows: "We were relaxing, resting, and eating well, when suddenly we heard news that the pagans had rebelled and were advancing on the Boma, weapons in their hands, pillaging the hamlets. We, for our part, treated the matter with some contempt; how could these folk act in such an outrageous way?"

33. Unless Jamalidinni did not consider them to be *waungwana* or civilized despite their being Muslims.

34. Whiteley's translation is as follows: "The pagans have persisted in destroying the world. Fools where will you go, tell me that? Clear your minds of any doubt, your pride endure this; we shall not leave a lean-to standing, we shall burn the lot. So, here I have put down some words, others I make a point of remembering, that I may set them down well."

35. Whiteley's translation is as follows: "The pagans have no intelligence; the pauper has no 'guts'. Everyone simply agreed with everything he said. The Makonde and the Yao, their hearts failed them, they and their children were daily killed by shooting. Not a single one of any importance managed to escape; they were all hanged Now all is peace and happiness."

36. Whiteley translates this verse as follows: "As for that bastard (sic) Kinjara of Songea, may God curse him!" Could Jamalidinni have cursed Omari Kinjalla because by killing Muslim Arab and Swahili traders he had contravened a Qur'anic injunction (chapter iv, verse 92) that says "It is not for a believer to kill another believer unless (it be) by mistake"?

37. According to Otto Stollowsky, Bokero was preaching to the people about a great snake-god who lived in the rapids of the Rufiji at Kibambawe. The god had told him (Bokero) that a great flood would come, inundating all the land, so that only the summits of the mountains would stand above it. On these then the black people alone would find a safe refuge, while all the foreigners - Europeans, the Arabs and the Indians - must perish. See: Otto Stollowsky, "On the Background to the rebellion in German East Africa," translated by John W. East, The International Journal of African Historical Studies, 21 (1988): 687.

38. Lodhi and Westerlund also note: "In the interior it is often hard to distinguish the dividing line between Islam and the local religions. Prayers, the fasting month Ramadan and other principles of 'official' Islam are seldom strictly adhered to. The knowledge of Arabic is very limited. Both religiously and culturally the Moslems of Tanzania have a very strong local African identity." Thus in the eyes of Muslim elites like Jamalidinni the poet African Muslims who joined Maji Maji belonged to the category of *washenzi* because in spite of being Muslim their cultural and religious practices did not qualify them as *waungwana* or civilized.

39. Anderson (1977:58) notes that in 1910 only one out of thirty Muslim teachers in Uzaramo had training or could even read the Qu'ran.

40. Anderson mentions that the Lutherans received valuable assistance from the Domets, a Syrian Christian family. Unfortunately not much is known about this family and their invaluable contribution to Christian proselytization in Dar es Salaam.

41. Much of what follows is gleaned from Sigvard von Sicard's book, The Lutheran Church on the coast of Tanzania (Almqvist & Wiksells: Uppsala, 1970).

42. Subsequently, on 28 April, 1888 an agreement signed by Sultan Seyyid Khalifa ceded all power to the German East Africa Company for a period of fifty years. The agreement sparked Arab and Swahili resistance popularly known as the Bushiri uprising. Hostilities abated in December 1889 after Bushiri was caught and hanged publicly.

43. The literal translation is: Serve an infidel if you must to get your sustenance.

44. Its trunk is used for building and its leaves for roofing or making straw mats. Its young fruit contains a tasty, cool juice while the milk of a mature one is used for cooking. The strong, almost colorless palm wine, *tembo*, drawn by tapping from the crown of the coconut palm is drunk by many.

45. Most of these were freed slaves some of which had been freed slave-children when Greiner first established the mission in 1887.

46. In 1868 the Holy Spirit Fathers moved from Zanzibar to Bagamoyo. From their new base they spread the Gospel to Mhonda, Mandera, Kilema, Morogoro and Kondoa.

47. For hundreds of years, the Ottoman Empire ruled over the Muslim world and, as is noted in chapter 5, Muslims in German East Africa were suspected of paying allegiance to the Ottoman Sultan in view of his claims to the Caliphate. After centuries of battle with Christian Europe, it is understandable how the symbols of the Ottoman Empire became associated with Islam. However, some Muslims reject using the crescent as a symbol of Islam.

48. The fact that Islam offered practical solutions to problems such as witchcraft may have rendered it attractive to potential African converts. Christianity, on the other hand, simply condemned such beliefs like witchcraft as "superstition." However, although Muslims began the practice of wearing *hirizi* to ward off evil, these amulets eventually became popular with Christians as well.

49. In Uganda when the late Idi Amin became president he decreed that Friday become a day of rest like Sunday. The decision was revoked following his overthrow in 1979.

50. A much feared evil spirit.

51. Dhikr is the reciting of God's excellent titles by a gathering of Muslims usually in the privacy of a mosque or a house. As practiced in colonial Tanzania, in place of a private assembly, Dhikr took the form of a gathering of people in the street outside a house, or, on the occasion of Maulid and other special occasions, of a public procession (TNA, file number 21715).

52. It is said that Muslims who are at the lowest degree of perfection in God's sight can remedy their imperfection and ascend to the dhikr of the heart by constantly invoking loudly and forcefully "La ilaha Illa Llah." This awakens them from distraction.

53. In his report the P. C. notes that the D. O. told him of the possibilities of further trouble arising out of acts by sympathizers of either side.

54. Government found it necessary to prohibit public performances of dhikr in Dar es Salaam on account of interference with the traffic. Supposedly even though the performance of such ceremonies in the public streets and residential quarters at night constituted a nuisance to residents, no complaints were registered, even by Europeans, for fear of incurring the displeasure of Muslim neighbors.

55. Translated on the title page as "Evidences of the Christian Religion, together with a short Examination of Muhammadanism, in Swahili. For the C. M. S. East Africa Mission."

56. The fact that the Gospels of Matthew and John were eyewitness accounts has been disputed by some Muslim scholars. See, for example, Muhammad Ata ur-Rahim, Jesus: A Prophet of Islam (MWH London Publishers, 1977), p. 43.

57. An entry in the Antiquities of the Jews reads: "There was about this time Jesus, a wise man, if it is right to call him man, for he was a doer of wonderful works, a teacher of such men as receive the truth with pleasure. He drew over to him both many of the Jews and many of the Gentiles. He was Christ. And when Pilate, at the suggestion of the principal men among us, had condemned him to the cross, those that loved at first did not forsake him, for he appeared to them alive again the third day, as the divine prophets had foretold these and myriad other wonderful things concerning him. The tribe of Christians, so named for him, are not extinct to this day" (Quoted by Sandmel, 1873: 17-18).

58. Other ancient authorities read all things (Holy Bible, New Testament, p. 107).

59. Mitchell does not address the Muslims' accusation that some parts of the Bible have been tampered with. This Muslim allegation is probably a misinterpretation of some verses in Chapter V of the Qur'an such as verse 13: "And because of their breaking their covenant, We have cursed them and made hard their hearts. They change words from their context and forget a part of that whereof they were admonished. Thou wilt not cease to discover treachery from all save a few of them. But bear with them and pardon them. Lo! Allah loveth the kindly"; verse 14: "And those who say: Lo! we are Christians," We made a covenant, but they forgot a part of that thereof they were admonished. Therefore, We have stirred up enmity and hatred among them till the Day of Resurrection, when Allah will inform them of their handiwork."

60. My translation is: "First, we can evaluate it by those things we know are of God, and see if indeed it comes from Him. Second, we can compare it to human ways that we know, and say whether it is the work of human beings or not."

61. Muslims must abide by the Shariah which covers every aspect of human life. This characteristic is ridiculed by Salman Rushdie in his The Satanic Verses (Viking Penguin Inc., 1989: 363).

62. Muslim and some Jewish scholars have disputed this assertion. According to Sandmel, whereas Matthew describes the appearance of the resurrected Jesus in Galilee; Luke describes it as happening in Emmaus, near Jerusalem; Mark does not contain an account of a resurrection appearance at all. Another contradiction concerns the route that Jesus took on his last journey to Jerusalem where he would be arrested and crucified. According to Matthew and Mark, the route that

Jesus took led him eastward across the Jordan, then southward; he re crossed the Jordan at Jericho and went north westward from Jericho to Jerusalem. According to Luke (9:51-18:14), the route that Jesus took led him due south, without the two crossings of the Jordan. See Sandmel, We Jews and Jesus, 19.

63. The view that the Gospels were written by the disciples of Jesus remains controversial. Recent Biblical scholarship suggests that the author of Mark's Gospel was not a disciple of Jesus. Mark was the interpreter of Peter and wrote the Gospel from recollections of what Peter said in his preaching which it is known he used to adapt to the needs of his hearers. The author of Matthew's Gospel was not the disciple Matthew but rather an anonymous evangelist. According to the New American Bible in its introduction to the Gospel of Matthew, "The attribution of the gospel to the disciple Matthew may have been due to his having been responsible for some of the traditions found in it, but that is far from certain." The New American Bible also suggests that since Luke was not part of the first generation of Christian disciples he could not possibly have written the Gospel. Likewise, the authorship of John's Gospel remains uncertain. The prevailing view is that it was not written by a single author named John, the son of Zebedee, the disciple whom Jesus loved (John 13: 23).

64. Mitchell's understanding of the pillars of Islam is seriously faulty. There are five pillars and not four, namely The Shahada, Prayer, Almsgiving, Fasting, and Pilgrimage. Moreover, Hadith and Sunna are not two different things but one and the same.

65. For a biography of Muhammad, see: Maxime Rodinson 1971. Mohammed, translated by Anne Carter (Pantheon Books).

66. Mitchell notes that another authority on Muhammad, Sahih Al-Bukhari, is said to have collected 600,000 oral testimonies about the Prophet's life. However, Al-Bukhari thought that only 4,000 of these were worth of recording. Other authors who recorded only 4,000 hadith are Muslim bin Hajjaj (d. 261 A H.) and Abu Daud (d. 275 A H.)

67. Other sources suggest that the Qur'an as we know it is only a third of the original. Supposedly the Prophet's Companions, and especially the Caliphs, either deleted or added what they wanted in the Qur'an. Caliph Omar is said to have said: "One of you could say that I have compiled the whole Qur'an but much of it is lost and what I have is only that which I could ascertain."

68. Some of the changes were supposedly done by Muhammad's official scribe who would substitute a word or phrase to see if Muhammad would notice. Muhammad did not notice the alterations.

69. The total of chapters revealed at Medina is twenty-eight, including al-Fatiha or Chapter One which is also included among those revealed at Mecca.

70. Ar. Ahmad. Pickthall's notes: "A name of the Prophet of Arabia. The promised 'Comforter' was believed by many Christian communities of the East to be a prophet yet to come, and most of them accepted Muhammad as that prophet." The Glorious Koran, 738.

71. Or Helper.

72. The role of the Advocate is further explained in John 16: 8-11 and verse 13 as follows: "And when he comes, he will prove the world wrong about sin and righteousness and judgement: about sin, because they do not believe in me; about righteousness, because I am going to the Father and you will see me no longer; about judgement, because the ruler of this world has been condemned." And "When the Spirit of truth comes, he will guide you into all the truth; for he

will not speak on his own, but he will speak whatever he hears, and he will declare to you the things that are to come."

73. I am grateful to John Omachonu, at William Paterson University, for these observations.

74. The most compelling are the following:1. Moses and Muhammad became the lawgivers, military leaders, and spiritual guides of their peoples and nations; 2. Moses and Muhammad were first rejected by their own people, fled into exile, but returned some years later to become the religious and secular leaders of their nations; 3. Moses and Muhammad made possible the immediate and successful conquests of the land of (sic) after their deaths by their followers, Joshua and Umar respectively.

75. Some of these are: 1. Moses and Jesus were Israelites - Muhammad is claimed to be an Arab (Arabs are believed to be descendants of Ishmael, son of Biblical Abraham through his slave girl, Hagir; 2. Moses and Jesus both left Egypt to perform God's work - Muhammad was never in Egypt; 3. Moses and Jesus forsook great wealth to share the poverty of their people which Muhammad did not.

76. The controversy about the "Arabs" and the "Ishmaelites" is dealt with in Chapter Nine.

77. Indeed, the Qur'an concedes the performance of miracles by Jesus (Chapter 5 verse 110) albeit with the emphasis that whatever Jesus did was by Allah's permission.

78. In 1925 Rev. Dale published an English version of *Khabari za dini ya Kiislamu* which he entitled Islam and Africa: An introduction to the study of Islam for African Christians. The book was written at the request of the Bishop and the Synod of the Diocese of Nyasaland. It was published under the auspices of the Society for promoting Christian knowledge. The main objective was to provide European teachers, especially those who were living in districts where Islam was aggressive, with a book which provided answers to thorny issues which were certain to be raised by Muslims who were hostile to Christianity.

79. "When Muslims say these words they think they are criticizing the religion of Christ, but they do not know that they are committing a mistake which is obvious to every Christian who knows his religion."

80. *Jizya* signifies the payment of money by a non-Muslim community to a Muslim authority in order to guarantee their security. A good case study is that by Abdellah Larhmaid who analyzes the payment of *jizya* by a Jewish community in Islamic Morocco: "Collecting *Jizya*: Commerce, Power and Religious Identity in Goulmime, 1859-1894." Paper presented at the Conference on Islam and Africa, Binghamton University, April 19-22, 2001.

81. The Hadith and Sunna are one and the same.

82. An interesting case is that of Abdullah Muhammad of Zanzibar, reported by Anderson-Morshead and quoted by von Sicard (1978). It appears that Muhammad had been impressed by Bishop Steere's preaching and started attending the services in the cathedral as an observer. But the day he became a participant in prayers with the Christians, he was taken to prison on the express orders of Sultan Barghash.

83. Other questions Muslims continue to ask to this day include the following: Why did God have to punish His only Son for the sins of others? Is that justice? And if dying on the Cross was a part of Jesus' mission on earth, why then, at the material time, did he pray and ask (Matthew 26: 37-39, 46) for help from his Father?

84. Rev. Dale gives the Arabic translation as "Kalimatu Ilahi" because of God's command which he translates as Kun fa yakun.

85. Rev. Dale's assertion that the Qur'an may not possibly have come from God is a serious matter because he was the first person to translate the Qur'an in Kiswahili.

86. Rev. Dale's reference to verse 21 is incorrect.

87. "That Jesus the Messiah had no sin whatsoever and therefore he was able to give us salvation and sacrifice himself for our sins, upholding justice for those without, and able to show the way to blessedness, because he was the way, and is able to intercede for us forever because he is with God, the Just."

88. The founder Mirza Ghulam Ahmad was born in 1839 at Qadyan in India. In 1889 he proclaimed himself a mahdi or Muslim savior. Keeping in view the principle of the finality of prophethood of Muhammad mainstream Muslims strongly rejected Ahmad to be a "prophet". One ardent critique of Ahmad was the highly learned Muslim scholar Muhammad Iqbal. How could Ahmad be a prophet, questioned Iqbal, when his message was not one of power, dignity and freedom to the Muslims who were then under British rule? Ahmad was accused of abrogating Jihad and for accepting British rule. Moreover, his private life was said not to be all worthy of a prophet or messenger of Allah.

89. Idioms are human ideas invented by Abdul-aswad, with the intention of making it easy to teach the Arabic language to people of other nations. Likewise, the Qur'an is the Word of God revealed long ago before idioms were invented. So, how could this heretic have the right to claim that any word from the Qur'an must be translated following the order of idioms, when the Qur'an is the Word of God? Idioms do not contradict the Qur'an nor does the Qur'an contradict the idioms.

90. i.e. Jews and Christians.

91. "A Christian who reads the Qur'an after knowing the Gospel, and chooses the Qur'an over the Gospels, is like a person who likes a hurricane lamp although he can have electricity."

92. You (Muslims) believe that the Qur'an is the Word of God. Then, why did God ask Isa (Jesus) about these things? If God knew that Isa did not say them, why ask him? If He did not know, He cannot be God. Furthermore, is that what God thought Christians believe in? If that is what He thought, God was not aware. If He knew that was not what they believed in, why ask?

93. Sheikh al-Amin was born at Mombasa in 1890. His father Sheikh Ali bin Abdallah Mazrui was an expert of Islamic jurisprudence (fiqh) and held the position of Kadhi. Sheikh al-Amin initially received his training in the Islamic sciences under Sheikh Suleiman bin Ali Mazrui, and later on studied under Sheikhs Ahmad bin Sumayt and Abdallah Bakathir in Zanzibar.

94. Dale is known to be a Christian priest. Therefore, no Muslim would engage himself in reading his translation. But once you start criticising it, you will be compelled to copy his words, and to include them in your translation so as to squash them. In that way, Dale's words and their errors will reach Muslims via your translation. And you cannot know who will be affected by his words. (Mazrui, 1990:xi).

95. *Dale's translation:*
    In the name of God, the Compassionate, the Merciful.
    All Praise be to God, Lord of all the world
    The Compassionate, the Merciful
    Ruler on the Day of Reckoning

You alone do we worship, You alone do we ask for help.

Guide us on the straight path,

The path of those who received your grace

Not the path of those visited upon by your wrath, nor those who wander astray.

Mazrui's translation:

In the name of the Almighty God, Full of Compassion, the Merciful.

Every good praise belongs to the Almighty God,

Lord of creatures.

Full of Compassion, the Merciful.

Who controls (owns) the Day of Repayment

You alone we worship and from you alone we ask for assistance.

Lead us on the straight path.

96. The author's efforts to get copies of these two works proved futile because no library, including that at the School of Oriental and African Studies in London, has any holdings.

97. Traders were also responsible for the spread of Islam to Uganda where the first Arabs arrived there in 1844, and to the eastern parts of what is now the Democratic Republic of the Congo where Tip Tippu (whose father was Arab) carved for himself a sizable chiefdom in the late 1870s.

98. The role of the tariqa (Muslim brotherhoods), especially the Askariyya, in the spread of Islam in central Tanzania is mentioned by Mario Azevedo and Gwendolyn S. Prater (1991) but is not fully explored. See: Azevedo and Prater, "The Minority Status of Islam in East Africa: A Historico-Sociological Perspective," Journal Institute of Muslim Minority Affairs, vol. 12, no. 2 (July 1991).

99. "For the whole of German East Africa, an area of 385,000 square miles containing seven million Africans, the Germans had, in 1914, an administrative staff of only 79 Europeans" (Hill, 1957: 102). Consequently, "The Germans always seemed to fear the natives and every Government station was virtually a fortified post..., and fear led to a form of rule notable for harshness and severity" (ibid. p. 103-4).

100. The proper opposite of "shenzi" which actually refers to someone who is "uncivilized" is "ustaarabu" which refers to Arab mannerisms that are equated with "civilization." For a discussion of this distinction see Jonathon Glassman, "Sorting out the tribes: The creation of racial identities in colonial Zanzibar's newspaper wars," Journal of African History, 41 (2000), 406.

101. What Axenfeld did not realize was that the conduct of the same Muslim officials, commonly known as akidas and jumbes, was at times inimical to the cause of Islam. From the native point of view coastal Muslims in the employ of government "were the curse of the country" because they "were allowed a license which degenerated into extortion and brutality..." (Hill, 1957: 104).

102. Of 3,494 pupils enrolled in lower schools in 1911, 2,337 were Muslim, 794 various African and Asian religions, and 85 Christian. According to Pike the figures are unreliable, and 278 pupils are unaccounted for. See Charles Pike "History and Imagination: Swahili literature and resistance to German language imperialism in Tanzania, 1885-1910," International Journal of African Historical Studies, 19 , (1986), footnote 71, p. 216.

103. Such Muslim monopoly appear to be incongruent with public-mission school ratios. The figures given by Laura Kurtz for 1903 are 8 Government and 15 Mission schools; for 1911, 83 Government and 918 Mission schools; and for 1914, 99 Government and 1,852 Mission schools. Enrolment for 1911 was 3,192 for Government schools and 63,455 for Mission schools. The figures for 1914 were 6,100 and 155,287 respectively. See Laura S. Kurtz, An African Education: The social revolution in Tanzania (Pageant-Poseidon Ltd: Brooklyn, 1972), Table 1, p. 22.

104. Bishop Weston warned missionaries and other Europeans to desist from the following:

(1) "Do not treat Africans as 'pals' at one moment and as 'animals' at another; treat them as human beings," (2) "Do not make them conscious that you think them inferior – if you so think. If you make a boy conscious of your contempt, either he will be embittered or he will ape the European, whose praise he desires. And, once he begins to imitate us, he sits loose to his own customs," (3) "Do not under-rate the African mind. It has possibilities beyond what many think and, if you judge their minds by their slowness to grasp European methods, the Africans will one day surprise you – unpleasantly" (CMS Acc. 262/Z 4/2, "White and Black," by Rev. Frank Weston).

105. Others who also took the opportunity of missionary education and later served their newly found faith included Yohana Lusinde, the father of Canon Petro Malecela and grandfather of John Malecela, former Ambassador and Prime Minister, Canon Naftali Lusinde, and former Minister and Ambassador Job Lusinde. Yohana was a traditional "medicine man" who not only recanted his "profession" to become Christian but was one of the first 13 students admitted at "Huron" College, Kongwa, for evangelical training.

106. The need to bridge their differences was in part due to the realization that competition between different missionary groups was detracting their effort to spread Christianity. The number of denominations operating in German East Africa was astounding. Besides missions from Britain, France and Italy, there was the German Protestant Mission and the German Catholic Mission each with its own mouthpiece namely *Pwani na Bara* for the Protestants and *Rafiki* for the Catholics.

107. Marcia Wright suggests that it was Axenfeld's initiative, and that the meeting took place in Edinburgh rather than London, see Wright, *German Missions in Tanganyika, 1891-1941: Lutherans and Moravians in the Southern Highlands* (Clarendon. Oxford, 1971), 124. However, Sigvard von Sicard notes that at the Edinburgh Conference Axenfeld met with the Africa secretary of the Church Missionary Society, Baylis, and the mission director of the Moravian Church, Bishop Hennig, to discuss co-operation especially in the field of preacher and teacher training. See S. von Sicard, "The First Ecumenical Conference in Tanzania, 1911," *The Bulletin of the Society for African Church History* (1960), 323.

108. To Protestants in the 20th century the term ecumenism applied not only to Christian unity but, more broadly, to the worldwide mission of Christianity. The World Missionary Conference of 1910, held in Edinburgh, marked the beginning of modern ecumenism from which flowed three streams of ecumenical endeavor namely evangelistic, service, and doctrinal. See "Ecumenical Movement," Microsoft@ Encarta@ Online Encyclopedia 2000, http://encarta.msn.com @ 1997-200, Microsoft Corporation.

109. In 1869 Director Josenhans intimated that "Only on the day when Englishmen come to us to study here and to serve our society will the barrier be broken. But as long as the British are too proud to come to us, we will be too proud to go to them... This is the right, the Godly kind of pride for Swiss and Germany." See Marcia Wright, German Missions in Tanganyika, 1971), 2.

110. From the standpoints of religion and politics there was a significant convergence of interest and perception about the "threat" presented by Islam in German East Africa. Becker was aware of the concerns of the Berlin Mission Society and had read the work of Karl Axenfeld, Die missionnarische Aufgabe in Deutsch-Ostafrika as well as Axenfeld's opinion which appeared in the 86th Jahresbericht of the Berliner Missionsgesellschaft for 1909, published in Berlin, May 1910, which Becker quotes from in his article "Materials for the Understanding of Islam in German East Africa."

111. Previous to this Habib Saleh had been preaching in Lamu since the mid-1880s. His style of celebrating maulidi was controversial but served to draw an increasing number of students. According to Lienhardt, the students studied the Qur'an,

Arabic, the traditions of the Prophet, law and, in the later stages a little sufism. Some stayed as little as two years and others five years or more. There were no examinations.

112. Since the German administration did not include religious statistics in its annual reports there is no way of ascertaining the number of mosques and Muslim communities in central German East Africa.

113. Most Gogo at the time may have hesitated to convert to Islam due to the strict Islamic dietary regulations such as eating halal meat.

114. Among the numerous Gogo practices and beliefs that the Ussagara-Ugogo Executive Committee resolved to prohibit at its meeting of August 1911, the following are especially interesting:
   a. The wearing of charms of all kinds,
   b. Finding out from a soothsayer the cause of illness,
   c. Finding out through a sacrifice to the dead the name a child should have,
   d. Witchcraft of all kinds,
   e. The placing of charms around a house, garden, kraal, &c., for protection,
   f. The consulting of oracles,
   g. Sacrificing to the dead.
   h. The placing of prohibitions accompanied by oaths and curses (CMS G3 A8/02).

115. For a comparison of ideas of sacrifice in African and Christian religions see: Gwinyai Muzorewa, Mwari: The Great Being God (University Press of America: Lanham . New York . Oxford, 2001), 154-5.

116. The same problem of Gogo "heathenism" prevented the Muslims from making any significant conversions among the Gogo.

117. The Gogo believed in a Creator, whom they called Mulungu. Their Mulungu, however, was a distant God and the only relationship the Gogo had with this Supreme Being was a personalized relation through a number of intermediaries which included diviners and one's ancestors.

118. In October 1925 the Tanganyika Government called upon the missions for co-operation in the education of Africans.

119. These figures are not official figures. They are from Sheikh Mswia's article in Mwongozi, 26 October 1956, p. 4.

120. "One of the sad things to those who are concerned about Islam is to see that Tanganyika has not done much to promote Islam. There is neither school to teach Muslim children Islamic higher education and other beneficial things so that later they may help advance Islamic studies in their country, nor is there effort to send students abroad for Islamic studies that would benefit them in this world and in their afterlife."

122. I am very grateful to Alhaj Yusufu Kalala, a former student of both Kitchwele and Mzumbe, for information about these schools.

123. Trans. "The light of Islam." This refers to Egypt which is explicitly mentioned in verse 7.

124. These are verses 1, 2, 10, and 14. The poem appeared in Mwongozi, 16 November, 1956, p. 6.

125. In your name the Beneficient
   Bismillah I say
   We beg you, the Merciful
   Daring to ask for Your urgent intercession
   Protect all Muslims in the world
   from destruction
   God the Generous,
   so they can destroy the infidels

God the Most Kind
In your name we cry
Give power to Muslims
the World over
let them meet their damnation

God the Most Kind
Destroy the infidels
Oh God the Most Kind
The Forgiver, the Merciful
Destroy their enemies
As those in bygone days
The light of Islam
Lord, let it not go off
Oh God the Most Kind
Destroy the infidels.

Dua
All say Amen
Let's pray to the Creator
Trust in his glory
And all the Prophet's companions

The evil of the insolent
Break it You, the Rock
Let them feel ashamed
of every thing they once enjoyed
Lord give great power
to the Good and gracious President
Protect him from humiliation;
From enemy oppressors.

Pray for us to the Almighty
Let Him bless us with happiness
So that we may win in our intentions

126. Arab policy in black Africa to this day remains pragmatic. It is primarily motivated by a concern for Arab rather African interests. Thus, despite much talk of friendship and solidarity oil rich Arab countries have been of little financial help to poor African countries. Arabs have less to gain from black Africa than, say, from western countries. Therefore, they would rather invest in the west than in black Africa because western economies use most of their oil than Africa does.

127. After the Zanzibar Revolution in 1964 Al-Barwani alleges that Karume and Nyerere made a special trip to Cairo, and there demanded the closure of East Africa House, the special house in which the young boys and girls from Zanzibar were staying. "In plain language they demanded the termination of the educational aid by Egypt to Zanzibar. The Tanzanian Embassy, under Ahmed Diria and cultural attachee Hija Saleh, saw to it that the students were returned to Zanzibar by force" (Al-Barwani, 1997: 109).

128. The candidates were Julius Nyerere, John Keto, Onesmo Eliufoo, John Mwakangale and Chief Abdallah Said Fundikira.

129. Said mistakenly calls *dua* an oath when in fact it is a special prayer for Allah's intervention. It is related in a hadith that the dua of three persons is not rejected, rather it is surely accepted. These are (1) He who remembers Allah profusely, (2)

205

A wronged person, and (3) A ruler who avoids tyranny. The dua, whether said in a group or alone, is performed with the palms of the hands open to heaven; at the end, the words al-Hamdu li-Llah ("praise to God") are said and the palms are drawn over the face and down, crossing over the shoulders, as if one were annointing oneself with a divine blessing. See Cyril Glasse. 2001. The New Encyclopedia of Islam. rev. ed. of the Concise Encyclopedia of Islam (Altamira Press), 125.

130. The first Council of Ministers was made up of the following: Julius Nyerere, Rashid Kawawa, Abdallah Fundikira, Tewa Said Tewa, Paul Bomani, Nsilo Swai, Oscar Kambona, Job Lusinde, George Kahama, Amir Jamal, Derek Bryceson, Ernest Vasey and Attorney-General Roland Brown. Of the nine Africans, six were Christians and three were Sunni Muslims. Amir Jamal was an Ismaili Muslim of Asian descent.

131. "God has given us this day of our country's independence. God has blessed us with this day, He who is the source of everything that is good and holy. A human being, unlike a beast, has been blessed by his Creator with the freedom and ability to be master of his own destiny according to the commandments imprinted upon everyone's soul..."

132. "The accolades due to you for enhancing political, economic and social development will be rendered by other citizens and leaders. As for us we want to thank and praise you for your evangelical labors. In your conversations and speeches as Party Chairman and as President you always reminded your listeners or readers about the Scriptures..."

133. These verses read as follows: "Now the whole group of those who believed were of one heart and soul, and no one claimed private ownership of any possessions, but everything they owned was held in common... There was not a needy person among them, for as many as owned lands or houses sold them and brought the proceeds of what was sold. They laid it at the apostles' feet, and it was distributed to each as any had need."

134. In the same year, according to Swantz, a Muslim society known as Dawa al-Islamiya, which was established in October 1963, also sent a letter to all Bishops and religious leaders complaining about the lack of parity in educational matters between Muslims and Christians. Swantz is quoted by Abdin Chande, "Radicalism and Reform in East Africa," in Nehemia Levtzion and Randall L. Pouwels (eds) The History of Islam in Africa (Ohio University Press . Athens, 2000), 360.

135. "Islam continues to cause problems. Muslims have succeeded to the highest echelons in their attempt to lodge their complaints at the same time they enjoy our [Christian] social services, without agreeing to the conditions for unity under a pluralistic model as expressed in 'Unity and Freedom.'"

136. "Tabligh" is the work done by Muslims to call others to Allah. It is a continuation of what Muhammad himself did when he conveyed the message of Islam to his companions, who then conveyed the message to the rest of the world. It is every Muslim's duty to learn more about Islam and then convey the knowledge first to one's family and then to one's neighbors. The Qur'an, chapter 61 verse 14, commands: "O ye who believe! Be Allah's helpers..."

137. Evidently Nyerere's memorandum on "The Problem of Education in Tanganyika" mentioned above was a response to this growing Muslim demand for secular education.

138. Opposition to the Aga Khan and his patronage was nothing new. In the early 1950s there was a rather shadowy organisation which called itself the Ismailia Democratic Party in Tanganyika. In a long memorandum to the Aga Khan dated 17 October 1953 the Party called for the abdication of the Aga Khan and criticized the Ismailia structure as a "money making machinery under the masquerade of

religion." The memorandum further reiterated that, "This cunning exploitation of the Ismailis is detrimental to their existence and this Organisation has been formed for the emancipation of the Ismailis" (CO 822/860, "Ismailia Democratic Party in Tanganyika").

139. For Tewa, what had happened was similar to the break up of the Jamiatul Islamiyah fi Tanganyika in 1940 when the liwali of Dar es Salaam fomented a crisis that led to the creation of Jamiatul Islamiyah Fi Tanganyika..

140. Tewa was referring to Alhaj Saleh Masasi, Sheikh Adam Nasibu, Sheikh Abdallah Chaurembo, Sheikh Juma Jambia, Mr. Abdi Matunga, and Alhaj Omar Muhaji.

141. I am grateful to Prof. Issa Shivji for informing me about the involvement of these members of the UDSM faculty.

142. Some writers put the date of the interview much earlier in 1970. However, based on the chronology of events the meeting could not have been earlier than 1974 which is the date that is hand written on a copy of the interview in the Maryknoll Mission archives at Ossining, New York.

143. The essence of liberation theology, as introduced by the Jesuits in Latin America, was derived from Thomas More's Utopia whose basic idea is the restoration of society to its Christian base by adopting as supreme guide the norms of natural rights. The Ujamaa villages that Nyerere was trying to establish were similar to communities called "reductions" introduced by the Jesuits in Latin America. The "reductions" were divided into the Fields of God and the Fields of Man. The Fields of God were collectively cultivated, whereas the Fields of Man were parceled out for individual cultivation. The crops produced in the Fields of God were owned by the community, whereas the crops grown in the Fields of Man were kept by the individual farmers.

144. Its membership was open to people of all faiths. No one could be turned down because of their religion.

145. Maryknoll Mission Archives, Ossining (NY), "Interview: President Nyerere/ Fr. Robert," dated 1974, p. 2.

146. We don't think it is against anything you Imams have been directed to do in the Qur'an ... If there is anything then you will declare it during this seminar. You will inform our leaders, places where what we are explaining contradicts the Qur'an ... if what we are saying contradicts the Gospel, honourable people don't feel shy, don't feel shy in these discussions; tell us that the Gospel is against, that the teachings of the Lord Jesus are against what you are saying; against these efforts to eliminate exploitation, for the Lord Jesus is so fond of exploitation!" (Nyerere, 1970, 38).

147. The Encyclical titled Atheistic Communism was written in 1937. Previous to Pope Pius XI's encyclical, Pope Leo XIII had also issued an Encyclical letter in which he criticized the remedy offered by Socialists to social and economic inequities as follows: "To remedy these evils the Socialists, working on the poor man's envy of the rich, endeavor to destroy private property, and maintain that individual possessions should become the common property of all, to be administered by the State or by municipal bodies. They hold that, by thus transferring property from private persons to the community, the present evil state of things will be set to rights, because each citizen will then have his equal share of whatever there is to enjoy. But their proposals are so clearly futile for all practical purposes, that if they were carried out the working-man himself would be among the first to suffer. Moreover they are emphatically unjust, because they would rob the lawful possessor, bring the State into a sphere that is not its own, and cause complete confusion in the community (emphasis added)(Quoted from George, 1965: 111).

148. In his 1891 encyclical letter Pope Leo XIII opposed socialism in the following

terms: "Let it be laid down, in the first place, that humanity must remain as it is. It is impossible to reduce human society to a level. The Socialists may do their utmost, but all striving against nature is vain. There naturally exist among mankind innumerable differences of the most important kind; people differ in capability, in diligence, in health, and in strength; and unequal fortune is a necessary result of inequality in condition. Such inequality is far from being disadvantageous either to individuals or to the community; social and public life can only go on by the help of various kinds of capacity and the playing of many parts; and each man, as a rule, chooses the part which peculiarly suits his case... To suffer and to endure, therefore, is the lot of humanity; let men try as they may, no strength and no artifice will ever succeed in banishing from human life the ills and troubles which beset it."

149. Maryknoll Mission Archives (NY), "Interview," p. 2.

150. Ibid., p. 3. It is this statement that Njozi (2000) gives as evidence that Nyerere was in alliance with the Church to marginalize Islam.

151. Maryknoll Mission Archives (NY), "Interview," p. 4.

152. All the data in this paragraph comes from an online article "The Tanzania Catholic Church" available at <http://www.rc.net/tanzania/tec/tzchurch.htm>

153. Alhaj Aboud Jumbe was born on 14 June 1920 at Mkamasini Ng'ambo, Zanzibar. He got his primary and secondary education at Mnazimmoja Government School (now Ben Bella) from 1930-1942. He first met Julius K. Nyerere at Makerere College, Uganda where both were students and members of the Debating Society from 1943-1945. In their final year at Makerere Jumbe and Nyerere were chairmen of student halls of residence, Ssejongo and Bamuja respectively. Jumbe was president of Zanzibar following the assassination of Abeid Amani Karume in 1972 until 1984 when he resigned all his posts after a political crisis in the ruling Party (CCM) over the nature of the Union between Tanganyika and Zanzibar. Jumbe insisted the Union was federal and not unitary in character.

154. The Muslim World League, founded in 1963, has head offices in Mecca, Saudi Arabia. The League deals mainly with the establishment of Islamic cultural centers and with the organisations of courses for religious leaders.

155. His book titled *Safarini*, intended for Muslims who want to reconcile themselves to their Maker, was published in 1988 after he had relinquished his positions as President of Zanzibar and Vice-President of Tanzania.

156. "Every one must be aware of how one uses the freedom of choice given to him, the will power endowed him of deciding and the power and responsibility handed to him of acting, keeping in mind his responsibility, as one will stand before his God to recount his earthly deeds on the Last Day," (Mwinyi, 1988:15).

157. "No one can criticise, put in a different way, change the Truth, the Correctness, the Assurance and the Genuineness of that Leadership, despite the many developments taking place, and that will continue to take place in worldly knowledge, resulting from any achievement and discovery by science!" (Mwinyi, 1988,31).

158. "To take human beings, creatures of the Almighty God, and to turn them into gods or children of gods, is not something new ... For people to blaspheme by believing in those fables and stories is an unforgivable sin."

159. On 10 January 1993, Zanzibar announced that it had joined the O.I.C. Following the protests against the decision in August President Salmin Amour announced that his government would withdraw its membership.

160. <http://www.op.org/Nigeriaop/kenny/Yale2.htm>
161. The expelled Sudanese were Secondary School teachers at Jabal Hira Secondary School in Morogoro. They were expelled by Hon Augustine Mrema, the then Minister for Home Affairs probably in an attempt to locate a foreign scapegoat for the pork butcheries riots of 1993. Also in the wake of those riots the authorities arrested some 250 Muslims over disturbances throughout the country and charged them with illegal demonstrations and incitement.
162. Osama bin Laden was initially trained, armed and financed by the CIA.
163. Reported by Rachel Lugoe via TANZANET <Tanzanet@news.parrett.net>.
164. The controversial issue on the re-emgernce of the Zanzibar's intention to join with the Organisation of Islamic Countries (OIC).
165. Halal (lawful) is the Arabic word which means "allowed or lawful." It is anything which is permitted with respect to which no restriction exists, and the eating of which Allah (God) has allowed. Slaughtering must be done according to Islamic code.
166. Haram (unlawful) is the Arabic word which means "prohibited or unlawful." It is anything the eating of which Allah (God) has prohibited . Any Muslim who partakes of such becomes unclean.
167. The prohibition of intoxicants (khamr) is more stringent and encompassing. The Prophet Muhammad is said to have said: "Truly, Allah has cursed Khamr and has cursed the one who produces it, the one for whom it is produced, the one who drinks it, the one who serves it, the one who carries it, the one for whom it is carried, the one who sells it; the one who earns from the sale of it, the one who buys it, and the one for whom it is bought." Thus he not only forbade the drinking of alcohol but also forbade trading in it, even with non-Muslims.
168. Taboos are usually animals and not plants. Among the Gogo, animals that are forbidden to be eaten by different clans include bush buck, civet cat, roan antelope, eland, pig (ngubi), badger, and sheep with short tail.
169. Baraza la Ukuzaji Kuran Tanzania.
170. At <http://www.islamtz.org/an-nuur/167/167-13.htm>
171. "In our neighborhoods pork is roasted and sold to passers-by, we have written to the authorities concerned but so far they have taken no action."
172. "What are the authorities doing when the environment and people's health are so much at risk."
173. Other legislation on food is found in the Qur'an in the following Chapters: 5 verses 3 ff., 96; 6 verses 119 ff., 146 f; 16 verse114 ff.; 22 verses 34, 36.
174. To the ardent believer God Almighty is all-knowing and our limited knowledge and science cannot as yet understand all the reasons for the prohibitions and recommendations contained in the Scriptures.
175. "If there is anything about slavery in the Qur'an, it explains how slavery was found, but not how it was started by the Qur'an." (Nyerere, 1970: 45-46).
176. <http://www.islamset.com/hip/pork/Abdussalam.html>
177. The Qur'an does not use the term hijab but rather uses the term khimar which translates as head cover. But hijab too translates as "cover, wrap, curtain, veil, screen, partition."For various names and meanings of Islamic Arabic male and female garments see Fadwa El Guindi, Veil: Modest, Privacy, and Resistance (Berg, 1999), 3-12.
178. The preceding verse 30 in Chapter 24, enjoins believing men to lower their gaze and be modest. This verse has been used by some commentators to explain the

practice of veiling among Tuareg men and male poets in pre-Islamic Mecca.

179. Azam Kamguian, "Against Hijab," at <http://www.isisforum.com/women/hijab.htm>

180. Naheed Mustafa, "Hijab (Veil) and Muslim Women," at <http:www.usc.edu/

ARCHIVAL SOURCES

I. Christian Missionary Society (CMS) Archives, University of Birmingham, England.

CMS Acc. 212 F12/9: Henry Cole, "The Story of Andereya Mwaka."

CMS Acc. 262/Z4/2 Rt. Rev. Frank Weston, Bishop of Zanzibar, "White Man and Black."

CMS C A6/O/1-5: Tanganyika Letter Book, 1907-20.

CMS CA 5O 16/1-161 Dr. John L. Krapf - Correspondence

CMS G3 A5/O - 1888: J. C. Price, Journal of second visit to Ugogo, Apr. 18 - May.

CMS G3 A5/30 - 1889: J. C. Price, Account of his last tour in Ugogo

CMS G3 A5/O/45 - Correspondence

CMS G3 A8/01, 1912, nos. 1 - 66, Karl Axenfeld, memo, "The joint Seminary for the Protestant Missions in German East Africa," dated 9th July 1912.

CMS G3 A8/02, 1910, nos. 1 - 66, E. Forsythe, "Annual Letter," dated 28th November 1910

CMS G3 A8/02, 1911, nos. 1 - 66, "Proceedings of the Executive Committee," held at Kiboriani, 26th August 1911.

CMS G 3 A8/02, 1911, nos. 1 - 62, D. J. Rees and E. J. Baxter, "General Report of the Ussagara-Ugogo Mission for 1910."

CMS G3 A8/02, 1912, nos. 1 -66, T. B. R. Westgate, "Annual Letter," dated 30th November, 1910.

CMS G3 A8/O - 1906 to 1920: Correspondence

CMS M/Y/A 8 - 1934 to 1947: Diocese of Central Tanganyika, "Memorandum on Medical Policy."

II. Public Record Office (PRO), Kew Gardens, London.

PRO, CO 822/859 - 1954-56, Activities of T.A.N.U.

PRO, CO 822/1375 - 1959, All Muslim National Union of Tanganyika.

PRO, CO 822/1584 - 1958, Representations by H. H. The Agakhan on Muslim Education in East Africa

PRO, CO 822/2130 - 1960, All Muslim National Union of Tanganyika.

PRO 822/3204- Zanzibar - Tanganyika: Political Relations

III. Rhodes House Library, Oxford University, England.

Conditions of Dar-es-Salaam during the early days," dated 1931.
      MSS Afr. s. 452, R. M. Bell, "The Maji Maji Rebellion in Liwale District,"
      dated 23 March 1941.
      MSS. Brit. Emp. S. 526/2, Fletcher-Cooke, "Interview given at Oxford to
      John Tawney, dated 9 February 1970."
      MSS. Afr. s. 1090, W. B. Helean, "Notes on the Gogo," not dated.
      MSS. Afr. s. 1471, Mwalimu J. Nyerere, "The Problem of Education in
      Tanganyika."
      MSS. Afr. s. 1604, British Council of Churches, "The Political Situation in
      Tanganyika, May, 1961" and "Tanganyika: Church and Political Situation,
      1961."

IV. New York Public Library, Schomberg Center, Harlem.

      Phelps-Stokes Fund, MG 162, Box 103,. "An Appraisal of the Situation
      Confronting the Church in
      Tropical Africa," by Max A. C. Warren, dated 1959.

V. Maryknoll Mission Archives, Ossining, NY.
      Oral History Project, "Interview: President Nyerere/Fr. Robert," dated
      1974.

VI. Tanzania National Archives (TNA), Dar-es-Salaam, Tanzania
      TNA 21715, Tanganyika Secretariat, "Affray between Mohammedans &
      Christians at Morogoro."

APPENDIX I

From *The Condition of Labor: An Open Letter to Pope Leo XIII*, by Henry George (1891)[1]

"To Pope Leo XIII.

YOUR HOLINESS: .

We hold: That—

This world is the creation of God.

The men brought into it for the brief period of their earthly lives are the equal creatures of his bounty, the equal subjects of his provident care.

By his constitution man is beset by physical wants, on the satisfaction of which depend not only the maintenance of his physical life but also the development of his intellectual and spiritual life.

God has made the satisfaction of these wants dependent on man's own exertions, giving him the power and laying on him the injunction to labor – a power that of itself raises him far above the brute, since we may reverently say that it enables him to become as it were a helper in the creative work.

God has not put on man the task of making bricks without straw. With the need for labor and the power to labor he has also given to man the material for labor. This material is land – man physically being a land animal, who can live only on and from land, and can use other elements, such as air, sunshine and water, only by the use of land.

Being the equal creatures of the Creator, equally entitled under his providence to live their lives and satisfy their needs, men are equally entitled to the use of land, and any adjustment that denies this equal use of land is morally wrong.

As to the right of ownership, we hold: That–
Being created individuals, with individual wants and powers, men are individually entitled (subject of course to the moral obligations that arise from such relations as that of the family) to the use of their own powers and the enjoyment of the results.

There thus arises, anterior to human law, and deriving its validity from the law of God, a right of private ownership in things produced by labor – a right that the possessor may transfer, but of which to deprive him without his will is theft.

This right of property, originating in the right of the individual to himself, is the only full and complete right of property. It attaches to things produced by labor, but cannot attach to things created by God.

To attach to things created by God the same right of private ownership that justly attaches to things produced by labor is to impair and deny the true rights of property. For a man who out of the proceeds of his labor is obliged to pay another man for the use of ocean or air or sunshine or soil, all of which are to men involved in the single term land, is in this deprived of his rightful property and thus robbed.

As to the use of land, we hold: That–

While the right of ownership that justly attaches to things produced by labor cannot attach to land, there may attach to land a right of possession.

In the rudest social state, while industry consists in hunting, fishing, and gathering the spontaneous fruits of the earth, private possession of land is not necessary. But as men begin to cultivate the ground and expend their labor in permanent works, private possession of the land on which labor is thus expended is needed to secure the right of property in the products of labor. For who would sow if not assured of the exclusive possession needed to enable him to reap? Who would attach costly works to the soil without such exclusive possession of the soil as would enable him to secure the benefit?

This right of private possession in things created by God is however very different from the right of private ownership in things produced by labor. The one is limited, the other is unlimited, save in cases when the dictate of self-preservation terminates all other rights.

The purpose of the one, the exclusive possession of land, is merely to secure the other, the exclusive ownership of the products of labor; and it can never rightfully be carried so far as to impair or deny this. While any one may hold exclusive possession of land so far as it does not interfere with the equal rights of others, he can rightfully hold it no further. To combine the advantages of private possession with the justice of common ownership it is only necessary therefore to take for common uses what value attaches to land irrespective of any exertion of labor on it...

We do not propose to assert equal rights to land by keeping land common, letting any one use any part of it at any time. We do not propose the task, impossible in the present state of society, of dividing land in equal shares, still less the yet more impossible task of keeping it so divided.

We propose – leaving land in the private possession of individuals, with full liberty on their part to give, sell or bequeath it – simply to levy on it for public uses a tax that shall equal the annual value of the land itself, irrespective of the use made of it or the improvements on it. And since this would provide amply for the need of public revenues, we would accompany this tax on land values with the repeal of all taxes new levied on the products and processes of industry – which taxes, since they take from the earnings of labor, we hold to be infringements of the right of property.

This we propose, not as a cunning device of human ingenuity, but as a conforming of human regulations to the will of God."

APPENDIX II

"National Property," by Julius K. Nyerere (1958).[2]
On land being God's gift to His living creation:-

1. All human beings, be they children brought up in poor or rich families, or belonging to sinners or saints, or even those whose parents are either slaves or free men, were born to find land in existence. They can neither add to it or reduce its extent. It is God's gift, given to all His creation without discrimination

2. What is the origin of the right to possess wealth? What prompts a person into declaring anything to be 'mine'?. . . This right originates from only one factor; the fact that man is nobody's property. . . If, therefore, man possesses himself, it is clear that his health, his intellect, and his ability cannot be someone else's property. So, whenever he uses his intellect, his health and ability to make anything, that thing becomes his property...

3. Land is a free gift from God to all His living things. . . When I use my energy and talent to clear a piece of ground for my use it is clear that I am trying to transform this basic gift from God so that it can satisfy a human need. It is true, however, that this land is not mine, but the efforts made by me in clearing the land enable me to lay claim of ownership over the cleared piece of ground... which will remain mine as long as I continue to work it.

On selling land:-

4. If we allow land to be sold like a robe, within a short period there would only be a few Africans possessing land in Tanganyika and all others would be tenants. . . We will get a group of people working to fulfil God's law of earning one's living through ones own labour. But there will be another group of idle people who will not be doing any work but will simply be waiting to exploit the energies, and suck the blood of the poor workers. . . by charging exorbitant land rents. . .

5. When a lot of people accept the introduction of a method which will enable a few people to claim ownership of a thing which is actually

God's gift to all His people, they are in actual fact, voluntarily accepting slavery. .

6. It is not God's intention that we should use His free gift to us — land and air and water — by permission of our fellow human beings.

On the genuine solution to landownership:-

7. It is that everybody should be given land under certain regulations. . . One of these vital regulations is that a man will return his land to the public immediately he stops using that land. This is a necessary condition needed to protect the rights of the public, and to prevent greedy people from accumulating land for themselves without being able to use it. . .

APPENDIX III

"The Problem of Education in Tanganyika." By the President of Tanganyika, Mwalimu J. Nyerere.

Among the political and economic problems facing the government of any developing country, none is more pressing than that of education.

At its simplest, that task of providing anything like an adequate number of teachers and schools is formidable. But the subject of this memorandum is a special aspect of our educational problem which is the result of history and religion.

For most of the forty years during which this country was administered - first under a League of Nations mandate and then as a Trust Territory under the United Nations - nearly all the education available to us was that provided by the Christian missionaries. The administering authority itself took very little interest in providing schools for our people. From their point of view, educating the African was not particularly important since the administration and public services were staffed by their own expatriates, and the mission schools were already turning out more than enough literate Africans to fill the handful of low-grade clerical posts for which it was not considered worthwhile to bring over expatriates.

The Christian missionaries, however, since they *were* missionaries, were primarily concerned with the work of spreading the Christian faith. That was what they had come for and naturally, therefore, the education they offered was a Christian education. This is not to say that non-Christians were not admitted to their schools, nor that conversion was forced on the children of any non-Christian parents who might send them there. Nevertheless, the very fact of their being missionary schools meant that, as a rule, only those parents who were themselves Christians - or who at least did not mind if their children became Christians - would make use of them. Moslems, who sincerely believed Islam to be the only true faith, were understandably reluctant to do so. And since there were no other schools available to them (such Moslem schools as there were taught only the Koran) the result was that the Moslem population lagged far behind in education.

Not only did the Moslems lag behind, but, lacking the stimulus which the opportunity for education would have provided, they took little interest or no interest in it. Thus, when at long last the administering authority began to see that it could no longer shrug off the responsibility for educating the people they were supposed to be preparing for self-government, and opened a few government schools, most of the pupils again came from among the Christians because that was the section of the population to which the advantages of education had already been demonstrated, and in which, therefore, the enthusiasm and demand for it had been whipped up. The Moslems, from long habit, remained apathetic. Moreover the administering government was not concerned with (possibly it was hardly even aware of) the religious factor underlying Moslem apathy towards education. So that its still very limited participation in the field of African education was not concentrated on providing secular schools and encouraging Moslems to attend them, but was divided - part of it taking the form of grants-in-aid to the existing voluntary agency schools "To him that hath" was indeed given; but it was still the Moslem who "had not".

Inevitably, then, when Tanganyika became independent, the majority of Africans who were qualified to fill positions of responsibility were Christians. But by now the Moslems had awoken to the fact that education was a very desirable thing after all. They saw that the people of Tanganyika, of whom they formed a considerable proportion, now had the opportunity to control their own affairs. They also saw that those of their fellow countrymen who were taking over the positions vacated by the expatriates had to be educated people - and they found this ruled out all but a very few Moslems. Their apathy towards education vanished almost overnight - but where were they to get it?

This is the situation which the Tanganyika Government has to face to-day; a situation in which the basic problem of educating the masses of our people is further complicated by the need to redress the present educational imbalance between Christians and Moslems. The only possible answer, indeed the only just answer, is to give priority to the provision of schools at which Moslems can be educated without offence to their religious scruples.

What we must do is provide secular schools. When we can do this we shall be able to make school attendance compulsory. At present we cannot. And we could not even if there were a mission school in every district of Tanganyika; for while it is our duty to see that, once we do have enough schools, no parents are allowed to deprive their children of the right to education through mere selfishness or prejudice, it is of course equally our duty to respect the conscience and the religious convictions of the parents.

But when we say that our policy is to provide secular schools in sufficient numbers to enable us to make attendance compulsory, this does not mean that the government intends to interfere with the existing mission schools. What it does mean is that when that stage is reached no parent will have any excuse for refusing to send his children to school; for those who wish to do so will continue to use the Christian schools, while those who have religious objections to them will be able to use the secular schools. I have explained this, and the reasons for it, many times during the years before and after this country became independent, but I am still not sure that we are always understood when we emphasize our need for secular schools.

I have said that, as a Government (unintelligible) ourselves to give priority to the provision of such schools. But even if we had not, it would make no difference. Our people are demanding them, and will insist on getting them somehow. Unfortunately you cannot expect uneducated ignoramuses to discriminate between one kind of 'secular' education and another. You cannot expect them to see through the motives of people who come to them with offers of a so-called 'secular' education which is really a calculated course of indoctrination in materialism. Those offers will be made; they are already being made. It would be a tragedy if the very sincerity of their desire to preserve their children's faith were to leave our unsophisticated Moslems at the mercy of people whose one aim is to destroy all faith. Yet, unless Government can get the help it needs to give them genuinely secular schools under its own control, the masses will not wait. They will seize the offers of that other kind of 'secular' education without realizing until too late the poison it conceals. Moslems and Christians alike believe in the same God. If the faith of Moslem children is destroyed by those who talk glibly of "brotherhood" while denying the very source of brotherhood - the Fatherhood of God - and if this happens because Christians were prepared to turn their backs rather than give help in a way which the Moslem conscience can accept, who will be to blame?

On the purely political level, the educational gap between Christian and Moslem in Tanganyika is, of course, potentially explosive. Indeed, there are people who are already trying to make political capital out of it. But this is not necessarily a bad thing. It may even prove a blessing in disguise. For there are all too many people in the world who will not recognize a moral obligation unless it is disguised as a political threat to their security! Then, and only then, will they do, for political considerations, what they should have done from purely moral considerations. Feeding the hungry , healing the sick, and instructing the ignorant are moral obligations. If those obligations are not met, and if there are individuals in our country who exploit the situation for vote-catching, who am I to say that such people are more immoral than those who gave them their opportunity by ignoring their moral obligations?

But the problem is not truly a political problem at all. Those who are trying to make it a political issue are an insignificant handful and, thank God, the vast majority of our people are not misled by the hypocrisy of the few who try to cloak political self-seeking under a mantle of pseudo-religious fervour. No; the problem as I have stated it is a moral one. And it is on the moral plane that I must seek the understanding and assistance of the Christian Church, and indeed of all those who are in a position to help.

I know the Church has always been reluctant to associate itself with education which is not directly Christian and under its own control. I am saying that it is urgently necessary for the Church to think again. Where the sincere religious beliefs of a Moslem, or other non-Christian, people make it impossible for them to use Christian schools, I cannot believe Christians are justified in doing nothing. On the contrary, I believe Christians in particular have a positive duty to go out of their way to give all the help they can - and to give it in a way which can be accepted. The relief of ignorance, even on the purely secular level, is as much a work of charity as the relief of sickness. Therefore I go as far as saying that I believe the Christian Church has a duty to help us clear away the undergrowth of ignorance and superstition which endangers the mind as much as any sickness can endanger the body.

We need all the help we can get. We need money; we need school buildings; we need teachers. But there are limits to the amount of help which a government can hope for in response to its own appeals - and this is particularly true in the case of charitable causes like education and health. One of the reasons for the almost hostile reaction to a government's appeal for help with its educational programme is the question of who is to benefit by that help. Even sincere Christians very often seem to feel that it is not enough to give help just because help is needed. They want to be sure their giving helps only their fellow Christians, or potential fellow Christians. So that many charitable individuals and organisations, who would be ready and eager to respond generously to appeals from the Christian churches are decidedly less ready to do so when a similar appeal is made to them directly by a government. Those sources the Church can, and I believe should, approach on our behalf. For surely what is supremely important is that the help should be given where it is needed. If the motive for giving is the love of God - the desire to help any of His children who need help, then the way in which the help is to be used should not form a condition of the giving. As long as the need is there, and the opportunity to help is there, the results can safely be left to God.

Dar es Salaam, November 12th, 1963.

NOTES TO THE APPENDICES

1. This is an abbreviation of a much longer letter. See: Henry George, *The Land Question* (Robert Schalkenbach Foundation, New York, 1965), "The Condition of Labor – An open letter to Pope Leo XIII," pp. 3-105.
2. Julius K. Nyerere, "National Property," in J. K. Nyerere, *Freedom and Unity* (London: Oxford University Press, 1967). The essay "Mali ya Taifa" (National Property) was published in 1958, by Nyerere as a comment on the Government's proposals for new legislation regarding land holding. Nyerere acknowledged that at about that time he was reading *Progress and Poverty* by Henry George and that the quality of the argument and writing greatly impressed him.

BIBLIOGRAPHY

Abdin N. Chande. 1998. *Islam, Ulamaa and Community Developemnt in Tanzania: A Case Study of Religious Currents in East Africa.* San Francisco: Austin & Winfield, Publishers.

Addison, James T. 1966. *The Christian Approach to the Moslem: A Historical Study.* New York: AMS Press, Inc.

Akrong, Abraham. 1999. "A Comparative Analysis of the Christian and an African Myth of Creation," in Esi Sutherland-Addy (ed) *Perspectives on Mythology.* Accra: Goethe-Institute.

Al-Barwani, Ali Muhsin. 1997. *Conflicts and Harmony in Zanzibar: Memoirs.* Dubai: n.p.

Allport, Gordon W. 1973. "The religious context of prejudice," in Benjamin Beit-Hallahmi (ed.) *Research in Religious Behavior: Selected Readings.* N.p.: Wadsworth Publishing Co.

Alpers, Edward A. 1972. "Towards a History of the Expansion of Islam in East Africa: the Matrilineal Peoples of the Southern Interior," in Terence O. Ranger and Isaria N. Kimambo (eds) *The Historical Study of African Religion.* Los Angeles and Berkeley: University of California Press.

Anderson, William B. 1977. *The Church in East Africa, 1840-1974.* Dodoma: Central Tanganyika Press.

An-Na'im, Abdullahi A. 1986. "The Islamic law of apostasy and its modern applicability," *Religion,* N.p.: n.p.

Antoun, Richard T. 1968. "On the Modesty of Women in Arab Villages: A Study in the Accommodation of Traditions," *The American Anthropologist,* vol. 70, Issue 4 (August), 671-697.

Arnold, T. W. 1913. *The Preaching of Islam: A History of the Propagation of the Muslim Faith.* New York: Charles Scribner's Sons.

Axon, William E. A. 1902. "On the Mohamedan Gospel of Barnabas." *Journal of Theological Studies* (April), 441- 451.

Baker E. C. 1947. "A Note on the Washomvi of Dar-es-Salaam," *Tanganyika Notes and Records,* Number 23 (June).

Bates, Margaret. 1957. "Historical Introduction" in *Utenzi wa Vita vya Maji Maji,* by Abdul Karim bin Jamalidinni, translated by W. H. Whiteley. Arusha: Beauchamp Printing Co. Ltd.

Becker, Carl H. 1968. "Materials for the understanding of Islam in German East Africa", trans. By B. G. Martin, *Tanzania Notes and Records,* no. 68. Carl Becker's "Materialen zur Kenntnis des Islam Deutsch-Ostafrika" was originally published in the German periodical *Der Islam,* II, 1911, pp.1-48.

Biersteker, Ann. 1996. *Kujibizana: Questions of Language and Power in Nineteenth-and Twentieth-Century Poetry in Kiswahili* (Michigan State University Press, East Lansing).

Blair, Sheila S. and Jonathan M. Bloom. 1999. "Art and Architecture: Themes and Variations," in John L. Esposito (ed) *The Oxford History of Islam.* Oxford: Oxford University Press.

Blyden, Edward W. 1994. *Christianity, Islam and the Negro Race*, first published 1888. Baltimore: Black Classic Press.

Carey: George. 1995. "Documentation: The Challenges Facing Christian-Muslim Dialogue." *Islam and Christian-Muslim Relations*, Vol. 7, No. 1, pp. 95-101.

Cerulli: Enrico. 1969. "Islam in East Africa," in A. J. Arberry (ed), *Religion in the Middle East: Three religions in concord and conflict*, vol. 2. Cambridge: At the University Press.

Chapman, Colin. 1995. *Cross and Crescent: Responding to the challenge of Islam*. Leicester: Intervarsity Press.

Cook, Michael. 2000. *Commanding right and forbidding wrong in Islamic thought*. Cambridge: Cambridge University Press.

Cragg, Kenneth. 1959. *Sandals at the Mosque*. New York: Oxford University Press.

Dale, Godfrey. 1909. *Khabari za dini ya Kiislamu*. London: Society for Promoting Christian Knowledge.

Dale, Godfrey. 1913. *The Contrast between Christianity and Mohammedanism: Four Lectures Delivered in Christ Church Cathedral, Zanzibar*, sixth edition. London: Office of the Universities' Mission to Central Africa.

Dale, Godfrey. 1923. *Tafsiri ya Kurani ya Kiarabu*. London: Society for Promoting Christian Knowledge.

Deedat, Ahmed H. 1987. *Missionary Christianity*. Lagos: IBRASH Islamic Industrial Press Ltd.

Deedat, Ahmed H. 1994. *The Choice*. Durban: n.p.

du Plessis, J. 1921. "Government and Islam in Africa," in *The Muslim World: a quarterly review of history, culture, religions and the Christian mission in Islamdom*, vol. 11, 2-23.

El Saadawi, Nawal. 1999. "Why Keep Asking Me About MY IDENTITY?". In E. Anthony Hurley, Renee Larrier, and Joseph McLaren (eds), *Migrating Words and Worlds: Pan - Africanism Updated*. Trenton: Africa World Press, Inc.

El-Guindi, Fadwa. 1999. *Veil: Modesty, Privacy, and Resistance*. Oxford: Berg.

Eliade, Mircea (ed). 1987. *The Encyclopedia of Religion*, vol. 4. New York: Macmillan Publishing Co.

Ephal, I. 1976. "'Ishmael' and 'Arab(s)': A Transformation of Ethnological Terms," *Journal of Near Eastern Studies*, vol. 35, Issue 4 (October), 225-235.

Esposito, John L. (ed). 1995. *The Oxford Encyclopedia of the Modern Islamic World*, vol. 3. New York: Oxford University Press.

Esposito, John L. (ed). 1999. *The Oxford History of Islam*. New York: Oxford University Press.

Farb, Peter and George Armelagos. 1980. *Consuming Passions: The Anthropology of Eating*. Boston: Houghton Mifflin Company.

George, Henry. 1965. *The Land Question, Property in Land and The condition of Labor*. New York: Robert Schalkenbach Foundation.

Gilchrist, John. *Is Muhammad Foretold in the Bible?* at http://www.answering-islam.org/ Gilchrist/muhammad.html

Gilchrist, John. 2002. *Facing the Muslim Challenge: A Handbook of Christian-Muslim Apologetics.* Claremont/Cape Town: Life Challenge Africa.

Glassman, Jonathon. 1995. *Feasts and Riot: Revelry, Rebellion, and Popular Consciousness on the Swahili Coast, 1856-1888.* Portsmouth: Heinemann.

Gray, Sir John. 1950. "Mikindani Bay before 1887." *Tanganyika Notes and Records,* no. 28 (January).

Haddad, Yvonne Y. 1996. "Islamist Depictions of Christianity in the Twentieth Century: the pluralism debate and the depiction of the other." *Islam and Christian-Muslim Relations,* Vol. 7, No. 1, pp. 75-93.

Hadjivayanis: Georgios G. 1999. "Pemba Nationalism and the struggle for the state in Zanzibar," Seminar paper presented at the University of Cape Town, 12 May.

Haider, A., "Amkeni Islamu wa Tanganyika," *Mwongozi,* 27 September, 1957, p. 8.

Hansen, Holger B. and Michael Twaddle. 1995. *Religion and Politics in East Africa: The Period Since Independence.* Oxford: James Currey: London.

Harries: Lyndon. 1954. *Islam in East Africa.* London: Universities' Mission to Central Africa.

Hekmat, Anwar. 1997. *Women and the Koran: The Status of Women in Islam.* Amherst, New York Prometheus Books.

Hill, M. F. 1957. *Permanent Way: The Story of the Tanganyika Railways,* vol. II, East African Railways and Harbours.

Hodge, Alison. 1971-1972. "The Training of Missionaries for Africa: The Church Missionary Society's Training College at Islington, 1900-1915," *Journal of Religion in Africa,* vol. 4, pp. 81-96.

Ismael, Tareq Y.. 1960. "Religion and U. A. R. African Policy," *The Journal of Modern African Studies,* vol. 6, no. 1, 49-57.

Jeffery, Patricia. 1982. "Indian Women in Purdah," *Current Anthropology,* vol. 23, Issue 2 (April), 195-196.

Joelson, F. S.. 1920. *The Tanganyika Territory - formerly German East Africa.* New York: Negro Universities Press.

Jumbe, Aboud. 1994. *The Partner-Ship Tanganyika - Zanzibar Union: 30 Turbulent Years.* Dar-es-Salaam: Amana Publishers.

Kaluta, Amri Abeid. N.d.. *Uwongofu wa Tafsiri ya Qur'an.* N.p.: n.p.

Kandoro, Abdu S.. 1961. *Mwito wa Uhuru.* Dar-es-Salaam: Thakers Ltd.

Kanisa la Kiinjili la Kilutheri Tanzania, Dayosisi ya Mashariki na Pwani. 1992. *Miaka Tisini ya Kanisa Kuu la Azania Front, 1902-1992* (Dar-es-Salaam, Tanzania).

Karen Blixen. 1980. *Out of Africa.* London: n.p.

Kasozi, A. B. K. 1995. "Christian-Muslim Inputs into Public Policy Formation in Kenya, Tanzania and Uganda," in Holger B. Hansen and Michael Twaddle (eds) *Religion and Politics in East Africa: The Period Since Independence.* Kampala, Nairobi, Oxford, Ohio: James Currey, EAEP, Fountain Publishers, University Press.

Kessel: Leo van (ed.) 1979. *Utenzi wa Rasi 'lGhuli,* by Mgeni bin Faqihi. Dar-es-Salaam: Tanzania Publishing House.

Kimambo, Isaria N. 1999. "The Impact of Christianity among the Zaramo: A Case Study of Maneromango Lutheran Parish," in Thomas Spear and Isaria N. Kimambo (eds) *East African Expressions of Christianity*. Oxford, Dar-es-Salaam: James Currey, Mkuki na Nyota Publishers.

Kimaro, Tumaini, "Bible quoted out of context", TANZANET@THOR.PARRETT.NET, 6 December, 2000.

Kopf, Jennifer. 2001. "German orientalism in East Africa," paper presented at the Islam and Africa Conference, Binghamton University, April 19-22.

Kurtz, Laura S. 1972. *An African Education: The social revolution in Tanzania*. Brooklyn: Pageant-Poseidon.

Lacunza-Balda, Justo. 1997. "Translations of the Qur'an into Swahili, and contemporary Islamic revival in East Africa," in Eva E. Rosander and David Westerlund (eds.) *African Islam and Islam in Africa: Encounters between Sufis and Islamists*. Athens: Ohio University Press.

Landau, Paul S.. 1995. *The Realm of the Word: Language, Gender and Christianity in a Southern African Kingdom*. Portsmouth: Heinneman.

Lester, Toby, "What Is the Koran?", *The Atlantic Monthly* (January 1999).

Lewis, B., V. L. Menage, Ch. Pellat and J. Schacht (eds). 1986. *The Encyclopedia of Islam*. London: Luzac and Co.

Lienhardt, Peter. 1959. "The Mosque College of Lamu and Its Social Background", *Tanganyika Notes and Records*, no. 53, pp. 228-242.

Lodhi, Abdulaziz Y. and David Westerlund. 1997. "African Islam in Tanzania," at http://www.islamtz.org/articles/islam2.htm

Lusinde, Naftali P.. n.d. "Miaka Kumi na Mitano Kutafsiri Biblia kwa Lugha ya Cigogo," Dayosisi ya Central Tanganyika (mimeograph, in author's possession).

Maddox, Gregory H. 1999. "The Church and Cigogo: Father Stephen Mlundi and Christianity in Central Tanzania," in Thomas Spear and Isaria N. Kimambo (eds) *East African Expressions of Christianity*. Oxford, Dar es Salaam: James Currey, Mkuki na Nyota Publishers.

Mallenkott, Virginia R. 2000. "Coping with Biblical Fundamentalism: Solutions." In Vernon McClean, ed., *Solutions for the New Millennium: Race, Class, and Gender*. Dubuque Kendall/Hunt Publishing Co.

Martin, Bradford G. 1976. *Muslim Brotherhoods in Nineteenth-Century Africa*. Cambridge: Cambridge University Press.

Marx, Karl. 1973. *On Society and Social Change*, edited and with an Introduction by Neil J. Smelser. Chicago and London: The University of Chicago Press.

Mazrui, Al-Amin Ali. 1980. *Tafsiri ya Qur'ani Tukufu: Al-Faatihah - Al-Baqarah*. Nairobi: Shungwaya Publishers Ltd.

Mazrui, Ali A. and Alamin M. Mazrui. 1999. *Political Culture of Language: Swahili, Society and the State*. Binghamton, New York: The Institute of Global Culture Studies.

Mazrui, Ali A.. 1985. "Religion and Political Culture in Africa," *Journal of the American Academy of Religion*, vol. 53, no. 4, 817-839.

Mazrui, Ali A.. 1986. *The Africans*. Boston. Toronto: Little, Brown and Company.

Mbele, Joseph. 1988. "Rasi 'lGhuli: Swahili classic", *Daily News* (Dar-es-Salaam), 19 March, p. 4.

Mbiku, Deogratias H. (ed.) 1985. *Historia ya Jimbo Kuu la Dar-es-Salaam.* Ndanda-Peramiho: Benedictine Publications.

Mbogoni, Lawrence E. Y. 1999. "Radio Broadcasting in Colonial Tanganyika," *Proceedings of the International Mass Communications Symposium,* Television Archive and School of Mass Communications. Texas: Tech. University.

McAuliffe, Jane D. 1996. "The Qur'anic Context of Muslim Biblical Scholarship."*Islam and Christian-Muslim Relations,* Vol. 7, No. 2, pp. 141-158.

Meagher, Paul K. (ed). 1979. *Encyclopedic Dictionary of Religion.* Washington, D.C: Corpus Publications.

Mitchell, J. Murray. 1905. *Shuhuda za Dini ya Kimasihia pamoja na Kupeleleza Kidogo Dini ya Isilamu.* London: Society for Promoting Christian Knowledge.

Mlahagwa: Josiah R.. 1999. "Contending for the Faith: Spiritual Revival and the Fellowship Church in Tanzania," in Thomas Spear and Isaria N. Kimambo (eds.) *East African Expressions of Christianity.* Oxford, Dar es Salaam, Nairobi, Athens: James Currey, Mkuki na Nyota, EAEP, Ohio University Press.

Mohamed, Ovey N. 1999. *Muslim-Christian Relations: Past, Present, Future.* Maryknoll, New York: Orbis Books.

Mohammed, Khalifa K. 2002. *Waislamu Amkeni.* Dar-es-Salaam: Sherman Publishers & Distributors.

Morrison, David R.. 1976. *Education and Politics in Africa: The Tanzanian Case.* Montreal: McGill-Queen's University Press.

Mortley, Raoul. 1981 *Womanhood: The feminine in ancient Hellenism, Gnosticism, Christianity and Islam.* Sydney: Declaoix.

Msamy, Hassan. N.d. "Kaluta Amehitilafiana Na Mtume Wake," *Mwongozi,* 22 February, 1957, p. 6.

Mswia, K.S. Kiangi, "Udhalili wa elimu kwa Waislamu Tanganyika," *Mwongozi,* 26 October 1956, p. 4.

Munir, Abu, "Ya Allahu Ya Karima Wahiliki Makafiri," *Mwongozi,* 9 November, 1957, p. 6.

Mwinyi, Aboud Jumbe. 1988. *Safarini.* Zanzibar: Al-Khayria Press Ltd.

Nafziger, George F. and Mark W. Walton. 2003. *Islam at War: A History* (Praeger).

Nasser, Gamal Abdel. 1955. *Egypt's Liberation: The Philosophy of the Revolution.* Washington, D. C.: Public Affairs Press.

Njozi, Hamza M. 2000. *Mwembechai Killings and the Political Future of Tanzania.* Ottawa: Globalink Communications.

Northrup, David. 2002. *Africa's Discovery of Europe, 1450-1850.* Oxford: Oxford University Press.

Nyerere, Julius K. 1967. *Freedom and Unity: A selection of writings and speeches, 1952-65.* London: Oxford University Press.

Nyerere, Julius K.. 1968. *Freedom and Socialism: A selection from writings and speeches, 1965-1967.* Dar-es-Salaam: Oxford University Press.

Nyerere, Julius K.. 1970. "Ujamaa wa Tanzania na Dini," A speech given at Tabora when opening a seminar for religious leaders of various persuasions, Monday 27 July, 1970.

Oded, Arye. 2000. *Islam and Politics in Kenya.* N.p.: Lynne Rienner Publishers, Inc.

Oded, Arye. 1987. "The promotion of Islamic activities by Arab countries in Africa - Contemporary Trends," *Asian And African Studies*, vol. 21, 281-304.

Okafor, Gabriel M.. 1992. *The Development of Christianity and Islam in Modern Nigeria.* Echter Verlag Wurzburg / Oros Verlag Altenberge.

Pakenham: Thomas. 1991. *The Scramble for Africa: White Man's Conquest of the Dark Continent From 1876 to 1912.* New York: Avon Books.

Parsons, Timothy. 2000. "Dangerous Education? The Army as School in Colonial East Afrca," in *The Journal of Imperial and Commonwealth History*, vol. 28, no. 1 (January),112-134.

Partner, Peter. 1998. *God of battles: Holy wars of Christianity and Islam.* Princeton, NJ: Princeton University Press.

Peters, Rudolph and Gert J. J. de Vries. 1976-77. "Apostasy in Islam," in *Die Welt des Islams* (Berlin: D. Reimer).

Pickthall, Marmaduke. 1976. *The Holy Qur'an.* Albany: State University of New York Press.

Pike, Charles, "History and Imagination: Swahili literature and resistance to German language imperialism in Tanzania, 1885-1910," *The International Journal of African Historical Studies*, vol. 19, no. 2.

Pope Pius XI. 1937. *Atheistic Communism (Divini Redemptoris): Encyclical Letter of His Holiness Pope Pius XI* (New York: The Paulist Press).

Porter, Andrew. 1977. "Evangelical Enthusiasm, Missionary Motivation and West Africa in the Late Nineteenth Century: The Career of G. W. Brooke," *The Journal of Imperial and Commonwealth History*, vol. 6, no. 1, 23 - 46.

Pouwels, Randall L.. 1981. "Sh. Al-Amin B. Ali Mazrui and Islamic Modernism in East Africa, 1875-1947," *International Journal of Middle East Studies*, vol 13, no. 3 (August): 329-345.

Pouwels, Randall L.. 2000. "The East African Coast, c. 780 to 1900 C.E.," in Nehemia Levtzion and Randall L. Pouwels (eds) *The History of Islam in Africa.* Athens: Ohio University Press.

Prasch, Thomas. 1989. "Which God for Africa: The Islamic-Christian missionary debate in late-Victorian England," *Victorian Studies*, vol. 33, no. 1, 51-73.

Raum, J. 1930. "Educational Problems in Tanganyika Territory," *International Review of Missions*, vol. 19, 563-575.

Rigby, Peter J. A.. 1966. "Sociological factors in the contact of the Gogo of central Tanzania with Islam," in I. M. Lewis (ed.) *Islam in Tropical Africa.* Bloomington and London: International African Institute in Association with Indiana University Press.

Robinson, D. W. 1963. "The Church in Tanganyika," *Afer*, vol. 5, no. 3 (July), 256-264.

Rodinson, Maxime. 1971. *Mohammed*, translated by Anne Carter. New York: Pantheon Books.

Rosander, Eva E. and David Westerlund (eds.). 1997. *African Islam and Islam in Africa: Encounters between Sufis and Islamists.* Athens: Ohio University Press.

Said, Mohamed. 1998. *The life and times of Abdulwahid Sykes: the untold story of the Muslim struggle against British colonialism in Tanganyika.* London: Minerva.

Sallam al-Manasyeh al-Btoush, Amin M.. 1994. *The Question of Abrogation (Naskh) in the Qur'an*. Amman: National Print.

Sanneh, Lamin. 1994. "Translatability in Islam and in Christianity in Africa: A Thematic Approach," in Thomas D. Blakely, Walter E. A. van Beek and Dennis L. Thomson (eds) *Religion in Africa*. Oxford: James Currey: London.

Schildknecht: Franz. 1969. "Tanzania," in James Kritzeck and William H. Lewis (eds) *Islam in Africa*. New York . Toronto . London . Melbourne: Van Nostrand - Reinhold Company.

Semaan, Khalil I. 1961. *Ash-Shafi'i's Risalah: Basic ideas with English translation of the Chapters on an-Nasikh wa-al-Mansukh*. Lahore: Sh. Muhammad Ashraf: Kashmiri.

Shorter Aylward. 1985. *Jesus and the Witchdoctor: An approach to healing and wholeness* London: Geoffrey Chapman.

Shorter: Aylward. 1988. *Toward a Theology of Inculturation*. London: Geoffrey Chapman.

Shorter: Aylward. 1997. "Secularism in Africa," *African Christian Studies*, vol. 13, no. 1 (March).

Simons, Frederick J. 1961. *Eat Not This Flesh*. Madison: The University of Wisconsin Press.

Sivalon: John C. 2001. *Kanisa Katoliki na Siasa ya Tanzania Bara, 1953 hadi 1985*. Ndanda – Peramiho: Benedictine Publications.

Smith, Jane I. 1998. "Christian Missionary Views of Islam in the Nineteenth and Twentieth Centuries." *Islam and Christian-Muslim Relations*, vol. 9, No. 3.

Stollowsky, Otto. 1988. "On the background to the rebellion in German East Africa,"

Sugirtharajah, R. S. 2001. *The Bible and the Third World: Precolonial, Colonial and Postcolonial Encounters*. Cambridge:Cambridge University Press.

Sunseri, Thaddeus. 1999. "Maji Maji and the Millennium: Abrahamic sources and the creation of a Tanzanian resistance tradition," *History in Africa*, vol. 26: 365-378.

Sunseri, Thaddeus. 2000. "Statist Narratives and Maji Maji ellipses," *International Journal of African Historical Studies*, vol. 33, no. 3.

Sunseri: Thaddeus. 1998. "Dispersing the Fields: Railway Labor and Rural Change in Early Colonial Tanzania," *Canadian Journal of African Studies*, vol. 32/3 , pp.558-583.

Taha, Mahmoud M.. 1987. *The Second Message of Islam*, translation and Introduction by Abdullahi A. An-Naim (Syracuse University Press, Syracuse).

Tariq, A. R.. 1973. *Speeches and Statements of Iqbal*. Lahore: Sh. Ghulam Ali & Sons.

Tertullian. 1956 [c. 1951]. *Treatises on penance: On penitence and On Purity*, trans. and annotated by William P. Le Saint (Westminster, Md.: Newman Press).

Tewa, Tewa Said. N.d. "A Probe into the History of Islam in Tanzania," a handwritten manuscript in the possession of the author. Translated by John W. East, *The International Journal of African Historical Studies*, 21.

ur-Rahim, Muhammad Ata. 1979. *Jesus: A Prophet of Islam*. London: MWH London Publishers.

von Sicard, Sigvard. 1970. *The Lutheran Church on the Coast of Tanzania, 1887-1914*. Uppsala Almqvist & Wiksells.

von Sicard, Sigvard. 1978. "Christian and Muslim in East Africa." *Africa Theological Journal*, 7, 2, 53-67.

von Sicard, Sigvard. 1991. "Islam in Tanzania," CSIC Papers, no. 5 (September).

Wafi, Ali Abdel Wahid. 1967. "Human Rights in Islam," in *The Islamic Quarterly*, vol. XI, nos. 1 & 2 (January - June), 64-75.

Walker, Benjamin. 1968. *The Hindu World: An Encyclopedic survey of Hinduism.* New York. Washington, D.C.: Frederick A. Praeger.

Watt, W. Montgomery. 1961. *Muhammad: Prophet and Statesman.* London . Oxford . New York Oxford University Press.

Welch, Alford T.. 1999. "Muhammad: Life of the Prophet," in John L. Esposito (ed), *The Oxford History of the Modern Islamic World.* Oxford: Oxford University Press.

Whiteley, W. H., trans. 1957. *Utenzi wa Vita vya Maji Maji*, by Abdul Karim bin Jamalidinni, with a Historical Introduction by Margaret Bates, Supplement to the East African Swahili Committee Journal No. 27 June, 1957.

Wright, Marcia. 1971. *German Missions in Tanganyika, 1891-1941: Lutherans and Moravians in the Southern Highlands.* Oxford Clarendon Press.

Lightning Source UK Ltd.
Milton Keynes UK
29 March 2010
152057UK00002B/101/A